Praise for A Very Chinese Cookbook

"I've been a Kevin Pang fan for years. I'm crazy about his writing and his clever, quirky way of coming at everything from XO Sauce (which he says delivers a 'knuckle sandwich of umami') to the primer on ingredients, which is a marvel. Now I'm in love with his father, his mother and the food they cook. Their book is an original—generous, wise, funny and chockablock with smart information and irresistible, meticulously tested recipes. If you can't decide what to make first—there are just so many gems—I'll understand: That's just how it was with me."

— **Dorie Greenspan**
New York Times best-selling cookbook author

"Kevin Pang and his father make a wonderful team— a dynamic duo in their kitchens and in their lives. This book is filled with traditional Chinese home-cooked recipes unknown to many. It's for everyone who has fond memories of cooking and sharing their lives with their parents. Way to go, Kevin, and, of course, Dad, too!"

— **Martin Yan**
Host of *Yan Can Cook* on public television, chef-restaurateur, author

"I love this father and son exploration of Chinese cuisine especially because it focuses so much on their Hong Kong heritage. The handing down of recipes is so rare and a powerful way to keep our culinary culture rich and vibrant. This work is an important addition for every Chinese cookbook library."

— **Grace Young**
Author of *Stir-Frying to the Sky's Edge* and *The Breath of a Wok*

"A gloriously accessible guide to the most delicious cuisine ever devised. Then—at no extra charge!—the moving reconciliation of a father and son. Try the Dry Chili Chicken!"

— **Will Tracy**
Co-writer of *The Menu*, executive producer of *Succession* and *The Regime*

"A Very Chinese Cookbook is the rare cookbook that is as joyous as it is instructional. Kevin and Jeffrey Pang are skilled and spirited guides into the world of not only Chinese food, but delicious meals, full stop. What a gift this book is: rich, enlightening, and just plain delightful."

— **Rachel Khong**
Author of *Goodbye, Vitamin* and editor of *All About Eggs*

"I love this book! And I adore this incredible food from Kevin and Jeffrey, and their very fun but no-nonsense approach to cooking Chinese food together. The love of sharing food doesn't start at the table; it starts in the kitchen, when we shop, when we meal-plan. This book is a joy to read and cook from and reminds us why family and food are inexorably linked."

— **Andrew Zimmern**
James Beard Award–winning TV personality, chef, writer, teacher

"A big-hearted, accessible guide to Chinese cooking in America rooted in a father and son's immigrant experiences, A Very Chinese Cookbook presents a broad range of incredible recipes with the Pangs' trademark passion, expertise, and goofball antics."

— **Dan Pashman**
James Beard Award–winning host of *The Sporkful* podcast, inventor of the cascatelli pasta shape

"This is the Chinese cookbook I didn't know I was waiting for all my life. I have multiple shelves of cookbooks, but none capture the joy of Chinese cooking like this one. More than a compilation of recipes, Kevin and Jeffrey fill each page with helpful information and unbridled joy."

— **Larry Fong**
Cinematographer of *300*, *Batman v Superman: Dawn of Justice*, *Watchmen*, *Lost*

"Kevin and Jeffrey nailed this! Such a beautiful book with incredible recipes. My house will be permanently smelling like these dumplings from now on if anyone needs me. Love the authenticity and accessibility!"

— **Renée Paquette**
Author of *Messy In The Kitchen*, All Elite Wrestling on-air personality

"I'm a sucker for collections of recipes that mean something. And—this may sound contradictory—I'm drawn to cookbooks that confidently present technical prowess. A Very Chinese Cookbook has both, which is a rare find. Plus, it's as much fun to read as it is to cook from. The Smashed Cucumbers and Sesame Noodles became instant go-tos in my house, and now I'm set on a path to mastering the Master Dumpling System. With its chapter on demystifying the Chinese grocery and its brilliantly curated collection of recipes, I'm thinking this may be the only Chinese cookbook I need."

— **Rick Bayless**
Best-selling cookbook author, host of public television's *Mexico: One Plate at a Time*, chef-owner of Frontera Grill and Topolobampo in Chicago

"Kevin and Jeffrey Pang's story is a recipe of its own, and one that features ingredients you'll probably find in your kitchen: family members arguing, cultures clashing, fights ending strictly because everyone just wants to eat, etc. In the Pangs' case, the final dish is this magnificent tome, one that has already made me both a better cook and a happier person. This is a cookbook made by people who love food so much because they love each other so much."

— **Drew Magary**
Author of *The Hike*, co-founder of Defector

"Smart. Funny. Delicious. Kevin and Jeffrey Pang's beautifully shot deep dive into Chinese food makes you want to step into the kitchen and get cooking."

— **Omar Mamoon**
Writer and contributor for *Esquire*, *San Francisco Chronicle*

"Kevin and Jeffrey Pang—and America's Test Kitchen—have a knack for making complex topics approachable and fun. No better example than A Very Chinese Cookbook, which is thoughtful, funny, and, above all else, delicious."

— **Abra Berens**
Chef at Granor Farm and author of the cookbooks *Pulp*, *Ruffage*, and *Grist*

"In the era of influencers, educating food lovers and guiding people to delicious food is almost a lost art. My buddy Kevin Pang is the last of a dying breed, and I've been trusting his knowledge and palate for years. I'm here to tell you, you should too! A Very Chinese Cookbook is Kevin and Jeffrey Pang's guide to understanding the wonderful world of Chinese cuisine. Through their expert eyes, experienced taste buds and thoughtful techniques, our horizons will expand and our bellies win!"

— **Alvin Cailan**
Chef, author of *Amboy: Recipes from the Filipino-American Dream*, host of *The Burger Show*

"I judge a cookbook by what I end up doing after looking through it. Usually I smile at the impossibly perfect photos and put it back on the shelf. Sometimes, I mark a few pages, thinking I'll try one of those recipes, someday. With A Very Chinese Cookbook from Kevin and Jeffrey Pang, I immediately started researching where I could get ingredients and tools, not to mention a very expensive rice cooker I suddenly realized I needed. My only frustration with this funny, useful, and heartwarming book of food and life is that I can't order up a father like Jeffrey to argue with, cook with, and learn from. Get on it, Etsy."

— **Peter Sagal**
Host of NPR's *Wait Wait . . . Don't Tell Me!*

A VERY Chinese COOKBOOK

100 Recipes from China & Not China

(but still really Chinese)

with Kevin Pang & Jeffrey Pang

AMERICA'S TEST KITCHEN

CONTENTS

Library of Congress Cataloging-in-Publication Data has been applied for.

ISBN 978-1-954210-47-9

— AMERICA'S —
TEST KITCHEN

AMERICA'S TEST KITCHEN
21 Drydock Avenue, Boston, MA 02210

Printed in Canada
10 9 8 7 6 5 4 3 2 1

Distributed by Penguin Random House Publisher Services
Tel: 800.733.3000

Pictured on front cover: **Shu Mai (page 107)**

Pictured on back cover (clockwise from top left): **Three-Cup Chicken (page 173), Taiwanese Pork Rice Bowl (page 188), Salt and Pepper Squid (page 302), Rice Cooker Chicken Rice (page 143), Hong Kong–Style Wonton Noodle Soup (page 90), Sesame Balls (page 60)**

Book Design & Art Direction by **Katie Barranger**
Photography by **Kevin White**
Food Styling by **Ashley Moore**
Image Processing by **Amanda Yong**

Editorial Director, Books: **Adam Kowit**

Executive Food Editor: **Dan Zuccarello**

Deputy Food Editor: **Leah Colins**

Executive Managing Editor: **Debra Hudak**

Senior Editors: **Camila Chaparro, Joseph Gitter, and Lan Lam**

Test Cooks: **Olivia Counter, Carmen Dongo, Hannah Fenton, Hisham Hassan, Laila Ibrahim, José Maldonado, Kelly Song, Faye Yang, and David Yu**

Design Director: **Lindsey Timko Chandler**

Art Director: **Katie Barranger**

Associate Art Director: **Molly Gillespie**

Photography Director: **Julie Bozzo Cote**

Senior Photography Producer: **Meredith Mulcahy**

Featured Photographer: **Kevin White**

Contributing Photographers: **Beth Fuller, Joseph Keller, Steve Klise, Carl Tremblay, and Daniel J. van Ackere**

Featured Food Stylist: **Ashley Moore**

Contributing Food Stylists: **Sāsha Coleman, Joy Howard, Catrine Kelty, Chantal Lambeth, Marie Piraino, Elle Simone Scott, and Kendra Smith**

Illustrations: **Jay Layman**

Project Manager, Publishing Operations: **Katie Kimmerer**

Senior Print Production Specialist: **Lauren Robbins**

Production and Imaging Coordinator: **Amanda Yong**

Production and Imaging Specialists: **Tricia Neumyer and Dennis Noble**

Copy Editor: **Jeffrey Schier**

Proofreader: **Ann-Marie Imbornoni**

Language Consultant: **Carolyn Phillips**

Indexer: **Elizabeth Parson**

Chief Creative Officer: **Jack Bishop**

Executive Editorial Directors: **Julia Collin Davison and Bridget Lancaster**

Watch *Hunger Pangs* on YouTube by scanning here

About the Authors

Kevin Pang is the Editorial Director of Digital at America's Test Kitchen. A James Beard Award winner and a five-time finalist, Kevin has contributed to *The New York Times*, *Vanity Fair*, *Esquire*, and was a longtime staffer at the *Chicago Tribune*. He is the co-director of the documentary *For Grace*, which premiered at South by Southwest Film Festival in 2015 and was acquired by Netflix. He lives with his wife and son in Chicago.

Jeffrey Pang is a retired businessman and cooking enthusiast. His YouTube cooking channel became an unexpected hit and was featured in *The New York Times Magazine* in 2016. He's now the co-host of *Hunger Pangs* for America's Test Kitchen. Jeffrey lives with his wife Catherine in Seattle.

What Makes America's Test Kitchen Different

The recipes in this book have been tested and edited by the folks at America's Test Kitchen, where curious cooks become confident cooks. Located in Boston's Seaport District in the Innovation and Design Building, it features 15,000 square feet of kitchen space, including multiple photography and video studios. It is the home of *Cook's Illustrated* magazine and *Cook's Country* magazine and is the workday destination for more than 60 test cooks, editors, and cookware specialists. Our mission is to empower and inspire confidence, community, and creativity in the kitchen.

We start the process of testing a recipe with a complete lack of preconceptions, which means that we accept no claim, no technique, and no recipe at face value. We simply assemble as many variations as possible, test a half-dozen of the most promising, and taste the results blind. We then construct our own recipe and continue to test it, varying ingredients, techniques, and cooking times, until we reach a consensus. As we like to say in the test kitchen, "We make the mistakes so you don't have to." The result, we hope, is the best version of a particular recipe, but we realize that only you can be the final judge of our success (or failure). We use the same rigorous approach when we test equipment and taste ingredients.

All of this would not be possible without a belief that good cooking, much like good music, is based on a foundation of objective technique. Some people like spicy foods while others don't, but there are measurable scientific principles involved in producing perfectly poached chicken, deep-fried shrimp, and stable beaten egg whites. Our ultimate goal is to investigate the fundamental principles of cooking to give you the techniques, tools, and ingredients you need to become a better cook. It is as simple as that.

Making *A Very Chinese Cookbook* took one year and a team of a dozen recipe developers (see page 6), plus these special folks: The editors on this project were Adam Kowit, Dan Zuccarello, and Leah Colins; Katie Barranger and Lindsey Chandler were the art directors, responsible for the design and look of this book; and food stylist Ashley Moore and photographer Kevin White made the food look good enough to eat off the page. The progenitor of this cookbook is the YouTube cooking series *Hunger Pangs*— Erik Freitas, Christie Morrison, and Simon Savelyev are the producers who brought the show to light.

The majority of recipes within were newly created just for this book. A handful of recipes first appeared in the pages of *Cook's Illustrated* and *Cook's Country* magazines, and some of those were updated to reflect current cooking techniques and ingredient availability (e.g., a few older recipes that originally called for molasses were developed at a time when dark soy sauce wasn't widely available). What were once hard-to-source ingredients are now just a two-day delivery away, and we've approached the development of these recipes accordingly, with minimal compromise in service of maximal deliciousness.

We understand that if you're not familiar with Chinese cooking, it can seem intimidating. Picking up this book is half the battle, and we're grateful you did. To make the recipes more accessible, we've included a 1- to- 4 difficulty scale with every dish. In "Meet the Kitchen Team" a few pages down, we'll reveal our staff picks for the dishes our team members suggest you cook first.

Finding certain ingredients can be a challenge, especially if the translation on the label is inadequate (it happens more often than you'd think). We suggest bringing this book with you and pointing out the corresponding Chinese characters to a friendly store clerk. Speaking of translation, a word about our approach: The characters are in traditional Chinese, the written script used in Hong Kong and Taiwan. The romanized pronunciations are in Mandarin, the dialect spoken by 70 percent of the population in China. Special thanks to Carolyn Phillips, a renowned Chinese cookbook author who was our language expert and consultant for this book.

Finally, a word about the dishes. The recipes in this book lean heavily toward the cooking traditions of Hong Kong, home to the Pangs before they immigrated to North America. Much of the American Chinese culinary canon is rooted in Cantonese cooking, so many dishes will be familiar. But we're also lucky that America's Test Kitchen employs a number of Chinese-speaking test cooks; their families come from Sichuan, Beijing, and Taiwan. You'll find their recipes and stories represented in this book, too.

To see what goes on behind the scenes at America's Test Kitchen, check out our social media channels for kitchen snapshots, exclusive content, video tips, and much more. You can watch us work (in our actual test kitchen) by tuning in to *America's Test Kitchen* or *Cook's Country* on public television or on our websites.

Listen to *Proof* (AmericasTestKitchen.com/podcasts), our flagship podcast, hosted by Kevin Pang, to hear engaging stories about people and food. Want to hone your cooking skills or finally learn how to bake—with an America's Test Kitchen test cook? Enroll in one of our online cooking classes. However you choose to visit us, we welcome you into our kitchen.

facebook.com/AmericasTestKitchen
instagram.com/TestKitchen
youtube.com/AmericasTestKitchen
tiktok.com/@TestKitchen
twitter.com/TestKitchen
pinterest.com/TestKitchen

AmericasTestKitchen.com
CooksIllustrated.com
CooksCountry.com
OnlineCookingSchool.com

Join Our Community of Recipe Testers
Our recipe testers provide valuable feedback on recipes under development by ensuring that they are foolproof in home kitchens. Help us investigate the hows and whys behind successful recipes from your home kitchen.

Thank you for reading all the way to the end of this introduction. You're among the 0.002 percent of people who do! To reward you for your diligence, we've tucked in this food joke as an Easter egg: What's the heaviest dumpling in the world? Won-ton.

GETTING STARTED

Before we embark on our Chinese cooking adventure, let's familiarize ourselves with some foundational ingredients, techniques, and equipment. Yes, there are 6,000 years of culinary tradition to cover, but we'll keep it breezy! Plus, we'll tell you the unlikely story of how this book came to be, and we'll introduce you to the team responsible for the very delicious recipes to come.

What This Is

Have you ever had a belligerent, arms-flailing, slam-the-door, screaming argument with your family? This cookbook is the product of that. It began with two headstrong Pangs coming to verbal blows every other week—the son, Kevin, desperately trying to fit into America; the father, Jeffrey, hanging on to his Chinese identity. There was a lack of communication. Matters lost in translation. Cultures clashing and tempers flaring. A tale as old as time for countless immigrant families.

Then the son became a food writer and found himself calling his dad often about how to make certain dishes. On his own the father had created a YouTube cooking channel of his Chinese recipes, and those videos took off. Then the son wrote a story about this for the *New York Times Magazine* (that story appears next page). The realization came that food was their lingua franca, something they could talk about without getting into verbal fisticuffs. And when the son got a job at America's Test Kitchen, he asked his father—his bickering dance partner— if he'd consider making a Chinese cooking show together.

It began with fighting. It ends with this cookbook in your hands.

Enough writing in the third person. The reason this book exists is we—Kevin and Jeffrey—don't want to lose the recipes within. Recipes are family photos, camcorder tapes, and faded postcards—years from now they're evidence we ever existed. When we cook these dishes, the past comes alive, like pressing "Play" on a home video from Christmas 1992.

Many of these recipes traveled with us in a dog-eared and tattered spiral notepad when our family emigrated from Hong Kong in 1988. We want you to experience the thrills of waking up to a hot mug of Hong Kong–style milk tea accompanied with toast slathered in butter and condensed milk. We want you to feel the succulent highs of soy sauce–poached chicken and the crispy comforts of scallion pancakes. We want to share our secrets of fried rice and pot stickers with you.

This book is our loving homage to Chinese cooking, an out-growth of *Hunger Pangs*, our YouTube series. *A Very Chinese Cookbook* is not intended to be comprehensive. It's just not possible, unless you want to lug around a 3,000-page tome.

Instead, we focus on our favorite dishes, many of which reflect our Cantonese heritage. You'll also find the food of Beijing noodle stalls, Shanghai dumpling houses, and American Chinese joints. All the recipes in this book were rigorously developed by a dozen of the finest staffers at America's Test Kitchen, spending on average nearly $11,000 to create each dish (that includes refining our Pang family recipes). We researched, cooked, taste-tested as a group, and went back to the drawing board, over and over, until we were satisfied with each recipe. As for the Pangs, the two of us talked on the phone practically every day, conferring on our notes for this book. The storm clouds began to lift.

The making of this book over the course of a dream year was like no other experience. The two of us, along with Catherine (editor's note: Jeffrey's wife/Kevin's mom), tasted dish after dish that always seemed to elicit a strong emotion. This wasn't some carbon paper triplicate version of our taste memories. The test cooks had astonishingly lifted Cheung Hing Coffee Shop in Hong Kong and Taihuang Chicken in Shanghai off their foundations and plopped them right into America's Test Kitchen's Boston headquarters. Our pasts had come alive.

We could replay in our minds the moments we experienced while working with our test kitchen colleagues to develop the recipes: everyone plucking a morsel of crispy chicken from David Yu's Dry Chili Chicken and gasping at its deliciousness; Joe Gitter refusing to give up perfecting his soup dumplings, then nailing it on attempt 251; Camila Chaparro tweaking dough hydration levels five percentage points at a time for the Shanghai Pan-Fried Pork Buns; folding har gow alongside Lan Lam; Faye Yang telling us how proud her parents were of her Taiwanese beef noodle soup recipe.

On and on we could go. But one memory throughout the making of this improbable book stands out most:

The two of us never fought once.

— Kevin + Jeffrey

My Father, the YouTube Star

By Kevin Pang

The first few emails were marked "Fwd: Jeffrey Pang sent you a video," so I ignored them. Statistics were on my side: In the history of parental email forwards, roughly 0.001 percent have been worth opening.

Later he followed up by phone. I told him I hadn't found time to watch whatever it was he sent. Several seconds of silence hung between us before my dad replied: "Oh."

This is how it had gone for 30-some years—a father-son relationship kept cordial and indifferent through habit and physical distance. I live in Chicago; he's in Seattle. Once a week, we'd talk on the phone for five minutes and exchange the least substantive of pleasantries: "How's the weather?" "Plans this weekend?" Not a meaningful conversation so much as a scripted set of talking points.

Only when my mom nudged did I open the video Dad had sent.

Fade in: the company logo for Creative Production, with the E-A-T in "Creative" highlighted. Cue soft piano melody, the type of royalty-free soundtrack that sounds like the hold Muzak when you call your dermatologist. Dissolve to title screen: "Catherine Mom's Shanghainese Green Onion Pancake," with its translation in Chinese. And then a photo of my mother (Catherine) and my grandma. A shot of our white kitchen island, and my mother's hands, her unmistakable wedding band, digging into and massaging wet dough. My virulently anti-technology Chinese parents were starring in their own internet cooking show.

Then one video turned into a few dozen, and now, somehow, my retired, 65-year-old father has nearly a million views on his YouTube channel.

As a child who immigrated from Hong Kong, I was raised as an American during the day and Chinese after school. I brought home Western ideas that confounded my parents: sarcasm, irony, recalcitrance. My father and I argued all the time. The grievances were usually benign, but they would erupt into battles between two headstrong males, each standing his cultural ground. It didn't help that I stubbornly refused to speak Cantonese at home. Or when, during college, I went home for Thanksgiving with newly bleached blond hair. My dad was apoplectic, screaming the moment he saw me in the driveway, accusing me of being ashamed of my Chinese heritage.

Our differences would burn hot, then smolder, then fizzle to a détente. Eventually we would acknowledge each other, and everything would stay cool until the next flare-up. Our relationship reached a plateau of cordial indifference: We lived 2,000 miles apart and talked on the phone once a week about nothing important at all.

But something changed in our relationship the day I switched jobs. I was working as a metro news reporter at the *Chicago Tribune* when I was offered a position on the paper's food writing staff. I had zero experience, but I did have one advantage: I was Cantonese. We Cantonese have a love of eating that borders on mania. Our people eat every part of almost every animal; we were the original snout-to-tail diners, long before hipsters hijacked the term. Hong Kong, where I lived until age 6, is a place where instead of asking "How are you?" we greet one another with "Have you eaten yet?"

Food was my dad's obsession. He had always been a marvelous cook. He dreamed of being one of those Iron Chefs in white toques who enter Kitchen Stadium through dramatic fog. Much of the joy of Chinese food for him seemed nostalgic:

He always lamented his decision to leave his beloved Hong Kong, to come here, to a foreign land, for the sake of his children.

So when I became a food writer, my father and I shared, for the first time, a mutual interest. I would call to ask about recipes and cooking techniques. He would school me on the world of Cantonese cuisine. The first time he visited me in Chicago, I took him to a dim sum restaurant for brunch, and as we ate shrimp dumplings and barbecued pork buns, he explained—gesticulating with his arms like a conductor—how the shiu mai's wrapper should caress its filling "like a dress on a woman, like petals of a flower, like prongs on a diamond ring." I had never heard him speak with such enthusiasm or eloquence. My father never taught me to swim, or to ride a bike, but he did teach me how to tell a good dim sum restaurant from a great one.

Food became something I could use to engage him and repair our relationship. When we talked on the phone about how to wrap Shanghai water dumplings or braise dong po rou pork belly, 30 minutes would fly by. Then, when the subject turned to anything else: "How's the weather? Plans this weekend? O.K., goodbye."

It's not doing "Carpool Karaoke" numbers or landing guest appearances by Michelle Obama, but the relative success of my dad's cooking videos has been, for me, almost unbelievable. Most people would kill to have these viewer metrics. The videos are earnest and adorably cheese-ball, bearing the production tropes of '80s VHS: There are spinning wipe effects, gratuitous zooms, saccharine background music.

His most-watched recipe, with nearly a quarter-million views, is for Chinkiang-style pork ribs. I remember eating these when I was growing up. He would use a cleaver to chop spareribs into two-bite cubes, wok-fry them, then sauce them with a viscous glaze of Chinese black vinegar. The result was fatty and sticky and crisp, and I would slurp the meat clean off the bone in one motion. Watching through nearly two dozen more videos, I realized every single dish had been served in my childhood home. Macau-style Portuguese chicken. Pan-fried turnip cake. Sweet-and-sour pork. This time, the wave of nostalgia washed over *me*: I was 12 again, sitting at the kitchen table, my family's mouths too preoccupied to squabble.

My dad makes enough in each month's ad revenues to take my mom out for a nice lunch. Making the clips is a lot of work. The two of them test each recipe a half-dozen times before committing it to film. Dad is behind the camera and editing the footage; it's usually my mom's hands demonstrating. They don't speak in the videos. They say they're embarrassed by their spoken English and feel more comfortable using onscreen text, in Chinese and English, for instruction. Writing and translating this adds several more hours of work.

"Why?" I asked during one of our weekly phone conversations. "Do you want a show on the Food Network or something?"

"You really want to know?" my dad asked in Chinese. "Your mom's great-grandmother used to cook amazing Shanghainese food for her. She would dream about it. But when your mom was finally old enough to ask for the recipes, her great-grandmother had already developed dementia. She couldn't even remember cooking those dishes. The only thing your mom had left was the memory of her taste. We're afraid that if you wanted to eat your childhood dishes, and one day we're both no longer around, you wouldn't know how to cook it."

"You know," he added, "you can be pretty uncommunicative."

Neither of us is likely to have the courage to sit down and hash out years of father-son strife; we're both too stubborn, and verbalizing our emotions would leave us squirming. I even waited until the last minute to send him a draft of this story, and waited nervously for the response. Soon enough, a reply arrived:

—

Hi Kevin,

This is a good and true story. Thank you. Call me sometime.

Dad

MEET THE KITCHEN TEAM

Say hello to the cast of characters responsible for creating, testing, and refining most of the recipes in this book. They're all superheroes who wear aprons for capes. We asked them each two questions:

Q1 *WHICH RECIPE ARE YOU PROUDEST TO HAVE WORKED ON?*

Q2 *WHICH RECIPE SHOULD SOMEONE PICKING UP THIS COOKBOOK TRY FIRST?*

Leah Colins, *Deputy Food Editor, Books*
A1 **Radish Cake (page 276):** "It was so much fun fine-tuning the ingredients, ratios, and techniques."
A2 **Sesame Noodles (page 144):** "Simple and quick to put together, and incredibly satisfying."

Dan Zuccarello,
Executive Food Editor, Books
A1 **Shanghai Soup Dumplings (page 117):** "Refining the shaping instructions for these dumplings was a rewarding challenge."
A2 **Stir-Fried Tender Greens with Garlic (page 209):** "A simple cooking technique yields perfect greens every time."

David Yu, *Test Cook, Books*
A1 **Sesame Balls (page 60):** "The balls come out so beautifully golden, and their texture is such a treat."
A2 **Taiwanese Pork Rice Bowl (page 188):** "This classic Taiwanese dish will definitely become a staple in my repertoire!"

Faye Yang,
Photo Test Cook, Cook's Country
A1 **Youtiao (page 346):** "I never thought I would be able to tackle such an iconic breakfast staple."
A2 **Condensed Milk Toast (page 333):** "An insanely delicious combination that almost everyone has in their pantry at home!"

Camila Chaparro, *Senior Editor, Books*
A1 **Shanghai Pan-Fried Pork Buns (page 123):** "For all their delicious textures in one bite: fluffy, bready, crispy, meaty, and juicy!"
A2 **Beef Ho Fun (page 156):** "I love the contrast of the chewy noodles, still-crisp onions, and tender beef."

Carmen Dongo, *Test Cook, Books*
A1 **Red-Braised Pork Belly (page 316):** "Serves up an abundance of luscious flavor and plenty of melt-in-your-mouth texture."
A2 **Sichuan Hot and Sour Potatoes (page 229):** "I'm in love with the potato's crispy texture and the mala-acidic combination."

Kelly Song, *Test Cook, Cook's Country*
A1 **Twice-Cooked Pork (page 186):**
"An homage to my father, who taught me the magic of this spicy, tantalizing dish. Thank you bàba!"
A2 **Winter Melon Soup with Meatballs (page 80):** "A simple bowl of comfort featuring my all-time favorite vegetable."

Joe Gitter, *Senior Editor, Books*
A1 **Shanghai Soup Dumplings (page 117):**
"For the sheer moment of joy when you burst one and out floods that supersavory broth."
A2 **Dry Chili Chicken (page 282):**
"You learn so much about making incredibly tasty and crispy fried chicken."

Hannah Fenton, *Test Cook, Books*
A1 **Egg Tarts (page 350):** "It was so fun making these quintessential Chinese bakery treats accessible to home cooks."
A2 **Spicy Cold Tofu (page 238):** "This dish solidified my love for tofu."

José Maldonado, *Test Cook, Books*
A1 **Homemade Tofu (page 234):**
"Incredibly gratifying making it from scratch, and it's surprisingly simple to do."
A2 **Mapo Tofu (page 240):** "Hooked since first bite, and it's left me longing for more."

Hisham Hassan, *Test Cook, Books*
A1 **Hakka Stuffed Tofu with Egg Dumplings (page 264):** "Such a great experience learning this dish from Jeffrey."
A2 **Salted Egg Fried Shrimp (page 300):**
"It's simply addicting!"

Olivia Counter, *Test Cook, Books*
A1 **Shu Mai (page 107):** "It was satisfying to learn this dim sum staple. I've never eaten less than five at once!"
A2 **Honey-Walnut Shrimp (page 258):**
"You'll obsess over the decadence of this recipe!"

Lan Lam, *Senior Editor, Cook's Illustrated*
A1 **Har Gow (page 112):** "Making these dumplings is almost as fun and satisfying as eating them."
A2 **Simple Fried Rice (page 133):**
"This tasty, easy, and versatile dish is a staple of my dinner rotation."

Laila Ibrahim, *Test Cook, Books*
A1 **Steamed Egg Custard with Ground Pork (page 260):** "It's simple and visually striking, as beautiful as it is delicious."
A2 **Beef Ho Fun (page 156):** "This Hong Kong staple is the perfect introduction to a stir-fried noodle dish. Plus, the chewy texture of the rice noodles is superfun!"

The Ingredients You Want

THE BASICS OF RICE

We kick off this book with a section on rice. This was not up for debate. The significance of rice to the Chinese—historically, culturally, practically—can't be overstated. We eat it for lunch and dinner, sometimes breakfast. (We're using "we" loosely; the northern Chinese diet is more wheat-based.) When referencing white rice in this book, we're talking mostly about long- or medium-grain varieties. Although nuances in texture and flavor abound depending on a rice's origin, these are the key aspects to keep in mind.

What makes rice sticky or fluffy? The texture of cooked rice depends on the rice's ratio of two starches, amylose and amylopectin. When rice cooks, it releases both starches onto the surfaces of the grains. Short-grain and glutinous types of rice contain high amounts of amylopectin, a bushy-shaped molecule with many branches that adhere to each other, causing grains to stick like Velcro. Long-grain types of rice, such as jasmine, contain more amylose, which is a straight chain rather than a sticky branching molecule; these grains cook up firm, fluffy, and distinct.

Chánglìmǐ 長粒米
Long-Grain Rice: Among the types of long-grain rice, jasmine rice is a staple in southeast regions of China, so you will often see it called for in the Cantonese recipes in this book. Praised for its delicate floral and buttery scent, it cooks up relatively soft and sticky compared with other long-grain varieties, though it maintains a slightly firm chew. It's classic in Clay Pot Chicken Rice (page 141). Day-old jasmine rice makes exceptional fried rice (page 133).

Zhōnglìmǐ 中粒米
Medium-Grain Rice: Shorter and squatter than long-grain rice, medium-grain rice is tender, with grains that clump together. Within this broad category we will focus primarily on Calrose, a variety grown predominantly in California, because it is an ideal rice for scooping up with your chopsticks to enjoy with stir-fried or braised dishes.

Duǎnlìmǐ 短粒米
Short-Grain Rice: With opaque, almost round grains, short-grain rice is softer and stickier than long- or medium-grain rice thanks to low amylose and high amylopectin. It's often sold as sushi rice (though many types of medium-grain rice have that label as well). Short-grain is the preferred rice in Taiwan and is traditional in Taiwanese Pork Rice Bowl (page 188).

Nuòmǐ 糯米
Glutinous Rice: Also called sticky rice or sweet rice (though it isn't sweet), glutinous rice is very low in amylose and high in amylopectin, making it quite sticky when cooked. There are myriad varieties of glutinous rice and both savory and sweet preparations. We use short-grain glutinous rice to make Stir-Fried Sticky Rice (page 272).

How Long Does Rice Last, Anyway?
Raw white rice will last in your pantry for at least one year. Rather than an expiration date, rice has a "best before" date. If you don't use it by this date, the rice might still be safe to eat although its flavor and smell may change. Cooked rice should be left at room temperature for no more than an hour and refrigerated for no longer than three to four days to prevent harmful bacterial growth.

ALL ABOUT NOODLES

The world of noodles within Chinese cooking is vast and, honestly, a bit dizzying. Within any given variety of noodles, such as egg, wheat, or rice, you'll have several options to consider: fresh or dried, thick or thin, round or flat. The good news is that despite our specific preferences for most dishes, we've rarely met a noodle we didn't like, and most recipes can accommodate several choices.

To help simplify shopping, we first focus on two main noodle characteristics: variety (wheat, egg, rice, or mung bean) and style (fresh or dried). From there we choose a shape. For our purposes, we consider thin noodles to be less than ⅛ inch wide and thick noodles to be greater than ⅛ inch wide. For many of the book's recipes we seek out the chewy texture of fresh noodles, but have found that substituting 12 ounces of a similarly shaped dried noodle for 1 pound of fresh noodles will work just fine. You can find fresh noodles in the refrigerator or freezer section of a Chinese or other market; thaw frozen noodles either in the refrigerator for 24 hours or on the counter for 30 minutes to 1 hour.

Miàntiáo 麵條
Wheat Noodles: Though humble in construction (just water and flour), these are heavy hitters. Distinguished by their pale color in comparison with egg noodles, plain wheat noodles come in a range of thicknesses and can be round or flat. They're sometimes labeled Shanghai-style, but we'll refer to them as white wheat noodles. Thin wheat noodles are ideal for Sesame Noodles (page 144), while chewy thick wheat noodles are used for Dan Dan Mian (page 150). One recipe where dried flat noodles (寬麵條) are traditional is Taiwanese Beef Noodle Soup (page 166).

Jīdànmiàn 雞蛋麵
Egg Noodles: Egg yolks give these wheat noodles their rich yellow color and flavor. We use two main styles of egg noodle: thin, ribbon-like wonton noodles (雲吞幼麵), which are excellent in Hong Kong–Style Wonton Noodle Soup (page 90), and thicker lo mein noodles (撈麵), which are ideal for stir-frying, such as for Pork Stir-Fried Noodles (page 152).

Mǐfěn 米粉
Rice Noodles: Dried Chinese rice noodles are available in several thicknesses. We use delicate thin-stranded mei fun (细米粉), often labeled rice vermicelli, to make Singapore Noodles (page 158). Mei fun is typically packaged in blocks; if you are buying a package labeled rice vermicelli, look for a Chinese brand, as these noodles are thicker than other varieties. Given their brittle nature it's best to soak the noodles in hot water to soften before using. Many Chinese markets also carry ho fun noodles (新鮮河粉). These chewy, fresh, wide rice noodles are the key to preparing Beef Ho Fun (page 156). They are sold presteamed in bags and don't need to be boiled or soaked before cooking. You'll also find rice roll noodles: flat sheets of ho fun rolled up like an area rug.

Soaking mei fun: After soaking mei fun in hot water until just tender, drain the noodles and transfer them to a greased wire rack set in a rimmed baking sheet.

Niángāo 年糕
Rice Cakes: Rice cakes come in a variety of shapes, though we most often use the thinly sliced, oval-shaped ones. They have an appealing chewy consistency and are excellent for stir-frying. They can be found fresh (refrigerated), frozen, or dried. We prefer the convenience of cooking with fresh or thawed frozen rice cakes, as they do not require any pretreatment before stir-frying.

Fěnsī 粉絲
Mung Bean Noodles: Made from mung bean starch, these translucent delicate noodles go by several names, including bean thread, cellophane, and glass noodles. (The latter two terms can also refer to noodles made from other starches, including potato, sweet potato, and tapioca.) Mung bean noodles soak up flavor from soups such as Winter Melon Soup with Meatballs (page 80), and add chewy texture to the fillings for spring rolls and egg rolls (pages 56 and 53).

Rice
Cakes

Rice Roll
Noodles

Ho Fun
Noodles

Lo Mein
Noodles

Wonton
Noodles

Thick Wheat
Noodles

Thin Wheat
Noodles

拉麵 (寬條)
Dry Noodles
Nouilles sèches (wide)

EXP.NOV/092024

g / 4LB

PRODUCT OF TAIWAN
PRODUIT DE TAIWAN
台灣製造

Wide Wheat
Noodles

NO PRESERVATIVES

SHANXI NOODLES

TOTAL NET WEIGHT: 2.5LBS/40oz/113

SINCLAIR FOODS CORPORATION

PRODUCT OF TAIWAN
PRODUIT DE TAIWAN

Mei Fun
(Rice Vermicelli)

WAI
WAI

健力

足旦系皮

江门排粉

RICE STIC

RICE VERMICELLI

Mung Bean
Noodles

WRAPPERS

The following wrappers are all sold fresh and can be found in the refrigerator or freezer section of the market. Thaw frozen wrappers either in the refrigerator for 24 hours or on the counter for 30 minutes to 1 hour.

Chūnjuǎnpí 春卷皮
Spring Roll Wrappers: These thin, square sheets, sometimes labeled spring roll pastry, skins, or shells, are crucial to creating the crisp, delicate exterior of a great spring roll (page 56). You want 8-inch square wheat-flour wrappers, not the Vietnamese-style translucent circular wrappers (both can be labeled "spring roll wrappers").

Měishì Chūnjuǎnpí 美式春卷皮
Egg Roll Wrappers: These 8-inch square wrappers are thicker than spring roll wrappers and contain egg in the dough, which leads to a crunchy, hearty shell that forms distinct surface bubbles once fried.

Yúntūnpí 雲吞皮
Wonton Wrappers: Also called wonton skins, wonton wrappers typically come in two varieties—egg (often labeled "Hong Kong–Style") and wheat—and are distinguished by their square shape and noticeably thinner structure compared with dumpling wrappers. Once cooked, they have a smoother, silkier mouthfeel than dumpling wrappers do.

Shuǐjiǎopí 水餃皮
Dumpling Wrappers: Dumpling wrappers also come in egg and wheat varieties but are distinguished by their round shape. While we will reach for these in a pinch, there is simply no replacement for homemade dumpling wrappers. We strongly encourage you to make your own using the recipe on page 95.

Egg Roll Wrappers

Spring Roll Wrappers

Wonton Wrappers

Dumpling Wrappers

Test Kitchen Tip

Recipe developer Joe Gitter notes: "Store-bought dumpling and wonton wrappers come tightly packed, and each must be individually peeled away from the stack. To save time when shaping dumplings, I like to separate the wrappers ahead of time, then restack and cover them with a dish towel. This helps the dumpling shaping go more expeditiously."

STARCHES AND SWEETENERS

Various starches and sweeteners each contribute their unique characteristics to the dishes in this book, whether you're looking for shattering crispiness or elastic chew. Buy them as you need them.

Tàibáifěn 太白粉
Cornstarch: The universal pantry starch is a thickener for sauces as well as a coating for meat, poultry, and fish—either to absorb moisture and encourage sauces to cling, or to create a velvety texture while stir-frying. It is also vital in coatings and batters used in frying, as it encourages browning and crispness.

Túdòufěn 土豆粉
Potato Starch: Used in similar ways as cornstarch, it is particularly good at creating a shatteringly crisp coating on fried items such as Beijing-Style Sweet and Sour Pork (page 290). Do not confuse it with potato flour.

Dìguāfěn 地瓜粉
Coarse Sweet Potato Starch: The coating of choice for many fried foods in Taiwan, coarse (sometimes labeled "thick") sweet potato starch fries up supercrisp thanks to coarser granules that are all of a slightly different size, making it ideal for achieving an exceptionally crisp, popcorn ceiling–like crust on Taiwanese Fried Pork Chops (page 292).

Mùshǔfěn 木薯粉
Tapioca Starch: This starch provides chew, elasticity, and structure to doughs such as the dumpling skins for Har Gow (page 112). Tapioca starch is sometimes labeled tapioca flour even though it is a pure starch.

Chéngfěn 澄粉
Wheat Starch: Containing minimal gluten, it is beneficial in creating soft, tender wrappers for har gow.

Zhǎnmǐfěn 粘米粉
Rice Flour: With a neutral flavor, light color, and somewhat sandy texture, rice flour is a good choice for creating a light and crisp coating for fried food, or for binding together filling. It's integral to the squishy, chewy texture in Radish Cake (page 276).

Nuòmǐfěn 糯米粉
Glutinous Rice Flour: High (98 percent) in amylopectin, the starch that makes rice sticky, this flour is key to achieving the chewy, elastic texture in Sesame Balls (page 60) and other desserts. It is sometimes labeled sweet rice flour or sticky rice flour.

Bīngtáng 冰糖
Rock Sugar: This is commonly used in Chinese cooking as a sweetener and to add shine to braised dishes such as Three-Cup Chicken (page 173) and Taiwanese Pork Rice Bowl (page 188). Flavor-wise, think granulated sugar with the roundness of honey. Although refined rock sugar, which is whiter and more translucent, is available, we use the less-refined versions, which have a golden hue. Because it is typically sold as irregular lumps, we recommend lightly crushing the rock sugar for easier measuring and quicker melting in the wok. You can substitute an equal amount of granulated sugar by weight for rock sugar if necessary.

Crushing rock sugar: Use a meat pounder or the side of a cleaver to lightly crush the sugar into small pieces that are easy to measure.

Màiyátáng 麥芽糖
Maltose: This thick, maddeningly sticky syrup with mild sweetness is produced from fermented barley or rice. It is used for roasting meats and creates a glossy glaze and hint of sweetness in dishes such as Char Siu (page 321) and Roast Duck (page 314). Honey can be used in place of maltose with similar results.

A Very Basic Chinese Pantry

Yes, there are a lot of ingredients listed in this chapter, but you won't need to take out a second mortgage to stock up your pantry. The bare minimum: Pick up light and dark soy sauce, Shaoxing wine, black vinegar, toasted sesame oil, five-spice powder, jasmine rice, dried Sichuan chiles, doubanjiang, cornstarch, and peanut oil. Have good chicken broth and chili oil on hand, too.

OILS, VINEGARS, COOKING WINES, AND BROTH

OILS

Càiyóu 菜油

Vegetable Oil: Neutral oils such as vegetable oil, canola oil, and grapeseed oil are good choices for stir-frying. While peanut is our preferred frying oil, vegetable oil is also a good option for shallow frying and for deep frying at temperatures below 400 degrees.

Huāshēngyóu 花生油

Peanut Oil: Refined peanut oil is the gold-standard for frying. Thanks to its relatively high smoking point (around 450 degrees), it can withstand periods of high heat without breaking down. We recommend it throughout the book but especially when frying at temperatures above 400 degrees.

Máyóu 麻油

Toasted Sesame Oil: Not for cooking, this fragrant oil, made from toasted sesame seeds, is a finishing oil for stir-fries, sauces, and dressings. Store it in the refrigerator to keep it from becoming rancid.

VINEGARS

Báimǐcù 白米醋

White Rice Vinegar: Also known as rice wine vinegar, it has a characteristic "malty" sweetness and mild acidity. While some rice vinegars come seasoned with sugar and salt, Chinese rice vinegar is always unseasoned.

Hēicù 黑醋

Black Vinegar: Of several black vinegars produced in China, the most widely available is popularly known as Chinkiang vinegar, a romanization of Zhenjiang, where it's made from rice and wheat bran as well as salt and sugar. Black vinegar brings earthy, complex flavors with hints of warm spice. It is used in dipping sauces and for braising meat. Balsamic and malt vinegars are (borderline) acceptable substitutes, though both lack Chinese black vinegar's complexity.

Hóngcù 红醋

Red Vinegar: Ranging from a pale red to a dark brownish-red, this vinegar has mild acidic flavor with a hint of sweetness. It is a favorite dipping sauce for dumplings and a finishing vinegar for Hong Kong–Style Wonton Noodle Soup (page 90).

COOKING WINE

Shàoxīngjiǔ 紹興酒

Shaoxing Wine: A staple in Chinese cooking, this amber-colored specialty of Zhejiang Province contributes distinctive nutty flavors to food. It's used in everything from marinades to stir-frying sauces to braises. While drinking-quality Shaoxing wine has a more complex flavor, at a Chinese grocer you are likely to find Shaoxing cooking wine, which contains added salt and can also be used. Dry sherry is a good substitute.

Táiwān Mǐjiǔ 台灣米酒

Michiu (Taiwanese Rice Wine): A clear rice cooking wine, it is milder than Shaoxing. Shaoxing wine and sake are suitable substitutes.

Méiguìlùjiǔ 玫瑰露酒

Mei Kuei Lu Chiew (Rose Cooking Liquor): Also called rose cooking wine, this sweetened rose-infused liquor is key in roast meats such as Char Siu (page 321). Chinese markets sell inexpensive versions suited for cooking.

BROTH

Jīgāotāng 雞高湯

Chicken Broth: While European-style broth often has vegetal flavors, Chinese-style broth emphasizes chicken, with hints of scallion and ginger. To make your own, see page 25. If using store-bought, try Swanson Chicken Stock; it has a richer, meatier flavor than other broths. Avoid bouillon pastes, which can have more vegetal flavors and add unnecessary sweetness.

SAUCES, CONDIMENTS, AND PASTES

SAUCES

Shēngchóu 生抽
Light Soy Sauce: Chinese light soy sauce, or sheng chou ("fresh extraction"), is a versatile, all-purpose soy sauce with a floral aroma. This is what we are referring to throughout the book when calling for "soy sauce." The term "light" distinguishes this type of soy sauce from dark soy sauce and is not an indication of flavor or sodium content.

Lǎochóu 老抽
Dark Soy Sauce: Lao chou ("old extraction") is made from soybeans that have been fermented longer than those used to make light soy sauce, and it sometimes also contains sugar. It's darker, more viscous, and less salty than light soy sauce, with a flavor that's a bit sweet, roasty, and wine-like. Given its concentrated flavor and dark hue, it is commonly used in marinades or to deepen the color of dishes such as Red-Braised Pork Belly (page 316) and Three-Cup Chicken (page 173).

Tiánjiàngyóu 甜醬油
Sweet Soy Sauce: Versions of sweet soy sauce exist across southern China and southeast Asia. Indonesian kecap manis, a sweet, glossy, viscous sauce, is particularly well known; we use ABC Brand as a dipping sauce for Hainanese Chicken Rice (page 307).

Háoyóu 蠔油
Oyster Sauce: A viscous briny-sweet seasoning integral to Chinese cuisine, oyster sauce is traditionally made by simmering oysters until caramelized, though more typically it's made from oyster extracts. The sauce adds salty tang and super-savory flavor to such dishes as Stir-Fried Beef and Gai Lan (page 184).

Hǎixiānjiàng 海鮮醬
Hoisin Sauce: A Cantonese staple, hoisin adds sweet and salty elements to stir-fries such as Pork Stir-Fried Noodles (page 152), as well as to meats, glazes, and sauces. Think of its flavor as a Chinese take on American barbecue sauce.

Huángdòujiàng 黃豆醬
Huangdoujiang (Soybean Sauce): Also called soybean paste, it has the savory qualities of other bean pastes but is distinguished by a thin yellow-brown sauce that contains floating whole and broken pieces of soybeans. It can be used to boost the savory flavor of a variety of stir-fries and braised dishes such as Zha Jiang Mian (page 154). You can also use ground bean sauce.

Sūméijiàng 蘇梅醬
Plum Sauce: This sauce is probably best known as a dipping sauce for spring rolls and egg rolls. Although its taste is mostly sweet, the pickled plums that are used to make it lend a slightly sour tang. Plum sauce is similar to "duck sauce," though the latter tends to be much more saccharine and less nuanced in flavor.

Choosing a Soy Sauce
Originating in China 2,000 years ago, soy sauce can be found in dozens of styles in many countries, and its flavor, aroma, and saltiness can vary. Chinese brands of light and dark soy sauce that we like include Pearl River Bridge and Lee Kum Kee. If you do use a soy sauce from Kikkoman (from Japan), the top-selling brand in the United States, know that it can be saltier than Chinese light soy sauce.

Oyster Sauces

Hoisin
Sauce

Light Soy Sauces   Dark
Soy Sauce   Sweet
Soy Sauce   Huangdoujiang
(Soybean Sauce)   Plum
Sauce

Tianmianjiang
(Sweet Wheat Paste)

Shrimp Paste

Sesame
Paste   Sweet Red
Bean Paste   Ganhuangjiang
(Dry Soybean Paste)   Doubanjiang
(Broad Bean Chile Paste)

PASTES

Májiàng 麻醬

Sesame Paste: A dark-brown paste from toasted sesame seeds, Chinese sesame paste is used to make flavorful dipping sauces and various noodle and salad dishes. It makes a rich, unctuous sauce for aptly named Sesame Noodles (page 144). Compared with tahini, Chinese sesame paste has a deeper toasted flavor that is distinctive.

Hóngdòuróng 紅豆蓉

Sweet Red Bean Paste: This sweetened paste made from adzuki beans is typically used as a filling in Chinese pastries and desserts, such as Sesame Balls (page 60).

Gānhuángjiàng 乾黃醬

Ganhuangjiang (Dry Soybean Paste): This fermented soybean paste is related to Japanese miso, though slightly coarser in texture and saltier. Fermentation breaks down the soybeans and creates complex, savory flavors that are beneficial to seasoning. Given the similarities, red miso is a good substitute.

Tiánmiànjiàng 甜麵醬

Tianmianjiang (Sweet Wheat Paste): This sweet, deeply flavorful sauce is used in northern Chinese cooking. Although it can also be labeled sweet soybean sauce or paste, its primary ingredient is fermented wheat (the ingredients should list wheat flour, sugar, and salt). We use it in Twice-Cooked Pork (page 186) and Zha Jiang Mian (page 154). Because of their similar flavors, hoisin is a decent substitute.

Dòubànjiàng 豆瓣醬

Doubanjiang (Broad Bean Chile Paste): An essential flavoring in Sichuan cuisine, this deep reddish-brown paste is made from red chiles, broad (fava) beans, salt, and wheat flour. It adds spicy, meaty depth to many dishes in this book, including Mapo Tofu (page 240). It's worth seeking out doubanjiang from the town of Pixian (look for Pixian on the label); bright red and chunkier than standard-fare doubanjiang, it has a more assertive and richer flavor.

Xiājiàng 蝦醬

Shrimp Paste: This pungent ingredient, also called shrimp sauce, is made from fermented shrimp that are then ground. Make sure to purchase Chinese shrimp paste, distinguished by its purplish-gray color, smooth texture, and assertive briny smell. Many Cantonese dishes, like Shrimp Paste Fried Chicken (page 254), rely on this ingredient for its distinctive flavor, beneficial in many applications when used sparingly. Let us repeat: *sparingly*.

Haam Choy

Yacai

Douchi (Fermented Black Beans)

Zhacai

A Very Intermediate Chinese Pantry

So you've procured the bare minimum for your starter Chinese pantry (page 14). Which ingredients to buy next? We suggest a package of dried wheat or rice noodles, hoisin and oyster sauce, Maggi seasoning, sesame seeds, star anise, chicken bouillon powder or MSG, dried shiitake mushrooms, whole Sichuan peppercorns, plus pickled mustard greens.

PRESERVES

Dòuchǐ 豆豉
Douchi (Fermented Black Beans): Salty, savory, and with a hint of funk to finish, fermented black soybeans add incredible depth of flavor to many dishes, including Twice-Cooked Pork (page 186) and Stir-Fried Clams with Black Bean Sauce (page 205). They are packed with a hefty amount of salt, so be sure to rinse before using.

PICKLED MUSTARD
Preserved mustard products represent a broad category of ingredients that all derive from the mustard plant. Each is distinguished by the variety of mustard plant used and the preparation method; the pickles can range in flavor, from tangy to funky and spicy to slightly sweet, as well as in appearance. In this book we use the three following types, though many more exist.

Yācài 芽菜
Yacai: Sometimes labeled suimiyacai 碎米芽菜 (meaning the vegetable has been chopped), it is made by sun-drying mustard stalks, rubbing them with salt, and applying spices and sugar, and then allowing the stalks to ferment for months. Its unique spice, tang, and complexity make it a perfect addition to the classic noodle dish Dan Dan Mian (page 150).

Zhàcài 榨菜
Zhacai: Sometimes labeled "spicy pickled mustard," "salted spicy radish," or "pickled mustard tuber," it can be sold whole or preshredded in vacuum-sealed packages. Zhacai is a great all-purpose table pickle as well as a tangy component to help contrast the richness in dishes such as Noodle Soup with Pork and Preserved Mustard (page 164).

Xiáncài 鹹菜
Haam Choy: Sometimes labeled "sour cabbage" or "pickled mustard greens," haam choy is typically sold as whole or halved heads with leaves in brine. This green is great for stir-frying—see Stir-Fried Pickled Mustard Greens (page 24)—and for serving as an accompaniment to Taiwanese Beef Noodle Soup and Taiwanese Pork Rice Bowl (pages 166 and 188).

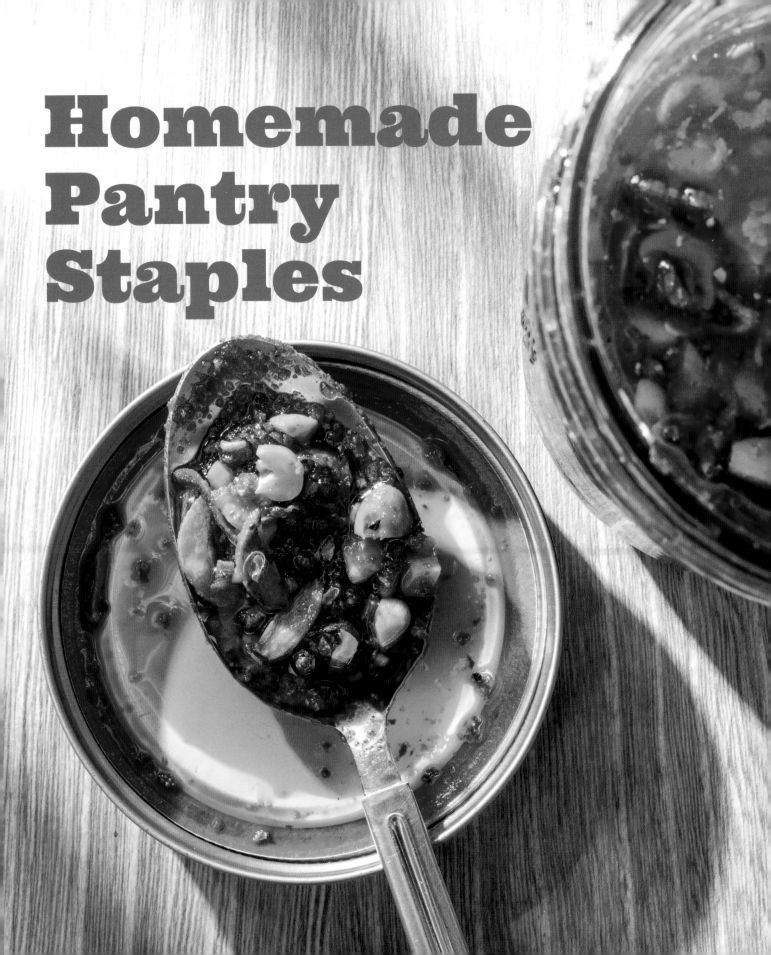

Homemade Pantry Staples

The Chinese table is always stocked with jars of condiments for dipping and drizzling. Here you will find recipes for some of our favorites.

Làjiāoyóu 辣椒油
Chili Oil

Makes: About 1½ cups
Total Time: 40 minutes, plus 12 hours resting

Although you can buy chili oil, making your own is easy and tastes fantastic as you infuse oil with freshly ground spices and aromatics. Once you have a jar on hand, you'll want to use it in everything from Smashed Cucumbers (page 67) to dumplings, soups, and beyond. It's super-fun to prepare and makes for a unique holiday gift.

- ½ cup Sichuan chili flakes
- 2 tablespoons sesame seeds
- 2 tablespoons Sichuan peppercorns, coarsely ground, divided
- ½ teaspoon table salt
- 1 cup vegetable oil
- 1 (1-inch) piece ginger, sliced into ¼-inch-thick rounds and smashed
- 3 star anise pods
- 5 cardamom pods, crushed
- 2 bay leaves

1 Combine chili flakes, sesame seeds, half of peppercorns, and salt in heatproof bowl. Cook oil, ginger, star anise, cardamom, bay leaves, and remaining peppercorns in small saucepan over low heat, stirring occasionally, until spices have darkened and mixture is very fragrant, 25 to 30 minutes.

2 Strain mixture through fine-mesh strainer into bowl with chili flake mixture (mixture may bubble slightly); discard solids. Stir well to combine. Let sit at room temperature until flavors meld, about 12 hours, before using. (Oil can be stored for up to 3 months; flavor will mature over time.)

Xiāngcuì Làjiāoyóu 香脆辣椒油
Chili Crisp

Makes: 1½ cups
Total Time: 50 minutes, plus 12 hours resting

Chili flakes, garlic, and nuts are fried and jarred in spiced oil. Popularized by the brand Lao Gan Ma, this condiment has a tingly crispiness that's superb on noodles, rice, greens, and eggs.

- ½ cup Sichuan chili flakes
- ½ cup salted dry-roasted peanuts, chopped
- 2 tablespoons Sichuan peppercorns, crushed
- 1½ teaspoons kosher salt
- ¼ teaspoon monosodium glutamate (optional)
- 1 cup vegetable oil
- 2 large shallots, sliced thin
- 4 large garlic cloves, sliced thin
- 1 (1-inch) piece ginger, sliced into ¼-inch-thick rounds and smashed
- 3 star anise pods
- 10 cardamom pods, crushed
- 2 cinnamon sticks
- 2 tablespoons toasted sesame oil

1 Combine chili flakes, peanuts, peppercorns, salt, and monosodium glutamate, if using, in heatproof bowl and set fine-mesh strainer over bowl. Cook vegetable oil and shallots in medium saucepan over medium-high heat, stirring frequently, until shallots are deep golden brown, 10 to 14 minutes. Using slotted spoon, transfer shallots to second bowl. Add garlic to hot oil and cook, stirring constantly, until golden brown, 2 to 3 minutes. Using slotted spoon, transfer garlic to bowl with shallots.

2 Add ginger, star anise, cardamom, and cinnamon sticks to vegetable oil; reduce heat to medium and cook, stirring occasionally, until ginger is dried out and mixture is very fragrant, 15 to 20 minutes. Strain ginger mixture through fine-mesh strainer into bowl with chili flake mixture (mixture may bubble slightly); discard solids. Stir well to combine. Once mixture has cooled, stir in shallots, garlic, and sesame oil. Transfer to container and let sit for at least 12 hours before using. (Chili crisp can be refrigerated for up to 3 months.)

Pang Shu Wing XO Jiàng 彭書榮 XO 醬
Jeffrey's XO Sauce

Makes: 2½ cups
Total Time: 1 hour, plus 30 minutes cooling

XO sauce is the greatest publicity Hennessy cognac could ask for. This ultrasavory seafood relish contains no cognac; the XO name comes from the fact that Hong Kongers associate Hennessy with opulence, and this condiment can be pricey to put together. (It just as easily could have been called Rolex sauce.) XO sauce is terrific over noodles, rice, or any dish that can use a knuckle sandwich of umami; think of it as a seafood version of bacon jam. Because the dried scallops are shredded in this recipe, we find the smaller, less-expensive scallops to be the best choice—unless, of course, you're the kind of person who can afford Hennessy X.O cognac.

2½	ounces (½ cup) dried scallops, rinsed
1	tablespoon Shaoxing wine
½	teaspoon toasted sesame oil
½	teaspoon white pepper
2½	ounces (⅔ cup) dried shrimp, rinsed and chopped
2½	ounces (⅔ cup) dried shredded radish, rinsed and chopped
1	cup vegetable oil
1	shallot, minced
1	Thai chile, stemmed, seeded, and minced
1	tablespoon black bean–garlic sauce
1	tablespoon chili-garlic sauce
2	teaspoons oyster sauce
1	tablespoon packed brown sugar

1 Combine scallops, 2 cups water, Shaoxing wine, sesame oil, and white pepper in bowl. Cover and microwave until steaming, about 7 minutes. Let sit until scallops are softened, about 10 minutes. Lift scallops from bowl with fork and discard liquid. Shred scallops into fine strands.

2 Add scallops, shrimp, and radish to empty 14-inch flat-bottomed wok and cook over low heat, stirring frequently, until aromatic and lightly toasted, 5 to 8 minutes; transfer to bowl.

3 Cook vegetable oil, shallot, and Thai chile in now-empty wok over medium-high heat, stirring frequently, until shallot is softened, about 2 minutes. Stir in black bean–garlic sauce, chili-garlic sauce, and oyster sauce and cook until fragrant, about 2 minutes. Stir in scallop mixture and sugar, bring to gentle simmer, and cook until flavors meld, about 5 minutes. Let mixture cool completely before serving, about 30 minutes. (Sauce can be refrigerated for up to 3 months.)

Soy-Vinegar Dipping Sauce

Makes: About ¾ cup
Total Time: 10 minutes, plus 30 minutes resting

This simple all-purpose dipping sauce has zip and zing, and works well as an accompaniment to a variety of dishes, including egg rolls and dumplings.

- ¼ cup soy sauce
- 2 scallions, sliced thin (optional)
- 2 tablespoons water
- 4 teaspoons Chinese white rice vinegar
- 2 teaspoons honey
- 2 teaspoons toasted sesame oil
- ⅛ teaspoon Sichuan chili flakes (optional)

Combine all ingredients in bowl. Let sit at room temperature until flavors meld, about 30 minutes. (Sauce can be refrigerated for up to 1 day; let come to room temperature before serving.)

Zhīmá Hǎixiān Zhànjiàng 芝麻海鮮蘸醬
Hoisin-Sesame Dipping Sauce

Makes: About ½ cup
Total Time: 20 minutes

Ginger, garlic, and cilantro add fresh flavor to this sauce, which pairs perfectly with roasted meats.

- 1 tablespoon vegetable oil
- 2 teaspoons grated fresh ginger
- 2 garlic cloves, minced
- 2 tablespoons hoisin sauce
- 2 tablespoons water
- 1 tablespoon Chinese white rice vinegar
- 1 tablespoon soy sauce
- 1 teaspoon toasted sesame oil
- 2 tablespoons chopped fresh cilantro

Heat vegetable oil in small saucepan over medium heat until shimmering. Add ginger and garlic and cook until fragrant, about 30 seconds. Stir in hoisin, water, vinegar, soy sauce, and sesame oil and cook until flavors meld, about 3 minutes. Off heat, stir in cilantro. Serve warm or at room temperature. (Sauce can be refrigerated for up to 4 days; let come to room temperature before serving.)

Jiāngcōngróng 薑蔥蓉
Ginger-Scallion Sauce

Makes: About 1 cup
Total Time: 30 minutes

Typically served alongside Hainanese Chicken Rice (page 307), this oniony relish is a great accompaniment to foods with lighter flavors such as steamed fish and Soy Sauce Chicken (page 175). We've also spooned this on noodles and rice and once, when no one was looking, over a hot dog. It was super.

- 5 scallions, sliced thin
- ⅓ cup minced fresh ginger
- ¼ teaspoon table salt
- ½ cup vegetable oil
- 2 teaspoons Chinese white rice vinegar

Combine scallions, ginger, and salt in heatproof bowl. Heat oil in small saucepan over medium-high heat until it reaches 400 degrees. Pour hot oil over scallion mixture (oil will crackle), and stir to combine. Stir in vinegar and let sit for at least 15 minutes to allow flavors to meld. (Sauce can be refrigerated for up to 4 days; let come to room temperature before serving.)

Suànróng Làjiāojiàng 蒜蓉辣椒醬
Chili-Garlic Sauce

Makes: About ¼ cup
Total Time: 25 minutes

Occupying one spot in the sauce trio traditionally served alongside Hainanese Chicken Rice (page 307), this bright and fresh sauce packs serious heat.

- 4 Thai chiles, stemmed and minced
- ¼ cup minced fresh ginger
- 4 garlic cloves, minced
- 2 teaspoons sugar
- ½ teaspoon table salt
- 1 tablespoon lime juice
- ¼ cup chicken broth or water

Using mortar and pestle (or flat side of chef's knife and cutting board) mash Thai chiles, ginger, garlic, sugar, and salt to fine paste. Transfer mixture to bowl and stir in lime juice and broth. Let sit for at least 15 minutes to allow flavors to meld. (Sauce can be refrigerated for up to 4 days; let come to room temperature before serving.)

Sūméijiàng 蘇梅醬
Plum Sauce

Makes: About 1 cup

Total Time: 30 minutes, plus 15 minutes cooling

Sour pickled plums offset the sweetness and mellow the acidity of this sauce. If pickled plums are unavailable, they can be omitted; add an extra 1 tablespoon vinegar to the sauce mixture before simmering. Dip your crispy egg rolls here.

  1 cup apricot preserves or jam
  ½ cup Chinese white rice vinegar
  ½ cup water
  2 salted pickled plums, pitted and mashed
    (2 tablespoons)
  1 (1-inch) piece ginger, sliced thin
  ⅛ teaspoon Sichuan chili flakes

Whisk apricot preserves, vinegar, and water together in small saucepan until combined. Stir in plums, ginger, and chili flakes. Bring to simmer over medium heat and cook, stirring occasionally, until slightly thickened and sauce coats back of spoon, about 15 minutes. Discard ginger. Let sauce cool to room temperature before serving, about 15 minutes. (Sauce can be refrigerated for up to 1 week; let come to room temperature before serving.)

Yóucōngsū 油葱酥
Microwave-Fried Shallots

Serves: 4 to 6

Total Time: 25 minutes

Fried shallots deliver bursts of crunch and savory flavor to Congee (page 336) and Taiwanese Pork Rice Bowl (page 188), but they're easy to overcook and require constant stirring. The microwave solves all that.

  3 shallots, sliced thin
  ½ cup vegetable oil

Combine shallots and oil in medium bowl. Microwave for 5 minutes. Stir and continue to microwave 2 minutes longer. Repeat stirring and microwaving in 2-minute increments until beginning to brown (4 to 6 minutes). Repeat stirring and microwaving in 30-second increments until deep golden brown (30 seconds to 2 minutes). Using slotted spoon, transfer shallots to paper towel–lined plate; season with salt to taste. Let drain and crisp, about 5 minutes.

Chǎoxiáncài 炒鹹菜
Stir-Fried Pickled Mustard Greens

Makes: About 1 cup

Total Time: 15 minutes, plus 30 minutes soaking

Think of this as supercharged Chinese relish—a bright, acidic contrast for rich and savory dishes such as Taiwanese Beef Noodle Soup (page 166) and Taiwanese Pork Rice Bowl (page 188). This topping has sweetness, tartness, spiciness, and a good kick of garlic. Haam choy is the pickled mustard green that's sold whole or halved in brine ("haam" in Cantonese means salty).

  4½ ounces haam choy, rinsed and chopped (1 cup)
  2 tablespoons vegetable oil
  2 garlic cloves, minced
  1 teaspoon minced fresh ginger
  2 Thai chiles, stemmed and sliced thin
  2 tablespoons sugar
  1 teaspoon soy sauce

1 Submerge haam choy in large bowl of water and let sit for 30 minutes. Drain haam choy, pressing on solids to extract as much liquid as possible.

2 Heat empty 14-inch flat-bottomed wok over high heat until just beginning to smoke. Reduce heat to medium, drizzle oil around perimeter of wok, and heat until just smoking. Add garlic, ginger, and Thai chiles and cook, stirring frequently, until fragrant, about 30 seconds. Add haam choy, sugar, and soy sauce and cook, stirring occasionally, until sugar has dissolved and liquid has evaporated, about 2 minutes. (Pickled mustard greens can be refrigerated for up to 4 days.)

Jīgāotāng 雞高湯

Chicken Broth

Makes: 8 cups
Total Time: 5½ hours

Good homemade chicken broth is liquid gold. In this recipe you'll coax out rich flavor and full body by using chicken wings, which are convenient as well as gelatin-rich, giving the broth a luscious consistency. Minimal additions ensure the broth tastes as chicken-y as possible. In the Pang family, we'll sometimes make broth with chicken and pork neck bones, the latter adding richness and depth of flavor to soups. If you have a large pot (at least 12 quarts), you can easily double this recipe to make 1 gallon.

4	pounds chicken wings
3½	quarts water
1	(1-inch) piece ginger, sliced into ¼-inch-thick rounds
2	scallions, cut into 2-inch lengths
1½	teaspoons table salt

1 Bring chicken and water to boil in large stockpot or Dutch oven over medium-high heat, skimming off any surface scum. Reduce heat to low and simmer gently for 3 hours.

2 Add ginger, scallions, and salt and continue to simmer for 2 hours. Strain broth through fine-mesh strainer into large pot or container, pressing on solids to extract as much liquid as possible; discard solids. Let broth settle for about 5 minutes, then, using wide, shallow spoon, skim excess fat from surface. (Cooled broth can be refrigerated for up to 4 days or frozen for up to 1 month.)

Variations

Enriched Chicken and Pork Broth

Substitute 2 pounds pork necks for 2 pounds of chicken wings.

Pressure-Cooker Chicken Broth

Add all ingredients to 6- or 8-quart electric pressure cooker. Lock lid into place and close pressure-release valve. Select high pressure-cook function and cook for 1 hour. Turn off pressure cooker and let pressure release naturally for 15 minutes. Quick-release any remaining pressure, then carefully remove lid, allowing steam to escape away from you. Strain broth as directed. (If using stovetop pressure cooker, bring cooker to high pressure over medium-high heat. As soon as indicator signals that pot has reached high pressure, reduce heat to medium-low and cook, adjusting heat as needed to maintain high pressure. Remove cooker from heat before allowing pressure to release.)

Scraps Today, Liquid Gold Tomorrow

Chicken wings are readily available at the market and are convenient for making this broth on demand, but you can also think ahead and put other resources to good use in making your broth. We like to hold on to leftover trimmings and carcasses from roasted or poached poultry (think Soy Sauce Chicken on page 175, Hainanese Chicken Rice on page 307, and Roast Duck on page 314) in our freezer. Once we have about a pound or more, we substitute them for an equal amount of wings.

SPICES AND SEASONINGS

Báihújiāo 白胡椒

White Peppercorns: White peppercorns are fully ripened black peppercorns that have been soaked in water to ferment, and their outer skin is removed. Lacking the sharp bite of black pepper, they instead have a complex floral and citrus flavor and a layer of funky earthiness. If you ask for ground pepper at a restaurant in China, white pepper is what you'll get. Do not substitute black pepper.

Huājiāo 花椒

Sichuan Peppercorns: A key Sichuan seasoning, these small reddish-brown husks (and more assertive green husks) aren't true peppercorns but rather the dried fruit rinds of the prickly ash. They don't contribute heat per se, but instead offer a unique tingling or buzzing sensation known as ma. The peppercorns are often ground before using—you can do this in a spice grinder or mortar and pestle.

Gānlàjiāo 乾辣椒

Dried Chiles: We call for Sichuan chiles but labeling can be inconsistent. What you're looking for are dried chiles with a moderate heat level. We use tien tsin chiles most often in this book, as these bright red chiles, 1 to 2 inches long and ½ inch wide at the stem, are readily available at the market and online. If tien tsin chiles are unavailable, arbols or other small medium-hot dried chiles can be used.

Sichuan chili flakes are made by crushing dried chiles and are a convenient option when a lot is required in a recipe, such as with the Chili Crisp (page 21) and the sauce for hand-pulled noodles (page 161). Sichuan chiles are also sold as a powder; however, we prefer the coarse texture of the flakes. Gochugaru (Korean red pepper flakes) are a suitable alternative.

Ròuguì 肉桂

Cinnamon: In addition to its use in five-spice powder, cinnamon (often whole pieces of bark) contributes a warming sweet spice in savory dishes such as Taiwanese Beef Noodle Soup and Red-Braised Pork Belly (pages 166 and 316).

Zīrán 孜然

Cumin: Most commonly used in northwest and northern China, cumin adds warm, toasty notes and a distinctive woodsy aroma to recipes like our Stir-Fried Cumin Lamb (page 178). For textural contrast in a dish, we often reach for cumin seeds for their pleasant crunch.

Zhīmá 芝麻

Sesame Seeds: Commonly used in both savory and sweet dishes, sesame seeds add nutty flavor as well as crunch. We prefer to buy untoasted seeds and toast them ourselves to preserve their shelf life.

Toasting whole spices and seeds: Toasting applies dry heat directly to spices and seeds, which brings their oils to the surface and results in a bolder aroma. Place whole spices or seeds in a dry skillet and cook over medium heat, stirring frequently, until fragrant. Quickly transfer to a bowl to prevent scorching.

Tingle All the Way

In China the Sichuan peppercorn contributed its woodsy fragrance and citrusy tang to food long before chiles arrived from the Americas. Though chiles were quickly adopted in the 15th or 16th century, people found that the tingling sensation created by Sichuan peppercorns on the lips and tongue complemented the chile heat, making it more tolerable. The interplay of Sichuan peppercorns and chiles is so foundational to Sichuan cuisine that it has a name, mala, or "numbing heat."

Bājiǎo 八角
Star Anise: Star anise has a warm, licorice-like flavor that works well in both sweet and savory recipes. We typically simmer or steep the star-shaped pods whole to extract their flavor, then discard them before serving. You don't want to eat them.

Wǔxiāngfěn 五香粉
Five-Spice Powder: This common Chinese seasoning blend imparts bitterness, sweetness, and pungency. Most traditional blends include cinnamon, star anise, cloves, fennel, and Sichuan peppercorns. Some versions substitute white peppercorns for the Sichuan peppercorns.

Měijí xiāngjiàngyóu 美極鮮醬油
Maggi Seasoning: Beloved in many parts of the world outside of the United States, Maggi seasoning tastes like a magically delicious version of soy sauce. Invented in 1886 by Swiss concentrated-soup magnate Julius Maggi, it's made from hydrolyzed wheat (and other protein sources) and is chock-full of glutamic acid, which packs an umami wallop. The seasoning is sold in liquid, powder, or paste form, though we always use the liquid in our recipes. Use it as a flavor enhancer in dishes such Hong Kong–Style Baked Pork Chop Rice (page 267). Many Chinese folks use Maggi as an everyday soy sauce.

Wèijīng 味精
Monosodium Glutamate (MSG): This sprinkle is the sodium salt of glutamic acid—the amino acid responsible for the super-savory, mouth-filling taste we know as umami. The use of MSG is a contentious issue in the United States (see page 297), but the seasoning is a common ingredient in many Asian countries. MSG works best on foods that are already savory, and it makes a great addition to seasonings of spicy foods such as Chili Crisp and Dry Chili Chicken (pages 21 and 282), but use it on any dish to give its savoriness a real kick.

Jīfěn 雞粉
Chicken Bouillon Powder: This pantry-friendly seasoning has concentrated chicken flavor as well as MSG, which helps boost the savory flavor of food in dishes such as Hong Kong–Style Portuguese Chicken (page 252). It's not unusual for Chinese chefs to sneak a pinch of chicken bouillon powder into dishes for a boost.

DRIED FISH AND SHELLFISH
Dried seafood products are used throughout Chinese cuisine to add sweet-savory flavor. Their dehydrated state makes them pantry-friendly, which is great because a little goes a long way. It's best to rehydrate dried shellfish before using. To do this quickly, place water and shellfish (roughly 1 cup of water per every ½ ounce of shellfish) in a covered bowl and microwave until steaming, then let soak until tender.

Dàdìyúfěn 大地魚粉
Dried Flounder Powder: This powder is made by pulverizing dried whole flounder carcasses. Both the powder and the whole carcass contribute savoriness and concentrated fish flavor to soups, though we prefer the compact nature of the powder and the fact that it doesn't require steeping. Avoid substituting flounder fish seasoning (which has added salt and flavorings) or powders made from other fish for this ingredient. The earthy savoriness of flounder powder is essential to Hong Kong–Style Wonton Noodle Soup (page 90).

Xiāmǐ 蝦米
Dried Shrimp: Although tiny, dried shrimp are power-packed with flavor. For the recipes in this book look for dried shrimp ½ to 1 inch in size with a pink-orange hue. We find rehydrating the shrimp before using helps their flavors come out.

Gānbèi 干貝
Dried Scallops: These golden medallions are considered a delicacy and pack a seafood-y punch in a variety of stir-fries, fried rice dishes, and condiments, including Jeffrey's XO Sauce (page 22). Dried scallops can vary widely in price based on quality and size (read: very pricey). In general we find that the smaller, less-expensive scallops work fine in most cooking applications. Because they're dried, you'll want to soak the scallops in hot water for about 30 minutes before using to remove excess salt and allow their flavors to bloom.

A VERY INCOMPLETE GUIDE TO THE CHINESE PRODUCE AISLE

Shēngjiāng 生薑
Ginger: One of the most distinct aromatics in Chinese cooking, ginger adds warm, spicy flavors and aromas. We purchase it in small quantities because, as ginger ages, it loses its pungency. If you're polishing off an older piece, be prepared to use more than the recipe calls for, and add it as close to the end of cooking as possible.

To peel and grate ginger: Scrape off a portion of the skin from a knob with the edge of a spoon (the bowl of which can easily be maneuvered around curves in the ginger). Use the unpeeled part of the piece as a handle while grating the peeled portion with a rasp-style grater.

Dàsuàn 大蒜
Garlic: An important aromatic in the Chinese kitchen, garlic gets its characteristic flavor from allicin, which is produced when garlic's cell walls are broken down. The more you slice, chop, or crush garlic, the more pungent the garlic will be. We use minced garlic when we want powerful garlic flavor, and sliced or lightly crushed garlic for milder garlic flavor.

Jiǔcéngtá 九層塔
Thai Basil (1): This basil variety brings slightly spicy, anise-like notes to dishes, especially ones from Taiwan. Its leaves are sturdier and stand up to heat better than those of Italian basil, so it can be added during cooking.

Yuánsuī 芫荽
Cilantro: This herb, which is also called Chinese parsley or fresh coriander, has a refreshing flavor and aroma. In general, delicate cilantro leaves and stems are used as a garnish before serving or added late in the cooking process because they quickly lose their aroma when heated.

Qīngcōng 青蔥
Scallions: Although not a hard-and-fast rule, we often cook the white section, which has a delicate, sweet taste, while thinly slicing the green portion, which has grassy notes and a peppery bite, to sprinkle as a garnish.

Xiǎobáicài 小白菜
Bok Choy (2): Regular bok choy has white stalks and dark green leaves with a crinkly texture, while Shanghai bok choy boasts jade-colored stalks. Both work equally well in recipes. Any variety picked at an early stage can be called baby bok choy. Be sure to thoroughly wash bok choy, as the tightly layered stems often retain a lot of grit.

Dàbáicài 大白菜
Napa Cabbage: This ruffled cool-weather brassica has been cultivated in China for almost 2,000 years. The leaves' mellow, sweet flavor and juicy crunch are key in countless applications, including soups, stir-fries like Hot and Sour Napa Cabbage (page 214), and dumpling fillings (page 96).

Jièlán 芥蘭
Gai Lan (3): Also known as Chinese broccoli or Chinese kale, gai lan has broad, waxy leaves that offer hints of minerality and bitterness and that branch from smooth, fleshy stalks (mature specimens may have started to flower), which are prized for their crispness and delicate nuttiness.

Kōngxīncài 空心菜
Ong Choy (4): Also called water spinach, this green is distinctive for its hollow stems, which become deliciously crunchy when stir-fried. Green ong choy, grown in damp soil, has larger leaves and vibrant green stems, while white ong choy, grown in water, has narrower leaves and lighter, wider stems. Look for firm stems and use within a day or two.

Xiàncài 莧菜
Amaranth (5): Sometimes called yin choy, among other names, this leafy green is often streaked with shades of red or purple. It has a sweet, slightly minerally flavor similar to flat-leaf spinach. Its stalks, leaves, and florets can be eaten raw when the plant is young and in its most tender state, while more mature versions are better suited for stir-frying and steaming. You can substitute flat-leaf spinach or watercress.

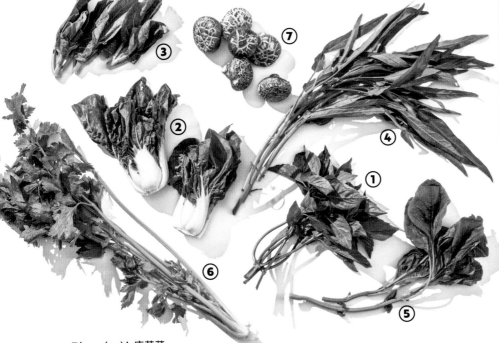

Tángqíncài 唐芹菜
Chinese Celery (6): A nearer relative of wild celery than North American celery, with a pungent, peppery flavor and bountiful leaves that look and taste somewhat like parsley, Chinese celery can be used in stir-fries as both an herb and a vegetable. North American common celery can be used in its place, sliced thinly to ensure proper cooking.

Qiézi 茄子
Chinese Eggplant: Long and slender, Chinese eggplant have thinner skin and fewer seeds than globe eggplant, along with a less bitter flavor and usually a paler purple color. They are similar in texture, shape, and flavor to Japanese eggplant, and the two can be used interchangeably. We enjoy their creamy texture when slow-cooked in our Braised Eggplant with Soy, Garlic, and Ginger (page 226).

Dōngguā 冬瓜
Winter Melon: A large vine-grown fruit with a hard green rind, this melon is typically sold in Chinese markets precut into long wedges. You'll need to remove the rind and seeds (see how on page 81). The mild-tasting flesh will absorb the flavors of the seasonings with which it is cooked. We enjoy this fruit simmered in Winter Melon Soup with Meatballs (page 80).

Xiānggū 香菇
Shiitake Mushrooms (7): Although we use both fresh and dried varieties, dried shiitake mushrooms deliver the most concentrated flavor to dishes such as Clay Pot Chicken Rice (page 141). Several varieties are available, and all will work in our recipes, though the most highly sought-after—and the type we recommend—is bai huagu (white flower mushroom 白花菇), which features caps with deep, white cracks resembling a flower.

To rehydrate dried mushrooms: Place water and mushrooms (1 cup water per ½ ounce of mushrooms) in a bowl, cover, and microwave until steaming, about 5 minutes, then let soak until tender, about 30 minutes. If using the soaking liquid for cooking, be sure to strain it through a coffee filter to remove the grit.

Common Vegetable Cuts for Stir-Frying

1 Bias Cut: Position knife diagonal to vegetable and slice oval-shaped pieces of desired thickness.

2 Matchsticks: Lay ovals flat on cutting board, then slice into matchsticks of desired thickness. For thinner matchsticks, start by slicing vegetable more thinly on bias.

3 Fine Chop: Bundle several matchsticks on cutting board and cut crosswise into dice of desired size.

PROTEINS

Zhūròu 豬肉

Pork: More than beef, pork is a staple in Chinese cooking. We utilize cuts from all over the pig. Ground pork is our go-to for dumpling fillings. Coarsely ground pork with a high percentage of fat is key to the juiciest fillings, so buy it at the butcher counter. Leaner chops and tenderloin are ideal for stir-frying. Pork belly is suited for slow braising, and pork butt is the base for Char Siu (page 321).

Làcháng 臘腸

Lap Cheong (Chinese Sausage): A thin cured sausage with a slightly sweet and spiced flavor, lap cheong is often cut into small pieces and rendered—just a small amount provides extra meaty flavor to fried rice and many other dishes. Look for good distribution of fat throughout the sausage and some alcohol in the ingredient list. Spam luncheon meat can be a good substitute in stir-fries and braised applications.

Làròu 臘肉

Lap Yuk (Chinese Cured Pork Belly): Lap yuk is similar to bacon, except it's not smoked but marinated and air-dried. Cantonese-style lap yuk typically includes soy sauce, rice wine, salt, sugar, and five-spice powder. Similar to lap cheong, it can be folded into stir-fries and other dishes for meaty flavor. Country ham can be used as a substitute.

Softening preserved meat: Because they have been preserved, lap cheong and lap yuk are quite firm. Just 10 seconds in the microwave softens them and makes them easier to slice.

Níuròu 牛肉, Yángròu 羊肉

Beef and Lamb: We often reach for beef flank steak, beef flap meat, lamb shoulder chops, or lamb leg for stir-frying, as they deliver great flavor and are plenty tender after quick cooking. For braising, you'll find several recipes calling for beef shank, which breaks down to become incredibly tender and luscious.

Jiāqín 家禽

Poultry: Whole chickens, particularly Buddhist-style chickens (see page 176 for more information), are praised in Chinese cooking for their succulent meat and skin when poached, while whole duck is revered for its crisp skin. Chicken pieces frequently include the skin and bones for both texture and flavor. A cleaver ably cuts chicken into bone-in pieces for gnawing in dishes like Soy Sauce Chicken (page 175).

Pídàn 皮蛋

Century Eggs (or Thousand-Year-Old Eggs): Despite what their name suggests, the curing process for these preserved chicken or duck eggs is closer to several weeks. The yolk turns a dark green and has a creamy consistency, while the white turns a translucent amber and is gelatinous. The eggs have a unique savoriness and can be eaten on their own or chopped and used as a garnish for Spicy Cold Tofu (page 238).

Xiándànhuáng 鹹蛋黃

Salted Duck Egg Yolks: With a firm texture, bright orange-red color, and rich and salty flavor, salted duck egg yolks need to be steamed to soften before being used as a topping for soup or congee or as the featured flavoring ingredient in Salted Egg Fried Shrimp (page 300). Salted yolks are often found vacuum-sealed and frozen or refrigerated.

Hǎixiān 海鮮

Seafood: The Chinese love being served whole fish. We like seeing heads and eyeballs; it's both a sign of respect for the animal and an indication of freshness. The late cookbook author Eileen Yin-Fei Lo wrote of fish not served whole as "white rectangles on ice, no head, no tail, no fins, no skin, no bones, no taste." At the fish counter look for whole fish that are well insulated with ice. The skin should be bright and reflective, without any sign of damage. When buying fillets, choose those that have been placed on (and not buried in) ice. In contrast, we often buy shrimp frozen because it's hard to know how long "fresh" (defrosted) shrimp have been sitting. Defrost only as many as you need. Look for shrimp that are preservative-free; shrimp should be the only thing on the ingredient list. If you're making Oil-Exploded Shrimp (page 202), it's worth seeking out head-on shrimp, which can be found at many Asian markets.

Dòufǔ 豆腐

Tofu: Made from coagulated soy milk, tofu is highly versatile and pairs with a variety of flavors. Ultracreamy silken tofu is ideal for soups and is excellent served chilled and sliced with a light dressing in Spicy Cold Tofu (page 238). It's quite delicate so should be handled carefully. Soft tofu is also creamy but holds its shape, making it well suited for braising in dishes like Mapo Tofu (page 240) and pan frying when you want a crisp exterior and silken interior. Firm and extra-firm tofu are good for stir-frying and deep frying—and for stuffing, as we do with Hakka Stuffed Tofu (page 264).

STICKY SCIENCE: MYOSIN DEVELOPMENT

If you've tasted a great meat dumpling, you may have noticed, in addition to juiciness, a certain snappy or bouncy texture. That pleasing springiness is represented by the letter Q, a term popularized by the Taiwanese. (Q can also describe the springy chewiness of noodles and bubble tea tapioca.) Some foods are QQ, a doubly springy version of Q.

In the case of meat, the Q texture comes from vigorously stirring ground or finely chopped meat, freeing up a sticky protein, called myosin, from the muscle. Kneading causes the myosin to cross-link and bind into a network (think of it like kneading bread dough to develop gluten). The more you mix, the more myosin gets released and cross-links. This network makes the meat cohesive, fine-textured, and springy. Myosin also grabs onto and traps water, fat, and other seasoning liquids, so that filling cooks up supremely juicy and flavorful. There are several ways to develop a strong myosin network. For small amounts, such as the filling for Hong Kong–Style Wonton Noodle Soup (page 90), use a wooden spoon or 4 bundled chopsticks to stir the pork. For larger quantities we turn to the stand mixer for recipes like Lion's Head Meatballs (page 194) and Shanghai Soup Dumplings (page 117).

Cutting Up Flank Steak for Stir-Frying

1 Cut steak with grain into 2½- to 3-inch-wide strips. To make slicing flank steak easier, first freeze it until firm, about 15 minutes.

2 Cut strips crosswise against grain into ⅛-inch-thick slices.

Halving Bone-In Chicken Thighs

1 Use cleaver or your heaviest (not your finest) chef's knife. Position cleaver at middle of thigh, perpendicular to bone. Slice through meat so bone is exposed.

2 Hold cleaver steady, with base of blade resting on top of bone, and use nondominant hand to press down on spine of cleaver to split thigh into two pieces.

Deboning Skin-On Chicken Thighs

1 Using sharp paring knife, cut slit along length of thigh bone to expose bone. Using tip of knife, cut meat from bone, being careful not to cut through skin.

2 Slip knife under bone to separate bone from meat. Discard bone and trim any remaining cartilage from thigh.

The Tools You'll Use

THE MIGHTY WOK

The majority of recipes in this book call for one pan, and it's a wok. Chinese cooks have briskly tossed, turned, and flipped food in this versatile vessel for centuries. A wok excels at stir-frying, of course, but it also brilliantly handles virtually any cooking task, from steaming to braising to deep frying. We highly recommend you use a wok to make these recipes, though you should be aware that not every wok is going to perform well on your stovetop. You can buy a reasonably priced quality wok, but choosing from the range of shapes, materials, and sizes can be confusing. Colleague Lisa McManus, ATK equipment expert, put an array of woks through their paces and shares some helpful advice.

Buy a Flat-Bottomed Wok

Round woks have traditionally been used on stoves with pit-shaped burners that cradle the wok and heat the entire outside surface, not just the bottom. But their shape isn't well suited to the flat heating element of a Western-style stove. Enter the flat-bottomed wok. While not traditional, the flattened bottom provides good contact with the heating element, so the wok gets hot and stays hot—even on electric and induction burners.

Look for a Broad Flat Surface

A 14-inch wok, from rim to rim, is well sized for the home kitchen. The diameter of the flat cooking surface matters, too: A wider flat interior space (up to 7 inches in diameter) means more area to sear food and evaporate moisture.

Go with Carbon Steel

Both carbon-steel and lightweight cast-iron woks are top choices among cooks. They transfer heat efficiently, so they sear foods more effectively than woks made of other materials. The metals in these woks also gradually acquire seasoning as you cook; over time, the polymerized oil naturally makes them increasingly nonstick. But even though cast-iron woks can stir-fry well, they are slower to heat up and also retain heat longer than carbon-steel woks, giving you less control over cooking (the thickest are also heavy and hard to lift). Thin carbon-steel woks are more responsive to temperature changes— they get smoking-hot fast, and cool down fast, too—which is important when shifting between steps in stir-frying.

Get a Good Handle

One of the biggest differences among woks is the handle. Because you grip it as you cook, its material, position, and shape greatly affect efficiency and comfort. We far prefer a wooden handle over a metal one, as wood won't heat up during cooking (so no need to grab a pot holder). The angle of the handle matters, too: Wok handles that are angled slightly upward offer the best leverage and make the wok feel lighter and more balanced than those with handles that are either nearly horizontal or tilted sharply upward.

Three Great Choices

Our three favorite woks are the **Taylor & Ng Natural Nonstick Wok Set** ($79.99), the **Joyce Chen Classic Series 14-Inch Carbon Steel Wok with Birch Handles** ($36.81), and the **IMUSA 14" Non-Coated Wok with Wood Handle, Silver** ($34.99). The lightest of the woks we tested, all three have wide, flat cooking surfaces, thin carbon-steel construction, and comfortable, stay-cool wooden handles that make them easy to maneuver. The Taylor & Ng wok costs more, but it comes with a lid. It is also preseasoned (the manufacturer calls it "natural nonstick"), a head start toward building up a nonstick surface— though the others quickly gain a nonstick coating after their initial seasoning, and the seasoning will continue to improve over time.

Wok Accessories

Wok Lid: Dome-shaped wok lids come in handy for steaming in your wok, including brief stretches during a stir-fry, and for containing splatters. If yours didn't come with a lid, you can buy one separately; just look for a lid 2 inches smaller than the wok so it can sit inside the wok's walls.

Spatula: The traditional tool here is a wok chuan, or wok "turner," a broad-edged, shovel-shaped spatula that is designed for tossing and flipping. However, we also like any spatula with a fairly thin, stiff edge and broad head such as a flat-edge wooden spatula, metal fish spatula, or wide-edge silicone spatula.

Wok Ladle: While a wok hoak, or ladle, is a mainstay in Chinese restaurant kitchens for cooking with larger woks and for scooping up larger amounts of sauces, we found that a wok ladle is not essential for home cooking. A Western-style ladle is an acceptable substitute when needed for basting meats or serving soups, or for braised recipes.

Wok Brush: Made of stiff bamboo strips, this tool is extremely helpful for scraping food from a wok without disturbing its patina.

Cooking Chopsticks: Although any pair of chopsticks can be used for beating eggs, mixing ground meat, and doing other prep work, if you're interested in using chopsticks while cooking (such as stirring food during frying or gently stirring noodles) you should buy a pair of cooking chopsticks, which are much longer (around 16.5 inches), made of solid wood, and uncoated so they can be exposed to hot oil or boiling water safely.

Do I Need a Wok Ring?

A wok ring is unnecessary when using a flat-bottomed wok, which is stable on the stovetop.

Will a Wok Perform Well on My Stovetop?

We tested a range of stir-fry recipes in a flat-bottomed wok across gas, electric, and induction stovetops. Dishes cooked on gas stoves did tend to cook slightly faster than dishes cooked on electric or induction stoves, but variations were small and all cooked within the recipes' stated time frames. The main differences related to how heat was transferred to the wok. With gas, the flames come up the sides of the wok and so the walls get hotter and do more of the cooking than when the wok is heated over induction or electric coils. Cleanup was easier when using induction or electric heat because there was less baked-on food up the sides of the wok. As long as your wok is not overcrowded, all stovetops will produce acceptable results.

Caring for Your Wok

With just a little TLC, a carbon-steel wok will reward you for years with its quick responsiveness and nonstick performance. To maintain this quality, a carbon-steel wok requires seasoning, just like a cast-iron skillet. Seasoning improves naturally every time you cook: Fats heated in a wok polymerize, or link together and bond to the surface, forming a coating that protects against rust and helps food release more easily. A new wok requires initial seasoning to kick-start the process (this is recommended even for woks that come preseasoned) and routine upkeep. Colleague Lan Lam devised the below method.

Initial Seasoning

1   Scrub off any protective wax or grease on the wok. Using very hot water and dish soap, scrub vigorously with a bristle brush. Dry the wok and set over low heat to finish drying.

2   Add ⅓ cup vegetable oil, 1 sliced onion, and ½ cup table or kosher salt to the wok. (The salt helps scrub any remaining wax or grease from the surface; the onion regulates the heat, preventing spotty polymerization of the oil.) Cook over medium heat, moving the mixture around the bottom and up the sides of wok. When the onion is very dark brown (almost burnt), remove the wok from heat and let cool. Discard the onion-salt mixture and clean the wok with a sponge and hot, soapy water. Dry the wok and return to medium heat to finish drying.

3   Using a wad of paper towels held with tongs, apply ½ teaspoon oil evenly over the wok's surface. Wipe away as much oil as possible with a fresh paper towel (excess oil won't fully polymerize and will instead lead to tackiness). Continue to heat the wok, wiping away any beaded oil that forms, until the wok smokes (indicating oil breakdown). Let the wok smoke for 2 minutes, wiping away beaded oil with a paper towel. Turn off the heat and let cool. (Note: Because the sides of the wok don't get as hot as the bottom, they will initially be less seasoned. With use, the upper portion will become more seasoned.)

Routine Maintenance

After you cook, rinse the wok with hot water, scrubbing gently with a wok brush (preferably) or a soft-bristled brush or, lastly, a sponge; avoid soap and abrasive scrubbers. Dry the wok over medium heat (but do not overheat, as that will weaken seasoning and detach it from the expanding steel) and repeat step 3 above, applying only ¼ teaspoon oil to darker, seasoned areas of the wok (you do not need to apply oil all the way up the sides).

Reseasoning

If the cooking surface feels bumpy or has tacky residue (caused by partially polymerized oil), or if the patina is chipped, scrub with a moderately abrasive sponge (also use a little soap if the wok is tacky) until the patina feels even to the touch (the color does not need to be even). Repeat step 3 above.

Why Is My Wok's Patina Uneven?

Lan Lam notes: "This question comes up a lot from new wok owners, who get concerned when their patina looks uneven and spotty after a few weeks of use. Be patient; let the patina develop on its own time. The more you use that wok, the faster the patina develops."

Can I Stir-Fry in a Skillet?

Any stir-fried recipe in this book can be made with good results in a 12-inch skillet that has some kind of nonstick surface. Your best bet is a carbon-steel skillet, which gets ripping hot and takes on seasoning just like our favorite woks. (But if you don't own one, why not just buy a wok?) Cast-iron skillets also work, though you'll have a bit less control over temperature changes. Skillets with nonstick coating can also be used to stir-fry, but you will need to modify the recipe to avoid heating a dry pan (without oil) over high heat to avoid any possible safety risks with the nonstick coating. If you use this type of skillet be sure to add the specified oil before heating the pan. Be careful when stirring and tossing food, as a skillet is far less roomy than a wok; some spilling may be inevitable.

STIR-FRYING 101

Stir-frying employs high heat and constant motion to cook food so rapidly that proteins brown uniformly and vegetables lose their raw edge but retain vibrant color and fresh crunch. As soon as food hits the wok, it's repeatedly pushed, flipped, and swirled all over the vessel's surface, allowing moisture to evaporate quickly and char to form. In researching the mechanics of woks and the act of stir-frying in them, Lan Lam came away with some informative guidance as to what makes cooking in a wok so unique.

Woks Are Precisely Designed for Stir-Frying

One obvious benefit of cooking in a wok is that its high, sloping walls allow you to move food around the surface easily, without spilling it over the sides. But a wok's tall sides also create two distinct heat zones that work in tandem to stir-fry food efficiently and evenly. The bottom of a wok, which makes direct contact with the heat source, is the sear zone; it can reach temperatures exceeding 750 degrees on a gas burner. A couple of inches above the wok's base is the steam zone, where moisture escaping from food is corralled by the vessel's tall sides. This steam heat helps food cook even more quickly as it's being tossed.

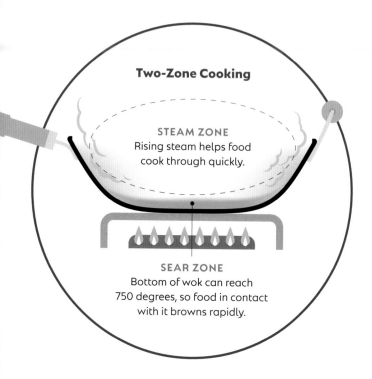

Two-Zone Cooking

STEAM ZONE
Rising steam helps food cook through quickly.

SEAR ZONE
Bottom of wok can reach 750 degrees, so food in contact with it browns rapidly.

What Is Wok Hei?

Food cooked in a well-seasoned wok can acquire wok hei 鑊氣, a Cantonese term for the charred and fragrant essence prized in some (not all) Chinese regional cuisines as the ultimate reward of a great stir-fry. Wok hei is colloquially translated as "the breath of the wok," and its flavor and aroma have been described as "smoky," "allium-like," "grilled," and "metallic." Think of burgers cooked over a charcoal grill—wok hei is the Chinese cooking analog of that exquisitely singed flavor.

Wok experts, including author Grace Young, attribute the unique flavor of wok hei to a few complementary factors, including aroma compounds that form when oil gets very hot, chemical interactions between food and a wok's seasoned steel, and the accelerated Maillard and caramelization reactions that happen when the heat is turned way up.

This electric flavor is most associated with dishes fresh from the flame-licked, blazing heat of restaurant woks. In professional kitchens oil sometimes even catches fire briefly when food is tossed into the air from the wok. But wok hei can be achieved at home—no pyrotechnics necessary, though you need proper technique, which you'll find on the next page. Make sure that your wok is very hot. (Lan's recipe for Stir-Fried Beef and Gai Lan, shown in the steps on the next page and found on page 184, is the perfect introduction to creating wok hei at home.) In a properly heated wok, modest amounts of food kept in motion pass through clouds of steam and smoke that rise from the sizzling-hot carbon steel, taking on the fleeting taste of wok hei, a savory, complex taste that no skillet can match.

10 Tips for Successful Stir-Frying

1. Cut Foods to the Right Size: Cutting ingredients uniformly and to the specifications of the recipe will ensure they cook evenly and within the time stated.

2. Have All Ingredients and Tools at Hand: The quick nature of stir-frying (often over high heat) makes it necessary to cook without interruption. With all the ingredients prepared ahead, and all the needed tools (and serving dishes) at the ready, you can add ingredients at the right time and cook without distraction.

3. Use the Right Oils: Neutral oils with high smoke points, such as vegetable, canola, and peanut, are the best choice for stir-frying. Sesame oil is not suitable for cooking and should be added just before serving.

4. Preheat Your Wok: Given that a wok has such a large cooking surface, it is important to provide enough time for it to heat up properly before cooking. To do this we often preheat an empty wok over high heat until the residual oils on the surface just begin to smoke—a reliable indication that the wok is ready for stir-frying. This can take 3 to 5 minutes, though subsequent heating between recipe steps will take less time. (Be aware that newer woks with less seasoning may not smoke as noticeably.) In certain cases—such as when blooming aromatics, toasting spices, or melting rock sugar—we will start heating food in a cold wok and use the extended time over a lower heat level to heat the wok slowly.

5. Swirl Oil Around the Wok's Perimeter: We purposely avoid adding oil to the wok while preheating to prevent the oil from overheating. Instead, we swirl it around the perimeter of the hot wok just before stir-frying. This allows for more of the wok's surface area to be coated in oil, creating a larger nonstick surface. The oil will also heat up faster.

6. Toss Slowly but Constantly: It may seem counterintuitive, but constant tossing cooks food faster. The movement brings new surfaces of the food into contact with the hot pan and releases steam—both of which expedite cooking. That evaporation also improves flavor; as water is driven away, flavor compounds concentrate and the solids that remain break down and form new flavor compounds. Using a tossing motion flips food more easily than stirring it (using a flat-edge spatula helps with this).

7. Cook in Batches: Just because a wok can hold a lot of food doesn't mean it can cook that food properly. Heat plays a large role in developing flavors while stir-frying, and a crowded wok is hard to keep hot. Cooking in small batches ensures that the wok stays properly heated and keeps more food in contact with the wok's surface, which is crucial for flavor development.

8. Cook to the Visual Cues: Since cooking times can vary depending on your cooking vessel—wok or nonstick skillet, for example—and your heat source (gas, induction, electric), it's a good idea to cook to the visual cues and use the times provided in the recipe as an overall guide.

9. Adjust Heat as Needed: Much of stir-frying happens over high heat, but if you notice foods cooking too quickly, particularly delicate aromatics, don't hesitate to lower the heat or even briefly remove the wok from the heat source.

10. Think About Ventilation: We've all been there: Right in the middle of cooking, the fire alarm goes off and pulls you away from the stove. With high-heat cooking, it's best to think ahead and make sure your stovetop hood fan (if you have one) is turned on and/or your kitchen window is open.

MORE USEFUL EQUIPMENT

Chef's Knife: A good chef's knife is invaluable for all kinds of tasks, from mincing garlic to slicing meat thinly for stir-fries. Our favorite knife, the **Victorinox Swiss Army Fibrox Pro 8" Chef's Knife** ($37.90), retains its edge well. Its textured grip feels secure for a range of hand sizes, and we can comfortably choke up on the knife for precise, effortless cuts.

Cleaver: Cleavers come in many styles. A meat cleaver will make simple work of hacking chicken and duck into small pieces and cutting up lobsters for stir-fry without concern for dulling your chef's knife. Our favorite meat cleaver is the **Masui AUS8 Stainless Meat Cleaver 180mm** ($90). That said, you may want to consider a Chinese cleaver—an all-purpose tool in many kitchens. Thinner, lighter, more precise, and more agile than a meat cleaver, and with a more rectangular blade, Chinese cleavers can chop and mince on par with a chef's knife, while their broad sides can smash garlic and ginger and scoop up food like a bench scraper. Flip them and use the blunt end to scrape the skin off ginger.

Kitchen Shears: This underrated tool handles a wide range of kitchen tasks, from snipping herbs and dried chiles to cutting soaked noodles and butchering poultry. Chinese scissors, which have short, sharp blades and large looped handles, are a common sight at dim sum restaurants, handy for halving hot fried spring rolls, sesame balls, and dumplings. Buy our favorite all-purpose kitchen shears, **Shun Multi Purpose Shears** ($49.95), or consider Chinese scissors instead.

Tongs: A good pair of tongs are a cook's best friend for turning hot food, tossing noodles, and more. They should feel like a natural extension of your hands. The **OXO Good Grips 12-Inch Tongs** ($12.95) are our favorite; they grip food well and are comfortable to hold. A pair of cooking chopsticks are useful for many of the same tasks, in addition to stirring, beating eggs, and gently separating foods as they fry.

Spider Skimmer: When we're deep-frying, blanching, or boiling we use a spider skimmer—a long-handled stainless-steel wire basket—to remove food from the pot. Spiders have larger capacities than slotted spoons and more open area for faster, safer drainage. We like the **Rösle Wire Skimmer** ($41.68).

Small Rolling Pin: We prefer to use a small, narrow rolling pin for rolling dumpling wrappers. They easily turn and pivot and allow you to feel the thickness of the dough and apply pressure as needed. Look for a pin that's about 8 inches long and 1 inch thick.

Thermometers: An instant-read thermometer is essential for testing food for doneness and for determining when oil is hot enough for frying. Our favorites are the **ThermoWorks Thermapen ONE** ($105) and the **ThermoWorks ThermoPop** ($29). For deep frying in a Dutch oven, a clip-on candy/deep-fry thermometer is a hands-off way to monitor temperature. We use the **ThermoWorks ChefAlarm** ($59).

Spice Grinder: Whole spices stay fresh and retain their flavor longer than ground spices. Sichuan peppercorns in particular should be bought whole and ground at home to preserve their flavor. We like the **Krups Coffee and Spice Grinder** ($17.99) for its relatively even grinding and easy-to-use design. You can also grind spices using a mortar and pestle.

Rimmed Baking Sheets and Wire Racks: Even when we're not baking, rimmed baking sheets see a lot of use in the kitchen, from corralling ingredients when prepping to acting as a holding surface when frying—often with a wire rack placed inside. We prefer baking sheets that are 18 by 13 inches and have a 1-inch rim all around; buy at least two. Our favorite sheet is **Nordic Ware Bakers Half Sheet** ($14.97), and our favorite rack—the **Checkered Chef Cooling Rack** ($12.95)—fits inside.

Rice Cooker: Rice cookers cook rice (duh) effortlessly and beautifully. Our favorite model, the **Zojirushi 5.5-Cup Neuro Fuzzy Rice Cooker & Warmer** ($250), produces excellent rice—in both small and large batches. This rice cooker employs an operating strategy, "fuzzy logic," that allows it to adjust cooking time and temperature as it cooks, making for a better pot of rice. It also automatically holds rice at a food-safe temperature for up to 12 hours so you can scoop up portions of hot rice when needed. The included cup measure and guided measurement lines make achieving perfect rice as foolproof as possible and free you up to focus on other tasks.

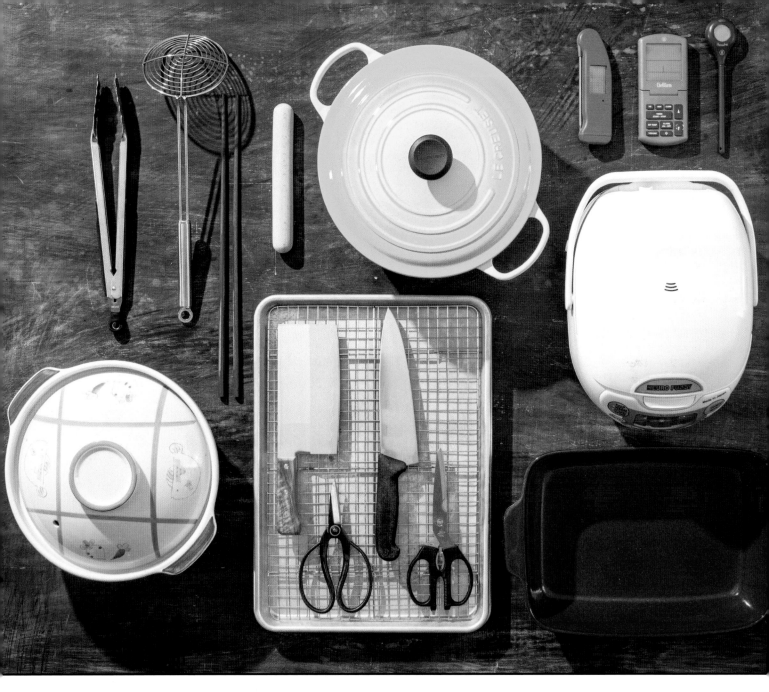

Dutch Oven: Although you can make almost any recipe in this book in a wok, we also turn to this kitchen workhorse for making soups, boiling noodles, braising, and deep frying—especially when we'll be using our wok to stir-fry as well. The most useful size is 6 to 8 quarts. Our winning Dutch oven at that size range is the **Le Creuset 7¼ Quart Round Dutch Oven** ($367.99), and our best buy is the **Cuisinart Chef's Classic Enameled Cast Iron Covered Casserole** ($83.70).

Broiler-Safe Baking Dish: Hong Kong–style dishes like Portuguese Chicken (page 252) and Hong Kong–Style Baked Pork Chop Rice (page 267) finish under the broiler. For a 13 by 9-inch baking dish that can handle the broiler (glass can't), opt for ceramic or porcelain. We like **Mrs. Anderson's Baking Lasagna Pan with Handle (Rose)** ($36.96), which has the best capacity and easy-to-grab looped handles.

Glazed Ceramic or Earthenware Pot: A traditional option for all kinds of braises and one-pot dishes, in addition to being an impressive serving vessel, glazed ceramic or earthenware pots are easier to care for and clean than unglazed. We use a 4½- to 7-quart glazed ceramic or earthenware pot to make Clay Pot Chicken Rice (page 141).

BAMBOO STEAMER

Last but certainly not least, a bamboo steamer is great for steaming lots of food efficiently. Our favorite, the two-tiered **Juvale 10 Inch Bamboo Steamer with Steel Rings for Cooking** ($23.99), has durable slats and steel-reinforced tiers. Wash your steamer with warm soapy water before using for the first time and after each use, then blot excess moisture with a dish towel and air-dry tiers before restacking.

How to Use a Bamboo Steamer

1 Fill wok or skillet with just enough water to be slightly below slats in bottom tier (4 to 6 cups for 14-inch wok, 3½ to 5 cups for 12-inch skillet). Bring water to rolling boil over high heat.

2 Line each tier you're using with 9-inch perforated parchment round (or poke 10 small holes in standard parchment round), and lightly coat with vegetable oil spray.

3 Place food on parchment in single layer, allowing some space between items so that steam can circulate. If cooking different types of food, place denser foods in lower tier. Cover with steamer lid.

4 Adjust heat to bring water to simmer, and place steamer in pan. You should see some wisps of steam coming from top of steamer and from water. If steaming for an extended period, keep kettle of water boiling to replenish without any interruption.

CHOPSTICKS 101

Is there anything a pair of chopsticks can't do? Beyond being a trusted table utensil, they are useful for stirring, mixing fillings, tossing ingredients while stir-frying, lowering and retrieving items when deep frying, sword fighting with siblings, and so much more.

Chinese chopsticks tend to be made from wood, bamboo, or melamine. You'll find wooden chopsticks at finer establishments; melamine (a type of plastic) in most homes because it's easiest to clean; and disposable bamboo chopsticks at street food stalls or takeout joints. Chinese chopsticks have tapered ends that are slightly more blunt than those of other cultures.

Cooking chopsticks, like we mentioned earlier, are made of wood and are uncoated, and are longer than chopsticks for eating, which makes them ideal for turning foods in hot oil or water.

Here's a fun activity to do with the kids on a Saturday night: Practice your chopsticks skills by picking up marbles. You're guaranteed to have minutes of fun.

How to Use Chopsticks

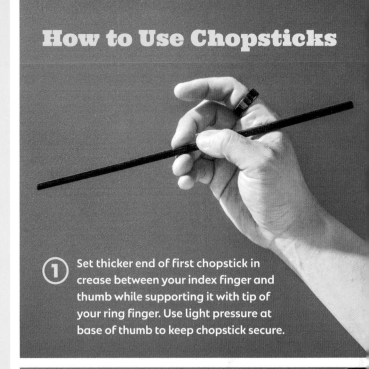

① Set thicker end of first chopstick in crease between your index finger and thumb while supporting it with tip of your ring finger. Use light pressure at base of thumb to keep chopstick secure.

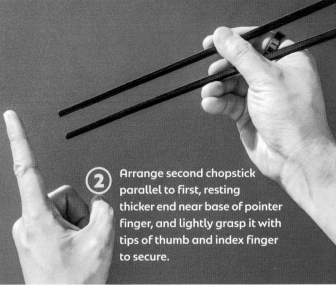

② Arrange second chopstick parallel to first, resting thicker end near base of pointer finger, and lightly grasp it with tips of thumb and index finger to secure.

③ To grasp food, keep bottom chopstick stationary while flexing index finger to open and close chopsticks.

FINGER FOODS AND SMALL PLATES

We'll ease into the world of Chinese cookery with simple
(and simple-ish) starters, all intended to prime you for
more ambitious dishes to come. But don't be fooled by their
relative ease. The recipes in this chapter contain some
all-time favorites, first-ballot inductees in the appetizer
hall of fame. If there's a through line in these dishes,
it's that you may find it hard to stop yourself at one.

Cháyè Dàn 茶葉蛋

Tea Eggs

Makes: 6 eggs — **Total Time:** 1 hour, plus 12½ hours resting and refrigerating   **Difficulty:** ●○○○

6 **large eggs**

¼ **cup dark soy sauce**

1 **tablespoon sugar**

3 **star anise pods**

1 **cinnamon stick**

2 **bay leaves**

¼ **cup black tea leaves**

My father grew up desperately poor in 1920s China. The way to a better life, then as now, was through education. Back then there was no public transportation where he lived. So like many of his generation he walked everywhere, no matter how distant. From his village in Chetianzhen in Southern China, it took him 14 hours to walk to school. (He stayed with relatives near his school in Longchuan and saw his mother only once a month.) What kept him going on those long walks was a pocket of hard-boiled eggs with a pinch of salt, which he ate for energy. My father wasn't the only person who did this.

Eggs were a fact of life in China then, and they remain so today. In time, we Chinese incorporated familiar flavors like tea and soy sauce, infusing the eggs in a pot of savory, smoky marinade. You'll now find tea eggs everywhere—sold hot and fresh at train stations, or in vacuum-sealed bags from a convenience store. It's not surprising that tea eggs became one of my father's favorite snacks.   — Jeffrey

We developed this recipe using oolong tea but you can also use black tea; any variety will work. You can substitute five tea bags for the loose-leaf tea. The longer the eggs sit in the marinade in step 4, the more distinct the marbling will be. The marinade can be reused for up to three batches of eggs. Refrigerate the marinade for up to one week, or freeze for up to one month; bring it to a brief simmer in a saucepan before adding the eggs in step 3.

1   Bring 1 inch water to rolling boil in large saucepan over high heat. Place eggs in steamer basket. Transfer basket to saucepan. Cover, reduce heat to medium (small wisps of steam should escape from beneath lid), and cook for 12 minutes.

2   When eggs are almost finished cooking, fill large bowl halfway with ice and water. Using tongs, transfer eggs to ice bath; let sit for 15 minutes. Discard water in saucepan. Using back of spoon, gently crack eggs all over, leaving shells intact.

Test Kitchen Tips

- If you don't have a steamer basket, use a spoon or tongs to gently place the eggs in the water. It does not matter if the eggs are above the water or partially submerged.

- You can double this recipe as long as you use a pot large enough to hold the eggs in a single layer.

3 Meanwhile, bring 2 cups water, soy sauce, sugar, star anise, cinnamon, and bay leaves to boil in now-empty saucepan over high heat. Reduce heat to low and simmer for 10 minutes. Off heat, stir in tea, then gently add cooked eggs. Let eggs sit in marinade until cool enough to handle, about 30 minutes, turning eggs occasionally.

4 Carefully transfer eggs and tea mixture to 1-gallon zipper-lock bag. Press out as much air as possible from bag, then seal bag. Set bag in bowl so eggs are fully submerged in liquid. Refrigerate for at least 12 hours or up to 24 hours. Remove eggs from marinade and peel. Serve.

Málà Huāshēng 麻辣花生

Sichuan Snack Peanuts

Makes: about 4 cups — **Total Time:** 20 minutes, plus 1 hour cooling — **Difficulty:** ●○○○

3¼ cups (1 pound) dry-roasted peanuts

2 tablespoons peanut or vegetable oil

10 small dried Sichuan chiles, stemmed and sliced ¼ inch thick on bias (optional)

1 tablespoon Sichuan peppercorns, plus 1 teaspoon ground Sichuan peppercorns

2 teaspoons Sichuan chili flakes

2 teaspoons sugar

1½ teaspoons table salt

½ teaspoon five-spice powder

½ teaspoon white pepper

I Feel Numb

Two ingredients are responsible for the signature mala 麻辣 (numbing spicy) flavor profile of these peanuts: Sichuan peppercorns, the "ma" that creates the numbing sensation, and dried Sichuan chiles, the "la" that brings the heat. Using these ingredients both whole and ground adds pops of texture plus robust flavor and aroma.

If there's a debate among Westerners about peanuts, it's usually in the context of peanut butter and whether you prefer it smooth or crunchy. (The correct answer, of course, is crunchy, full stop.) The Chinese version of that debate, however, just might be whether you prefer peanuts boiled or fried. *A Very Chinese Cookbook* is unabashedly Team Fried.

You might be surprised to learn that China is the world's top grower of peanuts. And wok-fried peanuts, particularly in Sichuan, are a beloved snack served with beer or something stronger. There's balanced heat from chiles and a delightful citrus-numb from Sichuan peppercorns, and the nuts are altogether savory, intense, and habit-forming.

Huang Fei Hong, the manufacturer that sells snack-size bags of these spicy peanuts, has popularized them around the globe. Though its version is available online, once you have the ingredients on hand it's cheaper, more satisfying—and, most important, easier—to make your own.

The classic method calls for skinning and slowly deep-frying raw peanuts until well-toasted before pouring off the oil and stir-frying them with spices. But you can achieve a similar outcome (using less oil and taking less time) by starting with unsalted dry-roasted peanuts, which are prepeeled.

Simply toast the nuts in a wok with a couple tablespoons of oil (to deepen their roasty flavors, intensify their crunch, and help the seasonings stick) and then vigorously stir-fry them with ample amounts of Sichuan peppercorns, Sichuan chiles and chili flakes, five-spice powder, white pepper, salt, and sugar for a brief time. Transfer them to a bowl and dig in.   — Kevin + Jeffrey

1   Combine peanuts and oil in 14-inch flat-bottomed wok over medium heat. Cook, stirring frequently, until peanuts begin to darken, 4 to 8 minutes.

2   Stir in sliced chiles, if using, whole and ground peppercorns, chili flakes, sugar, salt, five-spice powder, and pepper. Cook, tossing slowly but constantly, until peanuts are evenly coated and spices are fragrant, about 1 minute. Transfer peanuts to bowl and let cool completely, about 1 hour. Stir to redistribute spices before serving. (Peanuts can be stored in airtight container for up to 1 week; shake before serving.)

Prepping Sichuan Chiles

1 Cut top off of each chile to remove stem.

2 If you want to remove seeds, cut down sides of chile to split in half. Most seeds will shake right out.

3 Use small spoon to scrape off any additional seeds and pull off any dried veins.

Xiā Tǔsī 蝦多士
Shrimp Toast

Serves: 6 to 8 — **Total Time:** 1 hour — **Difficulty:** ●●○○

There's Cantonese food, and then there's Hong Kong food. For a century and a half, until 1997, Hong Kong was under British colonial rule. The result, gastronomically, was Chinese and British ingredients mismashed and coalesced into a fascinating fusion. Shrimp toast is one such example. White sandwich bread gets smeared with a puree of shrimp and speckled with sesame seeds, and then it is deep-fried until it becomes crispy golden finger sandwiches. That's why we entrusted British-born test cook Joe Gitter with developing this recipe, and he says this version (he calls them "sesame prawn toast") tastes exactly like the shrimp toast he grew up eating in London. The funny thing? We can say the very same growing up in Hong Kong.
— Kevin + Jeffrey

Serve with Miracle Whip, Worcestershire sauce, and/or Plum Sauce (page 24).

---

1 Finely chop half of shrimp. Cut remaining shrimp into ½-inch pieces. Using wooden spoon or 4 bundled chopsticks, vigorously stir all of shrimp, egg white, ginger, garlic, sugar, salt, and pepper in bowl until mixture tightens and becomes very sticky, about 3 minutes.

2 Remove crusts from bread and trim slices to measure roughly 3½ inches square. Spread shrimp mixture evenly over 1 side of each bread slice, then sprinkle with sesame seeds, pressing gently to adhere. (Coated bread can be covered and refrigerated for up to 24 hours.)

3 Set wire rack in rimmed baking sheet and line half of rack with triple layer of paper towels. Add oil to 14-inch flat-bottomed wok or large Dutch oven until it measures about 1½ inches deep and heat over medium-high heat to 350 degrees. Using spider skimmer or slotted spoon, carefully lower 3 slices of bread shrimp side down to hot oil and cook until edges of bread are golden brown, about 3 minutes. Adjust burner, if necessary, to maintain oil temperature between 325 and 350 degrees. Using tongs, flip toasts and continue to cook until bread is uniformly golden brown, 30 to 45 seconds.

4 Using spider skimmer, transfer toasts shrimp side up to paper towel–lined side of rack. Let drain for 1 minute, then move to unlined side of rack. Return oil to 350 degrees and repeat with remaining toasts. (Before cooking second batch, line rack with fresh paper towels.) Let toasts cool for 5 minutes. Halve toasts diagonally and transfer to serving platter. Sprinkle with scallions and serve.

1 pound shrimp (any size), peeled, deveined, and tails removed, divided

1 large egg white

2 teaspoons grated fresh ginger

1 garlic clove, minced

1 teaspoon sugar

½ teaspoon table salt

Pinch white pepper

6 slices hearty white sandwich bread

2 tablespoons sesame seeds

2 quarts peanut or vegetable oil for frying

2 scallions, sliced thin

The Miracle of Miracle Whip

Anytime there's a fried shrimp in sight, we Hong Kong folks love dipping it into an unexpected condiment: Miracle Whip. Our people's relationship with the sauce borders on unhealthy—it's used in fruit salads and is our stand-in for mayo (it's what the Cantonese mean when they say "salad dressing"). We understand if you're not ready for honeydew and Miracle Whip, but do try it with shrimp toast! The water is warm, folks.

Chinese Food vs. American Chinese Food

College is a time for discovering yourself. Some people meet the love of their life. They might attend a mind-altering lecture. Or realize one credit from graduation that they were meant for a completely different career.

For me, sophomore year at the University of Southern California was transformative.

It was the first time I tried orange chicken.

Until that moment, the Chinese food I grew up eating was wholly different from the Chinese food my friends in suburban Seattle consumed. It was like my friends and I lived in parallel food universes: They ate crab rangoon, empress chicken, chop suey—dishes not part of my vocabulary. When we ate Chinese food, we ate *Chinese food*—radish cake, winter melon soup, stir-fried clams with black beans. This was the proud cooking of our homeland.

Orange chicken?! It was as foreign a concept for us Hong Kongers as a Crunchwrap Supreme likely was for Mexicans.

We thumbed our noses at this gloppy, over-battered, sickly sweet stuff, which I later learned had a name: American Chinese food. It almost felt like a betrayal to our heritage. "That's not real Chinese food," aunties and uncles would scoff. In time, I realized this was about holding on to something over which we were slowly losing grip. Our family had moved halfway around the world, and this impostor food was breaking those ties with what we left behind, one fortune cookie at a time.

And so it was on that fateful day in college at a Panda Express near campus that orange chicken touched these lips for the first time.

I kept an open mind. And it was just... great. No qualifiers, no caveats, no asterisks. Just unapologetically delicious. I inhaled the whole plate like a maniac.

Instead of viewing my orange chicken scarf-down as a traitorous act, I saw it as finally appreciating American Chinese food as its own genre. It is the food of a diaspora with its own history and narrative, like Indian Chinese cooking (Chicken 65, Gobi Manchurian) or Peruvian Chinese (Arroz Chaufa, Tallarin Saltado).

It'd be easy to view people's food preferences as a purity test. I, and many immigrants, certainly furrowed eyebrows with disapproving judgment. But this business of assessing a dish's merit by its authenticity is a limiting belief. Like any good art, it evolves over time. It travels to new environments and adopts new hosts. Rock and roll crossed the ocean from Memphis to Liverpool and out sprang something different and magical.

The same can be said for Cantonese immigrants in the mid-19th century, lured to California by the Gold Rush, then sticking around when they realized restaurants were a viable business. The chefs quickly learned to tweak their dishes to please their diners' palates, and thus a new cuisine took root. These days there are more Chinese restaurants in America than McDonald's, Burger King, and Starbucks combined.

None of us Pangs dismiss American Chinese food today. We've come to embrace it and not view it as a threat, because it's not in competition with what we grew up cooking. Not to mention American Chinese cooking is dang delicious: Good food is good food, no matter the origin. And if you picked up this book because you've eaten orange chicken and enjoyed it, and are now curious about our cooking? Thanks for enrolling in Very Chinese Cooking 101.

— Kevin

Měishì Chūnjuǎn 美式春卷
American-Style Egg Rolls

Makes: 12 egg rolls — **Total Time:** 1 hour, plus 45 minutes resting — **Difficulty:** ●●●○

My favorite American Chinese restaurant is in Chicago and is called Chef's Special Cocktail Bar. The chefs behind the operation are not Chinese but instead are two White dudes with a fine-dining pedigree. Although the preceding sentences might be cause for permanent revocation of my Asian card, discovering this restaurant has helped evolve my previously dismissive stance on American Chinese cooking.

The culinary minds behind Chef's Special Cocktail Bar are Aaron Kabot and Jason Vincent, who have applied the precise execution of a Michelin-starred restaurant to dishes such as cashew chicken and walnut shrimp. You won't find highfalutin additions like foie gras or shaved truffles.

What they do serve are dishes cooked with incredible care and scholarship. Dining there has shown me the delicious possibilities of the American Chinese genre or, really, any misunderstood cuisine—source great ingredients, season properly, and cook at the right time and temperature, and the results can be glorious. And for that, this Chinese food writer says: "Respect."

The dish that especially wows me at Chef's Special Cocktail Bar is the egg roll. It's the best version I've ever tasted. The pork-shrimp filling is generous and flavorful, almost like the texture of shu mai. My attempts to pry the recipe were unsuccessful ("It took me two years to perfect the recipe," Vincent told me). So I did the only thing possible for an employee of America's Test Kitchen: Sample an unhealthy quantity of the restaurant's egg rolls and create a comparable version.

My sleuthing yielded a few clues about ingredients (fatty Berkshire pork shoulder, rock shrimp, five-spice powder). Mostly, though, I relied on my trained palate, honed through my many years as a newspaper restaurant critic.

In most American-style egg roll recipes, the ground pork filling and vegetables are cooked separately, then rolled into wrappers and fried. I kept going back to my tasting notes of "like a shu mai." My colleague Bryan Roof suggested whipping ground pork and lard in a stand mixer until the pork filling turns snow-white. I then added raw shrimp, seasoned with the marinade we use for shu mai, and combined the mixture with cooked cabbage and carrots, plus mung bean noodles.

After a dozen batches, I arrived at an egg roll recipe that's pretty dang delicious. Let's call it the second-best egg roll I've ever tasted.   — Kevin

Look for freshly ground pork sold at the butcher counter, which has more fat and a coarser texture than prepackaged pork. Adding a small amount of lard makes for even richer egg rolls. Serve with Plum Sauce (page 24) and/or hot mustard.

- 12 ounces ground pork
- 2 tablespoons lard, cut into 4 pieces, room temperature (optional)
- 4 ounces shrimp (any size), peeled, deveined, tails removed, and coarsely chopped
- 2 tablespoons soy sauce, divided
- 4 teaspoons sugar, divided
- 1 tablespoon oyster sauce
- 1 tablespoon chicken bouillon powder
- 1½ teaspoons toasted sesame oil
- 1½ teaspoons Shaoxing wine
- 1½ teaspoons Chinese white rice vinegar
- 1 teaspoon table salt
- ½ teaspoon white pepper
- ¼ teaspoon five-spice powder
- 1 teaspoon vegetable oil
- 2 cups chopped green cabbage
- 1 carrot, peeled and shredded
- 1½ ounces dried mung bean glass noodles
- 12 (8-inch) square egg roll wrappers
- 2 quarts peanut or vegetable oil for frying

recipe continues on next page

1 Using stand mixer fitted with paddle, beat pork and lard, if using, on medium speed until well combined and mixture has lightened in color, about 2 minutes. Reduce speed to medium-low and add shrimp, 1 tablespoon soy sauce, 1 tablespoon sugar, oyster sauce, bouillon powder, sesame oil, Shaoxing wine, vinegar, salt, pepper, and five-spice powder. Mix until just combined, about 30 seconds. Cover bowl with plastic wrap and refrigerate for 30 minutes.

2 Heat empty 14-inch flat-bottomed wok over high heat until just beginning to smoke. Reduce heat to medium-high, drizzle vegetable oil around perimeter of wok, and heat until just smoking. Add cabbage, carrot, remaining 1 tablespoon soy sauce, and remaining 1 teaspoon sugar and cook, tossing slowly but constantly, until cabbage is just softened, about 2 minutes. Transfer vegetable mixture to large plate, spread into even layer, and refrigerate until cooled slightly, about 15 minutes.

3 Meanwhile, soak noodles in 4 cups hot water in bowl for 15 minutes. Drain noodles and rinse under cold running water until chilled. Drain noodles again, then transfer to cutting board and chop into rough 1-inch lengths. Return bowl with pork mixture to mixer fitted with paddle. Add vegetable mixture and noodles and mix on low speed until well combined, about 1 minute.

4 Fill small bowl with water. Working with 1 wrapper at a time, arrange on counter so 1 corner points toward edge of counter. Place rounded ¼ cup filling on lower half of wrapper and mold it with your fingers into neat 4-inch-long cylinder parallel to edge of counter. Dip your fingertip in water and moisten entire border of wrapper with thin film of water.

5 Fold bottom corner of wrapper over filling and press gently along length of filling to remove air pockets. Fold side corners over to enclose filling snugly; gently roll to form tight cylinder and press edges to seal. Transfer egg roll seam side down to parchment paper–lined plate and cover with damp paper towel while shaping remaining egg rolls. Stack egg rolls as needed, separating layers with additional parchment. (Egg rolls can be frozen until solid, then transferred to zipper-lock bag and stored in freezer for up to 1 month. Do not thaw before frying; increase frying time by 2 minutes.)

6 Set wire rack in rimmed baking sheet and line rack with triple layer of paper towels. Add peanut oil to clean, dry, 14-inch flat-bottomed wok or large Dutch oven until it measures about 1½ inches deep and heat over medium-high heat to 350 degrees. Using tongs, carefully add 6 egg rolls seam side down to hot oil and cook until deep golden brown, 4 to 8 minutes, flipping egg rolls halfway through frying. Adjust burner, if necessary, to maintain oil temperature between 325 and 350 degrees. Using tongs, transfer egg rolls to prepared rack and let drain. Return oil to 350 degrees and repeat with remaining 6 egg rolls; transfer to prepared rack and let drain. Serve.

Test Kitchen Tips

- This recipe can easily be doubled; fry the egg rolls in four batches, keeping fried egg rolls warm in a 200-degree oven.

- Mung bean glass noodles are also called cellophane noodles or bean threads.

Assembling Egg Rolls

① Place rounded ¼ cup of filling on lower half of wrapper. Use your fingers to shape filling into 4-inch-long cylinder.

② Dip your fingertip in water, then moisten entire border of wrapper with thin film of water.

③ Fold bottom corner of wrapper over filling and press gently to remove air pockets. Fold side corners over to enclose.

④ Gently roll into tight cylinder and press edges to seal. Cover egg roll with moist paper towel while shaping remaining egg rolls.

Spring Rolls (Cantonese Egg Rolls)

Makes: 16 spring rolls — **Total Time:** 1¼ hours — **Difficulty:** ●●●○

1½ ounces dried shiitake mushrooms, rinsed

2 ounces dried mung bean glass noodles

2 tablespoons vegetable oil

6 scallions, white and green parts separated and sliced thin

4 garlic cloves, minced

4 teaspoons grated fresh ginger

2 tablespoons soy sauce

1 tablespoon Shaoxing wine

1 teaspoon toasted sesame oil

½ teaspoon table salt

¼ teaspoon white pepper

4 cups shredded napa cabbage

3 carrots, peeled and cut into 2-inch-long matchsticks

2 tablespoons cornstarch

16 (8-inch) square spring roll wrappers

2 quarts peanut or vegetable oil for frying

The First Cut Is the Deepest

Even after minutes out of the deep fryer, these spring rolls keep preposterously hot. Take a page from dim sum servers: Snip them in half with scissors and avoid having your day ruined.

Spring rolls the way we know of spring rolls are different from spring rolls most others recognize as spring rolls. Got all that? For us Cantonese, spring rolls are similar to what the Western world calls egg rolls—only thinner, with a smooth and crisp exterior, and in the same family as Filipino lumpia and Vietnamese cha gio. They are a staple of every dim sum parlor from Singapore to San Francisco. In this version, we've left out the pork to make them vegetarian. Make sure you get the correct spring roll wrappers (and here's where it gets confusing): The ones you want are square, flour-based wrappers, and not the translucent circular wrappers. Both might be labeled "spring roll wrappers." The easiest way to confirm is to look at the photo on the packaging—if the rolls look crispy and fried, those wrappers are the ones you want.   — Kevin + Jeffrey

This recipe can easily be doubled; fry the spring rolls in six batches, keeping fried spring rolls warm in a 200-degree oven. Serve with Worcestershire Sauce or Plum Sauce (page 24).

1   Microwave 1 cup water and mushrooms in covered bowl until steaming, about 1 minute. Let sit until softened, about 5 minutes. Lift mushrooms from bowl with fork and discard liquid. Squeeze mushrooms dry, remove stems, and chop. Soak noodles in 4 cups hot water in bowl for 15 minutes. Drain and rinse under cold water until chilled. Drain noodles again and chop into 1-inch lengths; set aside.

2   Heat empty 14-inch flat-bottomed wok over high heat until just beginning to smoke, about 3 minutes. Reduce heat to medium-high, drizzle vegetable oil around perimeter of wok, and heat until just smoking. Add mushrooms and cook, stirring constantly, until heated through, about 2 minutes. Add scallion whites, garlic, and ginger and cook, stirring constantly, until fragrant, about 1 minute. Stir in soy sauce, Shaoxing wine, sesame oil, salt, and pepper and cook until thickened to glaze, about 30 seconds.

3   Add cabbage and carrots and cook, tossing slowly but constantly, until cabbage is just softened, about 2 minutes. Off heat, add scallion greens and noodles and toss to combine. Transfer vegetable mixture to large plate, spread into even layer, and refrigerate until cool enough to handle, about 5 minutes.

4   Whisk cornstarch and 2 tablespoons water in bowl until combined. Arrange 1 wrapper on counter so 1 corner points toward edge of counter. Place 2 heaping tablespoons filling on lower half of wrapper and mold it with your fingers into neat 4-inch-long cylinder parallel to edge of counter. Using pastry brush, apply light layer of cornstarch slurry onto top corner of wrapper, being sure to coat edges.

5   Fold bottom corner of wrapper over filling and press gently along length of filling to remove air pockets. Fold side corners over to enclose filling snugly; gently roll to form cylinder. Transfer spring roll seam side down to parchment paper–lined platter. Press gently on spring roll to flatten slightly, and cover with damp paper towel while shaping remaining spring rolls; do not stack. Wipe any excess moisture from counter and repeat with remaining wrappers and filling. (Spring rolls can be frozen until solid, then transferred to zipper-lock bag and stored in freezer for up to 1 month. Do not thaw before frying; increase frying time by 2 minutes.)

6   Set wire rack in rimmed baking sheet and line half of rack with triple layer of paper towels. Add peanut oil to clean, dry, 14-inch flat-bottomed wok or large Dutch oven until it measures about 1½ inches deep and heat over medium-high heat to 375 degrees. Using tongs, carefully add 5 spring rolls to hot oil and cook until light golden brown, 5 to 7 minutes, turning as needed for even browning. Adjust burner, if necessary, to maintain oil temperature between 350 and 375 degrees.

7   Using spider skimmer or slotted spoon, transfer spring rolls to paper towel–lined side of prepared rack and let drain for 1 minute, then move to unlined side of rack. Return oil to 375 degrees and repeat with remaining spring rolls in 2 batches. (Before cooking each batch of spring rolls, line rack with fresh layer of paper towels.) Let cool for 5 minutes. Serve.

Sesame Balls
(page 60)

Jiānduī 煎堆

Sesame Balls

Makes: 8 balls — **Total Time:** 1½ hours — **Difficulty:** ●●●○

- 1½ **cups (8¼ ounces) glutinous rice flour**
- ½ **teaspoon baking powder**
- ⅛ **teaspoon table salt**
- ⅓ **cup (2⅓ ounces) sugar**
- 8 **teaspoons smooth sweetened red bean paste**
- ½ **cup sesame seeds**
- 2 **quarts peanut or vegetable oil for frying**

The Chinese are probably the world leaders in eating superstitious foods. The name of a dish might sound vaguely like a term of good luck, or it may resemble a bar of gold bullion . . . and so we must eat lots of it. Sorry, those are the rules.

We Cantonese always make fried sesame balls around Chinese New Year. We do so because of this one saying: 煎堆轆轆, 金銀滿屋. Loosely translated, it means sesame balls will have gold and silver rolling into your household.

In fact, because it's so important for us to make this dish perfectly, Cantonese home cooks have been known to ban children from the kitchen while making sesame balls, for fear they'll say something inauspicious and bring bad luck (or worse, imperfect balls).

For the record, we're legally obliged to say America's Test Kitchen is in no way promising gold or silver if you make these. What we can promise are irresistibly crisp and chewy fried balls with a sweet red bean paste center.   — Kevin + Jeffrey

---

Glutinous rice flour is also sold as sweet rice flour. We developed this recipe using Mochiko brand rice flour. Lotus seed paste, black sesame seed paste, and mung bean paste can be used in place of the red bean paste. This recipe can be easily doubled; fry the sesame balls in two batches.

---

1   Whisk flour, baking powder, and salt together in large bowl. Bring ¾ cup water and sugar to boil in small saucepan over high heat until sugar has dissolved. Using rubber spatula, stir hot syrup into flour mixture until combined and no dry flour remains. Transfer dough to clean counter and knead with hands until smooth, about 3 minutes. Return dough to bowl, cover tightly with plastic wrap, and let rest for 30 minutes.

2   Meanwhile, divide bean paste into 1 teaspoon portions. Using lightly moistened hands, roll each portion into ball and transfer to plate. Cover loosely with plastic and refrigerate until ready to use.

3   Divide dough into 8 equal pieces (about 2 ounces each). Cover with damp towel. Working with 1 piece of dough at a time, use hands to roll into ball. Place ball on counter and flatten with palm of hand into 2-inch-wide circle. Place 1 portion of bean paste in center of circle. Gather sides of dough around paste, pushing out air pockets, and pinch top to seal, enclosing paste in center. Remoisten hands and roll ball, smoothing any cracks with your fingertips. Cover with damp towel.

4   Place ½ cup water in small bowl. Place sesame seeds in shallow plate. Working with 1 ball at a time, roll in water, letting excess drip off, then coat with sesame seeds, pressing gently to adhere. Transfer to plate.

5   Line rimmed baking sheet with triple layer of paper towels. Add oil to 14-inch flat-bottomed wok or large Dutch oven until it measures about 1½ inches deep and heat over medium-high heat to 325 degrees. Using spider skimmer or slotted spoon, carefully add balls, 1 at a time, to hot oil. Cook, stirring constantly, until balls begin to float, about 4 minutes. Adjust burner, if necessary, to maintain oil temperature between 300 and 325 degrees.

6   Using spider skimmer, fully submerge each ball, gently pressing it against side or bottom of wok to deflate by about ½ inch, then release. Continuously submerge, press, and release balls until puffy and light golden brown, about 4 minutes. Using spider skimmer, transfer sesame balls to prepared sheet. Let cool for 5 minutes. Serve.

Test Kitchen Tip

Recipe developer David Yu notes: "To produce perfect balls every time, it is important to be active during the frying process. Keep the balls moving and rotating in the oil to ensure an even goldenness around the shell. The compressing and releasing may seem counterintuitive, but this technique is crucial for the expansion of the balls as well as their development into perfect spheres. Treat each ball gently and diligently and you'll be rewarded with an irresistibly crisp yet chewy snack!"

Shaping Sesame Balls

1   Place 1 portion of bean paste on dough circle, then gather sides of dough around paste, pushing out air pockets.

2   Pinch top of dough to seal, enclosing paste in center.

3   Working with 1 ball at a time, roll in water, letting excess drip off, then coat with sesame seeds, pressing gently to adhere.

Cōngyóubǐng 葱油餅
Scallion Pancakes

Serves: 4 to 6 — **Total Time:** 1¼ hours, plus 30 minutes resting — **Difficulty:** ●●○○

1½ cups (7½ ounces) plus 1 tablespoon all-purpose flour, divided

¾ cup boiling water

7 tablespoons vegetable oil, divided

1 tablespoon toasted sesame oil

1 teaspoon kosher salt, divided

4 scallions, sliced thin, divided

1 recipe Soy-Vinegar Dipping Sauce (page 23)

Jeffrey — The first recipe video I produced for my YouTube channel was for scallion pancakes. I learned the recipe from my wife Catherine's mother, who grew up in Shanghai, where these pancakes are sold as street food.

Kevin — Calling these "pancakes" doesn't do the dish justice. These are crispy flatbreads that pull apart to flaky layers, yielding a delicate chewy interior. The effort-to-yield ratio for scallion pancakes is exceptionally high—in fact, make a stack and freeze them to pan-fry on a rainy day.

Jeffrey — In this recipe, we use boiling water to form the dough. Not only does the hot water make it easier to roll the dough very thin without springing back, it is the secret to maximizing the alternating layers of dough and fat, creating those flaky layers. Make a small slit in the center of the pancake before frying. This prevents steam from building up underneath the pancake, ensuring it lays flat and cooks evenly.

1   Using wooden spoon, mix 1½ cups flour and boiling water in bowl to form rough dough. When cool enough to handle, transfer dough to lightly floured counter and knead until tacky (but not sticky) ball forms, about 4 minutes (dough will not be perfectly smooth). Cover loosely with plastic wrap and let rest for 30 minutes. Stir 1 tablespoon vegetable oil, sesame oil, and remaining 1 tablespoon flour together in bowl; set aside.

2   Divide dough in half. Cover 1 half of dough with plastic and set aside. Roll remaining dough into 12-inch round on lightly floured counter. Drizzle with 1 tablespoon oil-flour mixture and use pastry brush to spread evenly over entire surface. Sprinkle with ½ teaspoon salt and half of scallions. Roll dough into cylinder. Coil cylinder into spiral, tuck end underneath, and flatten spiral with your palm. Cover with plastic and repeat with remaining dough, oil-flour mixture, salt, and scallions.

3   Roll first spiral into 9-inch round. Cut ½-inch slit in center of pancake. Cover with plastic. Roll second spiral and cut slit in pancake. (Pancakes can be stacked between layers of parchment paper, wrapped tightly in plastic, and refrigerated for up to 24 hours or frozen for up to 1 month. If frozen, thaw pancakes in single layer for 15 minutes before cooking.)

Test Kitchen Tip

Use a cast-iron skillet if you can—an even, high heat is key for crispy browning. If you use a stainless-steel skillet, you may need to increase the heat slightly.

4 Meanwhile, place 10-inch cast-iron skillet over low heat and preheat for 10 minutes. Place 2 tablespoons vegetable oil in skillet and increase heat to medium-low. Place 1 pancake in skillet (oil should sizzle). Cover and cook, shaking skillet occasionally, until pancake is slightly puffy and golden brown on underside, 1 to 1½ minutes. (If underside is not browning after 1 minute, turn heat up slightly. If it is browning too quickly, turn heat down slightly.)

5 Drizzle 1 tablespoon vegetable oil over pancake. Use pastry brush to distribute over entire surface. Carefully flip pancake. Cover and cook, shaking skillet occasionally, until second side is golden brown, 1 to 1½ minutes. Uncover skillet and continue to cook until bottom is deep golden brown and crispy, 30 to 60 seconds. Flip and cook until deep golden brown and crispy, 30 to 60 seconds. Transfer to wire rack. Repeat with remaining 3 tablespoons vegetable oil and remaining pancake. Cut each pancake into 8 wedges and serve with dipping sauce.

turn to see how to shape pancakes

Shaping Scallion Pancakes

① Roll dough into 12-inch round.

② Brush round with oil-flour mixture; sprinkle with salt and scallions.

③ Roll up round into cylinder.

④ Coil cylinder, tucking end underneath, then flatten.

⑤ Roll out flattened spiral into 9-inch round; cut slit.

Pāi Huánggua 拍黃瓜

Smashed Cucumbers

Serves: 4 — **Total Time:** 35 minutes — **Difficulty:** ●○○○

Smashed cucumbers can be found on many Sichuan tables and are a refreshing and light starter that portends the spicy dishes to come. This is a fun dish for involving kids, because you get to place cucumbers inside a zipper-lock bag and bash them silly with a rolling pin. In addition to relieving stress, this step has a culinary benefit: It creates craggy, irregular pieces, helping the dressing cling to the cucumbers.   — Kevin + Jeffrey

We like using English cucumbers here because they are nearly seedless and have thin, crisp skins.

1   Cut cucumbers crosswise into 3- to 4-inch lengths and place in 1-gallon zipper-lock bag. Seal bag. Using small skillet or rolling pin, firmly but gently smash cucumbers until flattened and split lengthwise into 3 to 4 spears each. Tear spears into rough 1-inch pieces and transfer to colander set in large bowl. Toss cucumbers with salt and let sit for at least 15 minutes or up to 30 minutes.

2   Meanwhile, whisk vinegar and garlic together in medium bowl and let sit for at least 5 minutes or up to 15 minutes.

3   Whisk soy sauce, oil, and sugar into vinegar mixture until sugar has dissolved. Add cucumbers, discarding any extracted liquid, and sesame seeds to bowl with dressing and toss to combine. Drizzle with chili oil, if desired, and serve immediately.

2 (14-ounce) English cucumbers, ends trimmed

1½ teaspoons kosher salt

4 teaspoons Chinese black vinegar

1 teaspoon garlic, minced to paste

1 tablespoon soy sauce

2 teaspoons toasted sesame oil

1 teaspoon sugar

1 teaspoon sesame seeds, toasted

Chili oil (optional)

No. 1 Smash Hit

You want the cucumbers to achieve a crisp, pickle-like texture by shedding some of their liquid. The smashing process helps here by breaking down cell walls to release liquid, which speeds up the effects of a quick salting that pulls out even more moisture. If any seeds come loose during smashing, leave them in the bag, as they're mostly water.

Lǎohǔ Cài 老虎菜
Tiger Salad

Serves: 4 — **Total Time:** 25 minutes — **Difficulty:** ●○○○

The name comes from the idea that the bold spiciness of this salad is powerful like a tiger. Ironically, we find this vibrant salad rather refreshing, as it is served to stimulate the appetite at the beginning of a meal or to reset the palate between courses. We balance the bracing vinaigrette, piquant scallions, and hot chiles with the herbal freshness of cilantro and the juicy crunch of celery. The earthy sweetness of the nuts and seeds and the rich sesame oil further temper the dish. — Kevin + Jeffrey

For a spicier salad that'll make you roar, include the chile seeds.

1   In small bowl, stir vinegar, sugar, salt, and soy sauce until sugar and salt are completely dissolved. Add oil and Thai chile and stir to combine.

2   In large bowl, combine cilantro, celery, scallions, and serrano. Sprinkle with sesame seeds and dressing and toss to combine. Transfer salad to platter, sprinkle with peanuts, and serve immediately.

1 tablespoon Chinese white rice vinegar

1 teaspoon sugar

½ teaspoon table salt

½ teaspoon soy sauce

¾ teaspoon toasted sesame oil

1 Thai chile, stemmed, halved, seeded, and sliced thin

3½ cups fresh cilantro leaves and tender stems, chopped into 2-inch lengths

4 celery ribs, sliced on bias ¼ inch thick

3 scallions, sliced thin

1 serrano chile, stemmed, quartered, seeded, and sliced thin

2 teaspoons sesame seeds, toasted

2 tablespoons chopped salted dry-roasted peanuts

Mouthwatering Chicken

Serves: 4 to 6 — **Total Time:** 1 hour — **Difficulty:** ●●○○

4 (5- to 7-ounce) bone-in chicken thighs, trimmed

Table salt for poaching chicken

¼ cup vegetable oil

1 (½-inch) piece ginger, peeled and smashed

1 garlic clove, smashed and peeled

3 tablespoons Sichuan chili flakes

2 tablespoons soy sauce

1 tablespoon Chinese black vinegar

1 tablespoon toasted sesame oil

2 teaspoons sugar

2 teaspoons Sichuan peppercorns, toasted and coarsely ground

1 scallion, green parts only, sliced thin

2 tablespoons coarsely chopped fresh cilantro

2 tablespoons chopped dry-roasted peanuts

1 teaspoon sesame seeds, toasted

Test Kitchen Tip

Recipe developer David Yu notes: "Before slicing, make sure the chicken has cooled down so the skin has time to tighten up slightly. Use a sharp knife and slice confidently to ensure that each piece is a combination of skin and meat. Your plate will look beautiful and each bite will be mouthwatering."

If we're being technical, the correct translation of this cherished Sichuan dish would be "Saliva Chicken." Thankfully, we read a few marketing books before embarking on this cookbook and decided to label the dish "Mouthwatering Chicken" instead—it's so delicious it'll make you drool. Juicy dark meat chicken sits in a moat of tingly, spicy, savory sauce designed to activate taste buds.

The joys of the dish come in the delicate slices of poached chicken with cool fatty skin attached. Some Western palates get turned off by this texture, which might be described as slimy. The Chinese, however, savor the slipperiness, which we call waat 滑 in Cantonese. There's a certain luxuriousness with the slick mouthfeel we quite enjoy, like a freshly shucked oyster.   — Kevin + Jeffrey

1   Place 1 chicken thigh skin side down on cutting board. Using sharp paring knife, cut slit along length of thigh bone to expose bone. Using tip of knife, cut meat from bone, being careful not to cut through skin. Slip knife under bone to separate bone from meat. Discard bone and trim any remaining cartilage from thigh. Repeat with remaining thighs.

2   Whisk 4 quarts cool water and 2 tablespoons salt in Dutch oven until salt has dissolved. Arrange chicken skin side up in collapsible steamer basket in even layer, tucking thinner portions of meat under itself to form compact thighs. Submerge steamer basket in pot. Heat over medium heat, stirring occasionally to even out hot spots, until water begins to boil, 15 to 20 minutes. Remove pot from heat, cover, and let sit until chicken registers 175 degrees, 17 to 22 minutes. Transfer chicken skin side up to cutting board and let cool while preparing dressing.

3   Combine vegetable oil, ginger, and garlic in bowl. Microwave until oil is hot and bubbling, about 2 minutes. Stir in chili flakes and let cool for 10 minutes. Strain oil mixture through fine-mesh strainer set over large bowl; discard solids. Whisk soy sauce, vinegar, sesame oil, sugar, and peppercorns into strained oil. (Chicken and dressing can be refrigerated separately for up to 24 hours; bring chicken to room temperature before slicing, and whisk dressing to recombine before proceeding with recipe.)

4   Slice chicken crosswise into ½-inch-thick slices. Transfer chicken skin side up to shallow serving dish. Pour sauce over chicken and sprinkle with scallion, cilantro, peanuts, and sesame seeds. Serve.

Char Siu-Style Spareribs

Serves: 6 to 8 — **Total Time:** 2¾ hours — **Difficulty:** ●●●○

1 (6-inch) piece ginger, peeled and sliced thin

8 garlic cloves, peeled

1 cup maltose or honey

¾ cup hoisin sauce

¾ cup soy sauce

½ cup Shaoxing wine

2 teaspoons five-spice powder

1 teaspoon red food coloring (optional)

1 teaspoon white pepper

2 (2½- to 3-pound) racks St. Louis–style spareribs, trimmed and cut into individual ribs

2 tablespoons toasted sesame oil

Test Kitchen Tips

- Maltose is sometimes labeled "malt syrup." You can also use honey with little difference in flavor.

- Adding water to the baking sheet during roasting helps prevent smoking.

- Red food coloring enhances the color of the ribs; feel free to leave it out but note that your ribs will not look as red as restaurant versions.

If you're lucky enough to live near a Chinatown, you'll find these rich mahogany pork ribs hanging in the window of Cantonese barbecue shops, daring you not to stop and gawk with mouth agape. They get their distinctive sweet-spiced flavor from hoisin sauce, soy sauce, Shaoxing wine, five-spice powder, and maltose.

To cook the ribs, restaurants use a vertical roaster at very high heat, creating charred, crusty, tender meat. Although this fridge-size roaster is a commercial piece of equipment not found in homes, we think that our method mimics the restaurant process faithfully (see page 321 for our advanced-level char siu recipe).

We slice the ribs into individual pieces to speed up cooking and create more surface area, then braise them in a highly seasoned liquid to help the flavor penetrate thoroughly and quickly. That liquid then gets reduced to a full-bodied glaze in which we toss the ribs before roasting them to color and crisp their exteriors. For sheer effort-to-impressiveness, few recipes in this book are as crowd-pleasing as this one. — Kevin + Jeffrey

1   Pulse ginger and garlic in food processor until finely chopped, 10 to 12 pulses, scraping down sides of bowl as needed; transfer to Dutch oven. Whisk in maltose, hoisin, soy sauce, ½ cup water, Shaoxing wine, five-spice powder, food coloring, if using, and white pepper. Add ribs and toss to coat (ribs will not be fully submerged). Bring to simmer over high heat, then reduce heat to low, cover, and cook for 1¼ hours, stirring occasionally.

2   Adjust oven rack to middle position and heat oven to 425 degrees. Using tongs, transfer ribs to large bowl. Strain braising liquid through fine-mesh strainer set over large container, pressing on solids to extract as much liquid as possible; discard solids. Let braising liquid settle for 10 minutes. Using wide, shallow spoon, skim fat from surface and discard.

3   Return braising liquid to pot and add oil. Bring to boil over high heat and cook until syrupy and reduced to 2½ cups, 16 to 20 minutes.

4   Set wire rack in aluminum foil–lined rimmed baking sheet and pour ½ cup water into sheet. Transfer half of ribs to pot with braising liquid and toss to coat. Arrange ribs bone side up on prepared wire rack, letting excess glaze drip off. Roast until edges of ribs start to caramelize, 5 to 7 minutes. Flip ribs and continue to roast until second side starts to caramelize, 5 to 7 minutes. Transfer ribs to serving platter and tent with foil. Repeat with remaining ribs. Serve.

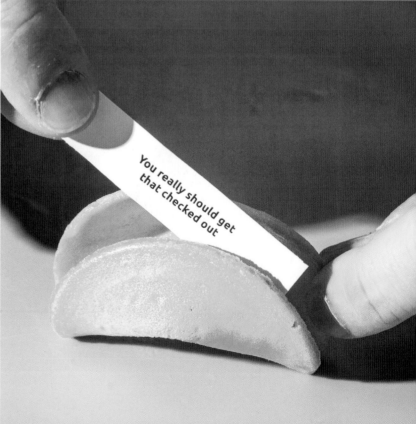

How to Hack a Fortune Cookie

When I was young, I bought a book by the magicians Penn & Teller that came with a page of fake fortune cookie fortunes, things like "The chef spat in your food." The 10-year-old me thought it was stupid-hilarious. Now that I've matured into a grown-up and father, I find it just as stupid-hilarious.

I've since learned how to open up a fortune cookie and switch out the paper slip with something far more nefarious, all without the cookie breaking.

Promise you'll use this newfound knowledge for good, not evil.

1. On your word processing program of choice, print out a sheet of fake messages in seven-point type, such as: "Will you marry me?" or "Your card is the three of hearts" or "The doctor says it shouldn't be that color." Cut into fortune cookie–appropriate lengths.

2. Procure fortune cookies from your favorite Chinese restaurant or Asian supermarket. Take one; carefully open one end of the plastic wrapper. Remove the cookie and place on a microwave-safe dish.

3. Fold a damp paper towel into a small package and place it on the dish next to the cookie. Microwave for 20–25 seconds.

4. Time is of the essence: The cookie will momentarily be warm and pliable enough to pry open. Take out the existing fortune and slip in your fake one. Shape the rapidly cooling cookie back to its fortune cookie shape.

5. Place the cooled cookie back into its plastic wrapper. Use an electric hair straightener to seal the opened end.

— Kevin

SOUPS AND DUMPLINGS

If you're seeking maximal food comfort, the gastronomic equivalent of a throw blanket, you've arrived at the right chapter. Here you'll find everything from a cozy soup that comes together in a snap (page 78), to the secrets of a sturdy and crisp pot sticker crust (page 103), all the way to the most impressive recipe in this book—and the most challenging to master (page 117). These dishes are the ones we rely on most to warm bellies and souls.

Jīróng Lìmǐ Gēng 雞蓉粟米羹
Corn and Chicken Soup

Serves: 4 to 6 — **Total Time:** 45 minutes — **Difficulty:** ●○○○

- 1 (3- to 4-ounce) boneless, skinless chicken thigh, trimmed and cut into ¼-inch pieces
- 5 teaspoons plus ½ cup water, divided
- 1 teaspoon plus 3 tablespoons cornstarch, divided
- 1 teaspoon soy sauce
- ⅛ teaspoon baking soda
- 2 large eggs
- 4 cups chicken broth, divided
- 5–7 ears corn, kernels cut from cobs (5 cups), divided
- 2 tablespoons finely chopped deli ham
- ¾ teaspoon table salt
- ¼ teaspoon white pepper
- 1 scallion, sliced thin

A Secret from Egg Drop Soup

It can be hard to achieve consistent and even egg ribbon strands instead of soupy scrambled eggs. Our solution was to add a touch of water to thin out the eggs, then pour the mixture in a thin, steady stream into the swirling soup. The result: perfectly delicate egg ribbons.

When I first took my American-born wife to Hong Kong, she was surprised to find ham macaroni soup on a diner menu. She never imagined something that sounded so Midwestern Americana could be so Chinese. Because Hong Kong is a port city on the South China Sea, it's easy to find food from far-flung places on our supermarket shelves. That includes canned creamed corn imported from the United States, which became something of a pantry staple in homes. Corn and chicken soup grew out of our geography and trade, in time becoming a practical dish of homey comfort. Funnily enough, this soup would make the return transoceanic trip and achieve popularity in American Chinese restaurants.

Our recipe, developed by Sandra Wu for *Cook's Illustrated*, takes the soup's homestyle appeal and uses in-season fresh corn cut from cobs for peak sweetness. (Thawed frozen corn works in a pinch.) To replicate the creaminess of the canned stuff, we puree half the kernels and leave the rest whole. Chicken thigh meat is marinated in that traditional Chinese way to achieve silky tenderness, and we finish the soup with chopped smoked ham and feathery egg ribbons. In the canon of warm, soothing soups for cold nights, this one's tough to top.   — Kevin

1   Combine chicken, 1 tablespoon water, 1 teaspoon cornstarch, soy sauce, and baking soda in bowl. In 2-cup liquid measuring cup, beat eggs and 2 teaspoons water with fork until thoroughly combined; set aside. Mix ½ cup broth and remaining 3 tablespoons cornstarch in small bowl until thoroughly combined; set aside.

2   Process 2½ cups corn and remaining ½ cup water in blender on low speed until thick puree forms, about 30 seconds. Increase speed to high; process until smooth, about 1 minute. Strain through fine-mesh strainer set over large saucepan, pressing with rubber spatula to extract as much liquid as possible; discard solids.

3   Add ham, salt, pepper, remaining 3½ cups broth, and remaining 2½ cups corn to corn puree. Bring to boil over medium-high heat. Reduce heat to maintain simmer and add chicken mixture, stirring to break up any clumps. Partially cover and simmer for 5 minutes (broth may look curdled as it comes to simmer). Stir broth-cornstarch mixture to recombine. Add to soup and cook, uncovered, stirring occasionally, until soup has thickened slightly, about 2 minutes.

4   Off heat, use 1 hand to stir soup with fork or chopsticks while using other hand to pour egg mixture in slow, steady stream into swirling soup. Continue stirring soup until cooked thin egg ribbons appear, about 1 minute. Season soup with salt and pepper to taste. Sprinkle individual portions with scallion before serving.

Dōngguā Ròuwán Tāng 冬瓜肉丸湯
Winter Melon Soup with Meatballs

Serves: 4 to 6 — **Total Time:** 1 hour, plus 45 minutes resting and soaking — **Difficulty:** ●●○○

Meatballs

- 1 pound ground pork
- 2 scallions, minced
- 1 tablespoon Shaoxing wine
- 1 tablespoon soy sauce
- 2 teaspoons grated fresh ginger
- 1 teaspoon toasted sesame oil
- ½ teaspoon table salt
- ⅛ teaspoon white pepper

Soup

- 2 ounces dried mung bean glass noodles
- 1 pound winter melon
- 1 teaspoon vegetable oil
- 2 scallions, white and green parts separated and sliced thin
- 4 cups chicken broth
- ½ teaspoon table salt

Test Kitchen Tip

Recipe developer Carmen Dongo notes: "These meatballs develop a coveted snappy texture through vigorous mixing, which develops myosin. Even if they crack as they cook, their texture will hold up!"

The winter melon is a very versatile gourd. By itself its white flesh doesn't taste like much (maybe a little like zucchini). Only when you cook it in a soup or stew does it turn translucent, soften to meltingly tender, and take on the flavor of its surroundings. This is why, for this dish, the quality of the broth matters. Try to use homemade chicken broth if you can; otherwise use store-bought bone broth. Some very flavorful pork meatballs make this dish something more substantial than a simple, modest soup. — Jeffrey

Mung bean glass noodles are also called cellophane noodles or bean threads. Winter melon is typically sold precut in large wedges. Look for freshly ground pork, which is typically sold in bulk at the butcher's counter, where it has a higher percentage of fat and a coarser texture than prepackaged pork.

1 **For the meatballs:** Using stand mixer fitted with paddle, beat all ingredients on medium speed until well combined, mixture has stiffened and started to pull away from sides of bowl, and pork has slightly lightened in color, about 2 minutes. Using wet hands, roll heaping 1-tablespoon portions (about 1½ ounces each) into meatballs and transfer to large plate. (You should have 12 meatballs.) Cover and refrigerate for at least 30 minutes or up to 24 hours.

2 **For the soup:** Soak noodles in 4 cups hot water in bowl for 15 minutes. Drain noodles and rinse thoroughly; set aside. Meanwhile, use spoon to scrape seeds from melon wedge. Cut wedge lengthwise into 1½- to 2-inch-wide wedges. Remove outer green rind and cut melon crosswise into ½-inch-thick slices. Set aside.

3 Heat oil in Dutch oven over medium heat until shimmering. Add scallion whites and cook until fragrant, about 30 seconds. Stir in broth, 4 cups water, melon, and salt and bring to boil. Gently add meatballs to soup. Bring to simmer over medium heat and cook, stirring occasionally, until edges of melon are translucent, 8 to 10 minutes. Stir in noodles and continue to cook until noodles are cooked through but still very chewy, and meatballs are fully cooked, about 4 minutes. Using wide, shallow spoon, skim off any scum. Season with salt to taste. Sprinkle individual portions with scallion greens before serving.

Cutting Winter Melon

1 Using sharp knife, cut seeded melon lengthwise into 1½- to 2-inch wedges.

2 Steady melon wedge by placing it skin side down on cutting board. Slice off rind in sections, following contours of melon as closely as possible.

3 Slice melon wedges crosswise ½ inch thick.

West Lake Beef Soup

Xīhú Níuròu Gēng 西湖牛肉羹

Serves: 4 to 6 — **Total Time:** 1 hour — **Difficulty:** ●●○○

Ingredients

- 10 ounces beef blade steak, trimmed
- ¼ teaspoon baking soda
- 1 tablespoon Shaoxing wine
- 1 tablespoon soy sauce
- ½ teaspoon table salt
- ¼ teaspoon white pepper
- 3 egg whites
- ½ cup water
- ⅓ cup cornstarch
- 6 cups chicken broth
- 4 ounces soft tofu, cut into ¼-inch pieces
- ⅓ cup water chestnuts, chopped fine
- 1 teaspoon grated fresh ginger
- ½ cup chopped fresh cilantro leaves and tender stems

Test Kitchen Tip

Recipe developer Joe Gitter notes:
"Of all things, this soup is most about texture—silky, starch-thickened broth; lacy egg whites; soft tofu; and silk-tender meat. We found that hand-minced steak, rather than ground beef, was vital to achieving this. I had the best luck using a sharp knife, slicing the partially frozen meat thin, and then running my knife over the slices until the pieces were no larger than ⅛ inch."

Imagine the most picturesque Chinese scenery you can in your mind's eye: a serene lake by which pagodas and temples are enshrouded in low fog as wooden boats glide past, inspiring poets to compose their most beautiful verses. This is West Lake, in the city of Hangzhou in eastern China. The lake is so arresting in its beauty it's painted on Chinese paper currency.

West Lake inspired this humble soup, velvety with delicate drifts of egg ribbons and subtly seasoned with tender beef morsels. The egg whites and the cilantro's green color, so they say, resemble the verdant surface of this freshwater lake.
— Kevin + Jeffrey

Sirloin steak tips or beef chuck steak can be used in place of blade steak. Soft tofu is traditional; however, if unavailable you can substitute firm tofu.

1   Place steak on large plate and freeze until firm, about 15 minutes. Using sharp knife, slice steak against grain as thin as possible, then finely chop. Combine steak and baking soda in medium bowl and let sit for 5 minutes. Stir in Shaoxing wine, soy sauce, salt, and pepper; set aside.

2   Lightly beat egg whites in 2-cup liquid measuring cup until combined but not foamy; set aside. Stir water and cornstarch in small bowl until thoroughly combined. Bring broth, tofu, water chestnuts, and ginger to boil in large saucepan over medium-high heat. Stir cornstarch mixture to recombine, then add to soup and cook, stirring occasionally, until thickened, about 2 minutes.

3   Reduce heat to simmer, then stir in beef mixture and cook, stirring constantly with fork or cooking chopsticks to break up meat, until no longer pink, about 2 minutes. Remove saucepan from heat. Use 1 hand to stir soup with fork or chopsticks while using other hand to pour egg whites in slow, steady stream into swirling soup. Continue stirring soup until cooked thin egg ribbons appear, about 1 minute. Stir in cilantro and season with salt and pepper to taste. Serve.

Suānlà Tāng 酸辣湯

Hot and Sour Soup

Serves: 4 to 6 — **Total Time:** 1 hour — **Difficulty:** ●●○○

7 ounces extra-firm tofu, cut into ½-inch cubes

1 (6-ounce) boneless pork chop, trimmed

6 cups chicken broth

3 tablespoons soy sauce, plus extra for seasoning

1 (5-ounce) can bamboo shoots, sliced thin lengthwise

4 ounces shiitake mushrooms, stemmed and sliced ¼ inch thick

3 tablespoons plus 1 teaspoon water, divided

3 tablespoons plus ½ teaspoon cornstarch, divided

5 tablespoons Chinese black vinegar

1 teaspoon white pepper

1 teaspoon toasted sesame oil

1–3 teaspoons chili oil

1 large egg

3 scallions, sliced thin

You Seem Like a Fungi

Instead of shiitakes, seek out wood ear mushrooms for a true hot and sour soup experience. They add a crunchy, gelatinous texture. They're often sold dried, in which case you'll have to soak them in water first.

This soup is a warm hello. Many small family-run restaurants I've frequented greet customers with a complimentary bowl of hot and sour soup—it's the Chinese equivalent of bread and butter at a French bistro. Because I've always thought of this soup as a restaurant dish, our family rarely made it at home. Turns out, it's easier to make than you'd think.

Although it's tempting to substitute ingredients for this soup, it's such a specific taste that I strongly suggest you don't: Be sure to use extra-firm tofu and not soft, which will disintegrate in the soup; Chinese black vinegar, because its malty sweet flavor is integral to this soup; and white pepper, whose floral headiness just can't be replicated with black pepper. Don't compromise on those ingredients, and you'll make a superb hot and sour soup I'll want to come over for sometime. — Jeffrey

Serve with extra chili oil, black vinegar, and white pepper.

1 Spread tofu over paper towel–lined plate and let drain for 20 minutes, then gently press dry with paper towels. Place pork chop on separate plate and freeze until firm, about 15 minutes. Transfer pork chop to cutting board and, holding knife parallel to cutting board, slice into 2 thin cutlets. Slice each cutlet crosswise into thin strips.

2 Bring broth and soy sauce to simmer in large saucepan over medium heat. Add bamboo shoots and mushrooms and cook until mushrooms are just tender, about 2 minutes. Stir in tofu and pork and cook until pork is no longer pink, about 2 minutes.

3 Whisk 3 tablespoons water, 3 tablespoons cornstarch, vinegar, and pepper together in bowl, then stir mixture into soup. Increase heat to medium-high and cook, stirring occasionally, until soup thickens and turns translucent, about 1 minute. Remove soup from heat, but do not let cool down. Stir in sesame oil and chili oil, and season with extra soy sauce to taste.

4 Whisk remaining 1 teaspoon water and remaining ½ teaspoon cornstarch together in 2-cup liquid measuring cup, then whisk in egg until combined. Off heat, use 1 hand to stir soup with fork or chopsticks while using other hand to pour egg mixture in slow, steady stream into swirling soup. Continue stirring soup until cooked thin egg ribbons appear, about 1 minute. Sprinkle individual portions with scallions before serving.

The Dumplings That Changed My Life

Dumpling #1

It was 1958 and I was seven years old. We were living in a poor, densely packed neighborhood of Hong Kong called Diamond Hill. My father paid me 10 cents each time I shined his shoes. My mother paid me 10 cents to rub her aching shoulders. When I saved enough, I headed out into the bustling Hong Kong evening (yes, my parents let me go out at night at age seven). Everywhere you looked, there were hawkers selling street food: congee, rice dumplings, fish ball noodles. The smell was pungent and incredible. My favorite vendor was the man who pushed the wonton noodle soup cart down the street. "Wonton mein! 雲吞麵!" he'd yell. This pushcart was an amazing feat of engineering: One section held hot water to cook noodles and wontons. The other section held warm broth. The cart also carried a number of wooden stools and had a compartment for bowls and chopsticks, plus a bucket for dirty dishes. It was a rickety but self-contained moving restaurant. I remembered watching the man squat over the street curb, toasting whole flat pieces of dried flounder, which he used to flavor the broth, over a gas grill. I'd pay the man 30 cents and he'd hand over a bowl of his famous shrimp-and-pork wontons with chewy alkaline noodles. The sight, the sound, the taste, that smell . . . those memories will never fade.

Dumpling #2

It was 1983. I ate many xiao long bao growing up, but never ones from Shanghai, where those dumplings originated. Then I had to travel to Shanghai for a business trip. A perfect opportunity! At that time the most famous soup dumpling in Shanghai was from a shop called Nanxiang Bun Shop in the City God Temple area. The first time I visited, I remember seeing two lines to get in: one to dine inside the restaurant, and a much longer line for takeout. People must have had to wait an hour to bring home xiao long bao. I dined in, of course, and the dumplings exceeded my high expectations. These xiao long baos had pork and crab meat and were supremely juicy. But the most memorable dumplings were the ones with crab roe. The dough wrapper was so thin and delicate you could practically see the vivid orange of the buttery crab roe inside. Every time I've returned to Nanxiang Bun Shop (it's still open, thank goodness), it's somehow even better than the previous visit.

Dumpling #3

It was 2010 and I was in the seaport city of Tianjin, just southeast of Beijing. I visited a wonderful Chinese Muslim restaurant, the name of which unfortunately escapes me. But I'll never forget a dumpling I ate there: It had a filling of lamb and dill. The dumplings, simply boiled and served as is, had a luscious dough skin with an appealing toothsome chew.

But it was that flavor of lamb and dill, a strong meat matched with a strong herb, that wowed me. Boiled dumplings typically have inexpensive fillings, a blue-collar food for the working man. So to taste such a sophisticated version made me appreciate this classic dish in a whole new light.

Dumpling #4

It's the present day. There are many places in North America considered Chinese food hubs: Flushing in New York City, the San Gabriel Valley in Southern California, the Bay Area. But I can't think of a more vibrant city for eating Chinese cuisine than the Canadian city of Richmond, just outside Vancouver. Nearly half of the more than 230,000 people living there speak Cantonese or Mandarin; you can throw a stone in any direction and hit one of the world's great Chinese restaurants. We've eaten at many of them in Richmond, but the only dim sum parlor that's become a regular is called Kirin. It's as good as any we've had in Hong Kong. The shu mai is the best I've ever had. You can tell that the chefs mix the pork and shrimp with chunks of pork fat, which give the dumpling richness and flavor. The size is generous, the texture is bouncy, and the taste is perfect.

— Jeffrey

Photo Descriptions (from top to bottom): *Photo 1: Jeffrey at age 5; Photo 2: Jeffrey picking up a remarkable xiao long bao in Shanghai; Photo 3: Admiring his all-time favorite shu mai from Kirin in Richmond, British Columbia.*

Hong Kong–Style Wonton
Noodle Soup (page 90)

Hong Kong-Style Wonton Noodle Soup

Serves: 4 to 6 — **Total Time:** 1 hour — **Difficulty:** ●●●○

1 teaspoon vegetable oil

12 large shrimp (26 to 30 per pound), peeled and deveined, shells reserved

4 cups chicken broth

¼ teaspoon plus ⅛ teaspoon table salt, divided

1 teaspoon dried flounder fish powder, divided

1 tablespoon soy sauce, divided

¼ teaspoon white pepper, divided

4 ounces ground pork

1 scallion, minced

1 tablespoon Shaoxing wine

½ teaspoon toasted sesame oil, plus extra for serving

2 teaspoons oyster sauce

24 (3-inch) square Hong Kong–style wonton wrappers

2 heads baby bok choy (4 ounces each), greens separated

6 ounces fresh thin wonton noodles

The financial heart of Hong Kong is called Central, an area surely with more bankers per square mile than anywhere on Earth. I spent a summer there working as an intern for my aunt's law firm. You won't be surprised to hear my fondest memories weren't alphabetizing legal briefs, but instead spending lunchtime at nearby Mak's, a legendary shop serving Hong Kong–style wonton noodle soup.

Mak's is old school in every way. My enduring memory remains sitting around a cheap wooden table with three strangers, neckties slung over shoulders, all deliberately slurping noodle soups with silent efficiency.

Wontons in Hong Kong mean something different from wontons everywhere else. The problem is that the word "wonton" has become a catchall term for any Chinese-sounding meat-filled dumpling. In Hong Kong wontons are a very specific construct. The word translates to "swallowing clouds"—plump, bouncy, cumulus-shaped dumplings of fresh prawns and pork. They are always served in a seafood-sweet and savory broth with thin egg noodles and a splash of red vinegar.

Good luck trying to score a weekday lunch table at Mak's. If you do, you'll witness wonton noodle soup as the great Cantonese culinary equalizer: construction workers and investment bankers sitting shoulder to shoulder, swallowing clouds in happy silence.   — Kevin

---

Look for freshly ground pork, which is typically sold in bulk at the butcher's counter, where it has a higher percentage of fat and a coarser texture than prepackaged pork. If flounder powder is unavailable it can be omitted, though the soup will not be as full-bodied. Don't substitute flounder fish seasoning (which contains added salt and flavorings) or powders made from other varieties of fish. Serve with Chinese red vinegar.

---

1   Heat vegetable oil in large saucepan over high heat until shimmering. Add reserved shrimp shells and cook, stirring frequently, until shells begin to turn spotty brown, about 2 minutes. Add broth, 2 cups water, and ¼ teaspoon salt and bring to boil. Off heat, stir in ½ teaspoon flounder powder and let steep for 15 minutes. Strain broth through fine-mesh strainer and return to empty saucepan; discard shells. Stir in 2 teaspoons soy sauce and ⅛ teaspoon pepper. Cover to keep warm.

Shaping Wontons

1 Place heaping ½ teaspoon pork filling in center of each square, then top with 1 piece shrimp and gently press into filling.

2 To form wontons, gather corners of wrapper around filling.

3 Pinch dough tightly just above filling to seal, leaving ends of wrapper unsealed.

2 Halve each shrimp crosswise; set aside. Using wooden spoon or 4 bundled chopsticks, vigorously stir pork in medium bowl until it has stiffened and started to pull away from sides of bowl and has slightly lightened in color, about 5 minutes. Stir in scallion, Shaoxing wine, sesame oil, oyster sauce, remaining 1 teaspoon soy sauce, remaining ½ teaspoon flounder powder, remaining ⅛ teaspoon salt, and remaining ⅛ teaspoon pepper until well combined.

3 Lightly dust parchment paper–lined rimmed baking sheet with flour. Working with 6 wrappers at a time, place heaping ½ teaspoon pork filling in center of each square, then top with 1 piece shrimp and gently press into filling. Form wontons by gathering corners of wrapper around filling and pinching dough tightly just above filling to seal; leave ends of wrapper unsealed. Transfer wontons to prepared sheet, cover with damp dish towel, and repeat with remaining wrappers and filling in 3 batches. (Wontons can be refrigerated for up to 24 hours or frozen on sheet until solid, then transferred to zipper-lock bag and stored in freezer for up to 1 month. Do not thaw frozen dumplings before cooking; increase simmer time to about 6 minutes.)

4 Meanwhile, bring 4 quarts water to boil in Dutch oven. Add bok choy and cook until tender, about 1 minute. Using spider skimmer or slotted spoon, transfer bok choy to plate. Return water to boil, add wonton noodles, and cook until just tender. Using spider skimmer, transfer noodles to colander and rinse thoroughly; divide noodles among serving bowls. Return water to boil, add wontons, and cook until wontons turn translucent and tender and float to top, about 4 minutes. Using spider skimmer, divide wontons among bowls and top with bok choy.

5 Return broth to boil over high heat, then ladle over bok choy, noodles, and dumplings. Serve, passing extra sesame oil separately.

Do I Really Need Flounder Powder?

Surveying our recipe testers, we found that the top complaint about this dish was the flounder powder. These are all true: 1) It's expensive. 2) It reeks. 3) You're buying a lot to use only 1 teaspoon. Look, we have no argument here. But we also didn't want to exclude it, as its unique flavor is bound up in the identity of Hong Kong wontons. Why not start *A Very Chinese Cookbook* book club and split costs?

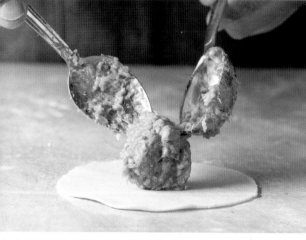

The Master Dumpling System™

A dumpling by any other name—pierogi, momo, kreplach—would taste as delicious. But we Chinese seem to have created an entire ecosystem around the dumpling category, with an endless number of fillings stuffed in an endless number of shapes and folds, and cooked an endless number of ways. But no need to be intimidated. It's a bit like IKEA furniture: modular and adaptable, and, in most cases, easy to put together.

We've developed a system that allows you to create your own dumpling adventure. We'll first make a dough with just two ingredients—flour and boiling water—to yield a wrapper that's easy to roll out and that remains moist but not sticky. Next, we'll offer three different fillings to start (though once you know the marinade, you'll be equipped to explore different proteins). Then we'll show you how to fold four traditional and beautiful dumpling shapes, step by step. Finally, we'll turn them into luscious boiled dumplings, delicate steamed ones, or irresistibly crispy pot stickers.

Your dumpling adventure awaits . . .

Dumplings Your Way

Think of making dumplings as like ordering at a Chipotle. Pick your filling, pick your fold, pick your method of cooking, eat, leave us a 5-star review.

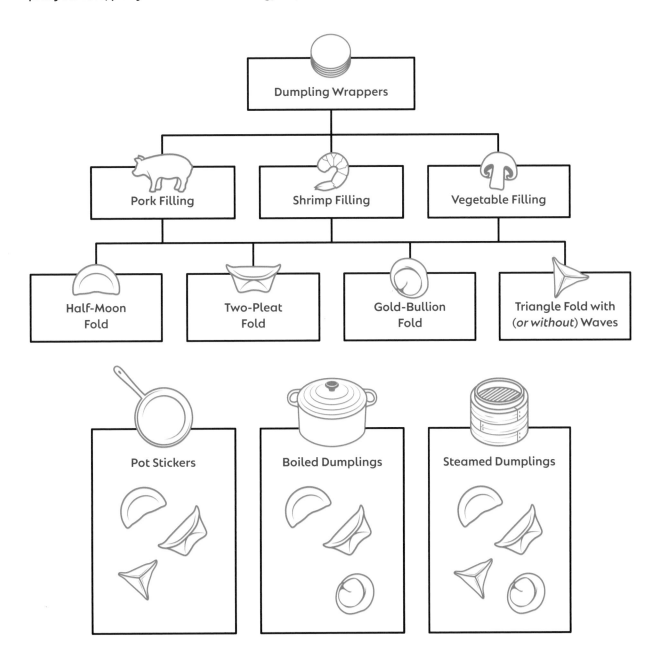

Dumpling Wrappers

Pork Filling

Shrimp Filling

Vegetable Filling

Half-Moon Fold

Two-Pleat Fold

Gold-Bullion Fold

Triangle Fold with (*or without*) Waves

Pot Stickers

Boiled Dumplings

Steamed Dumplings

1. Dumpling Wrapper

Homemade dumpling dough is soft and slightly stretchy, easy to roll and pleat, and chewier than store-bought wrappers. Boiling water hydrates the flour quickly, yielding a moist but not sticky dough that's less prone to snapping back. Rolling wrappers with tapered edges and a slightly thicker center prevents dough from getting too thick at the seams. The more dumplings you make, the better you'll get at this, and the shapes in this section are forgiving. Using a smaller-diameter rolling pin is very helpful here, but a conventional pin will also work.

Tàngmiàn Jiǎozipí 燙麵餃子皮
Hot Water Dough Dumpling Wrappers

Makes: 40 wrappers
Total Time: 20 minutes, plus 30 minutes resting

For dough with the right moisture level, we recommend weighing the flour. Use minimal flour when kneading, rolling, and shaping so the dough stays slightly tacky. Cover dough with a damp dish towel except when rolling and shaping.

2½ cups (12½ ounces) all-purpose flour
1 cup boiling water

1   Place flour in food processor. With processor running, add boiling water. Continue to process until dough forms ball and clears sides of bowl, 30 to 45 seconds longer. Transfer dough to counter and gently knead until smooth, 2 to 3 minutes. Wrap dough in plastic wrap and let rest for at least 30 minutes or up to 4 hours.

2   Transfer dough to lightly floured counter and roll into 12-inch cylinder. Cut cylinder into 4 equal pieces. Set 3 pieces aside and cover with plastic. Roll remaining piece into 8-inch cylinder. Cut cylinder in half and cut each half into 5 equal pieces; roll each piece into ball. Place dough balls on lightly floured counter and lightly dust with flour. Using pie plate or palm of your hand, press each ball into 2-inch disk. Cover disks with damp dish towel.

3   Roll 1 disk into 2½-inch round. Continue rolling outer 1-inch edge of dough to create 3½-inch round wrapper with tapered edges. Re-cover wrapper with damp dish towel. Repeat with remaining wrappers and dough; do not overlap wrappers.

Forming Dumpling Wrappers

1   Using pie plate or palm of your hand, press dough ball into 2-inch disk.

2   Roll dough disk into 2½-inch round. Continue rolling outer 1-inch edge of dough to create 3½-inch round wrapper with tapered edges. Roll from center toward you while rotating dough with other hand.

2. Dumpling Fillings

Dumpling wrappers (homemade or store-bought) can hold an array of juicy filling. Here are three popular options. The filling keeps for three days (and must sit for 30 minutes) so we suggest making the filling first so it's ready to use while you're rolling your wrappers.

Zhūròu Xiàn 豬肉餡
Pork Filling

Makes: about 4 cups
Total Time: 30 minutes, plus 30 minutes chilling
Look for freshly ground pork, typically sold at the butcher's counter, which has a higher percentage of fat and a coarser texture than prepackaged pork.

     5 cups 1-inch napa cabbage pieces
     ½ teaspoon table salt, plus salt for salting cabbage
    12 ounces ground pork
    1½ tablespoons soy sauce
    1½ tablespoons toasted sesame oil
     1 tablespoon vegetable oil
     1 tablespoon Shaoxing wine
     1 tablespoon hoisin sauce
     1 tablespoon grated fresh ginger
     ¼ teaspoon white pepper
     4 scallions, chopped fine

1 Pulse cabbage in food processor until finely chopped, 8 to 10 pulses. Transfer cabbage to medium bowl and stir in ½ teaspoon salt; let sit for 10 minutes. Using hands, squeeze excess moisture from cabbage. Transfer cabbage to small bowl and set aside.

2 Pulse pork, soy sauce, sesame oil, vegetable oil, Shaoxing wine, hoisin, ginger, salt, and pepper in now-empty food processor until blended and slightly sticky, about 10 pulses. Scatter cabbage over pork mixture. Add scallions and pulse until vegetables are evenly distributed, about 8 pulses. Transfer pork mixture to small bowl and, using rubber spatula, smooth surface. Cover with plastic wrap and refrigerate for at least 30 minutes or up to 3 days.

Xiānxiā Xiàn 鮮蝦餡
Shrimp Filling

Makes: about 4 cups
Total Time: 30 minutes, plus 30 minutes chilling

     5 cups 1-inch napa cabbage pieces
        Table salt for salting cabbage
    12 ounces shrimp (any size), peeled, deveined, and tails removed
    1½ tablespoons soy sauce
    1½ tablespoons toasted sesame oil
     1 tablespoon vegetable oil
     1 tablespoon Shaoxing wine
     1 tablespoon grated fresh ginger
     ¼ teaspoon white pepper
     6 scallions, chopped fine

1 Pulse cabbage in food processor until finely chopped, 8 to 10 pulses. Transfer cabbage to medium bowl and stir in ½ teaspoon salt; let sit for 10 minutes. Using hands, squeeze excess moisture from cabbage. Transfer cabbage to small bowl and set aside.

2 Pulse shrimp, soy sauce, sesame oil, vegetable oil, Shaoxing wine, ginger, and pepper in now-empty food processor until blended and slightly sticky, about 10 pulses. Scatter cabbage over shrimp mixture. Add scallions and pulse until vegetables are evenly distributed, about 8 pulses. Transfer shrimp mixture to small bowl and, using rubber spatula, smooth surface. Cover with plastic wrap and refrigerate for at least 30 minutes or up to 3 days.

Shūcài Xiàn 蔬菜餡
Vegetable Filling

Makes: about 4 cups
Total Time: 50 minutes, plus 30 minutes chilling

 1 carrot, peeled and coarsely chopped
 5 cups 1-inch napa cabbage pieces
 ¼ teaspoon table salt, plus salt for salting vegetables
 12 ounces shiitake mushrooms, stemmed and halved
 2 tablespoons vegetable oil, divided
 6 scallions, chopped fine
 1 garlic clove, minced
 2 large egg whites
 1 tablespoon soy sauce
 1 tablespoon toasted sesame oil
 ¼ teaspoon white pepper

1 Pulse carrot in food processor until finely chopped, about 5 pulses. Add cabbage and pulse until finely chopped, 8 to 10 pulses. Transfer cabbage mixture to medium bowl and stir in ½ teaspoon salt; let sit for 10 minutes. Using hands, squeeze excess moisture from cabbage mixture; transfer to small bowl and set aside.

2 Pulse mushrooms in now-empty processor until finely chopped, about 15 pulses. Heat 1 tablespoon vegetable oil in 12-inch nonstick skillet over medium-high heat until shimmering. Add mushrooms, scallions, garlic, and salt and cook until mushrooms begin to brown, 5 to 7 minutes; transfer to large bowl and let cool slightly, about 15 minutes. Stir in cabbage mixture, egg whites, soy sauce, sesame oil, pepper, and remaining 1 tablespoon vegetable oil. Using rubber spatula, smooth surface of filling. Cover with plastic wrap and refrigerate for at least 30 minutes or up to 3 days.

3. Dumpling Folding

There are many different dumpling shapes and folds, and some serve as the base for other, more elaborate shapes. Here we highlight four common folding methods, with a couple of embellishments. Using our homemade Hot Water Dough Dumpling Wrappers will make for easier shaping and sealing, but store-bought dumpling wrappers will work as well.

Half-Moon Fold

Difficulty: ●○○○

Our simplest fold is good for boiling and steaming and can be adapted for pot stickers, too.

1 Place scant 1 tablespoon filling in center of wrapper. Brush away any flour clinging to surface of wrapper.

2 Fold wrapper in half to make half-moon shape.

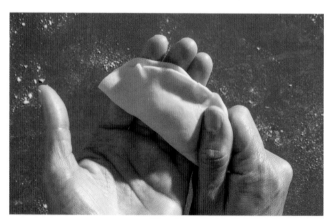

3 Using index finger and thumb, pinch dumpling closed, pressing out any air pockets from filling.

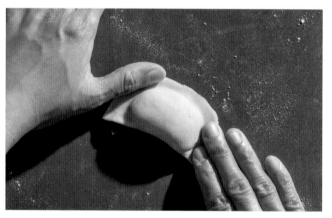

4 For pot stickers, lay dumpling on counter and press gently to flatten 1 side for even browning.

Two-Pleat Fold

Difficulty: ●●○○

By pleating the wrapper, the dumpling curves so that it stands up and browns on its flat side.

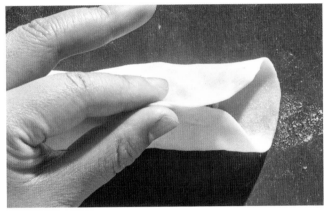

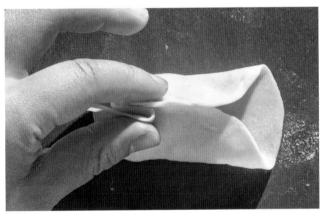

1 Place scant 1 tablespoon filling in center of wrapper. Brush away any flour clinging to surface of wrapper. Pinch together top and bottom edges to form 1½-inch-wide seam.

2 Lift left corner closest to you and bring to center of seam. Pinch to seal. Pinch remaining dough on left side to seal.

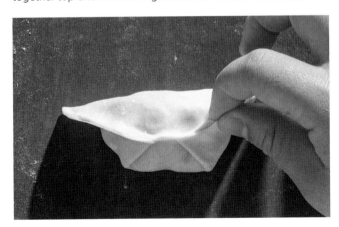

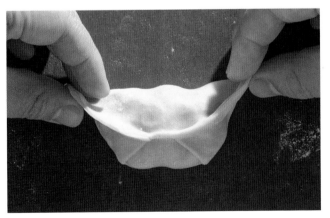

3 Repeat pinching on right side.

4 Gently press dumpling into crescent shape, with seam on top.

more folding methods on next page ☞

Gold-Bullion Fold

Rich with symbolism, this ornate dumpling shape is terrific for boiling and steaming.

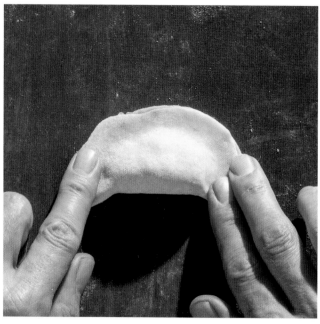

1 Fill and shape dumpling using Half-Moon Fold (page 98) through step 3.

2 Begin pulling corners together below filling, using finger to crease folded side of dumpling to aid in shaping.

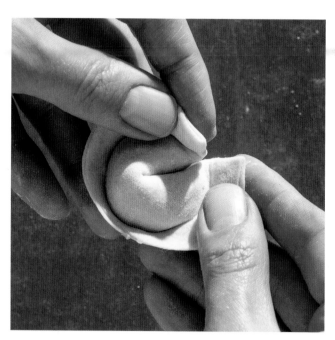

3 Overlap corners slightly to create bullion shape, with cupped outer edge and dimpled center.

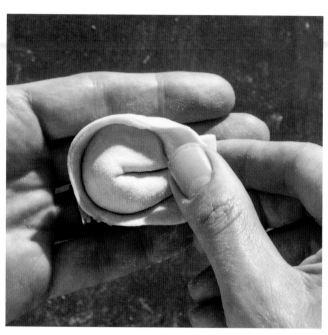

4 Press to seal overlapping edges.

Triangle Fold

Lots of surface makes this shape good for steaming and especially great for pan frying.

1 Place scant 1 tablespoon filling in center of wrapper. Brush away any flour clinging to surface of wrapper, then lightly mark 3 evenly spaced points around edge with finger.

2 Lift marked points of wrapper to center and pinch to seal, creating triangle shape with 3 open ends.

3 Pinch open ends to seal, pressing out any air pockets from filling.

4 If desired, pinch along sealed edges with thumb and index finger in ¼-inch increments to create wavy pleats.

4. Cooking Methods

How you cook your dumplings depends on your mood. Want something crispy and crowd-pleasing? Pot stickers all the way. Want to show off your ornate folds and keep the dumplings delicate? Steam them. For an easy, filling weeknight meal, boil your dumplings. These recipes accommodate all the fillings and folds we've covered, so have fun with it.

Guōtiē 鍋貼
Pot Stickers

Makes: 40 dumplings
Total Time: 1½ hours (15 minutes with preshaped dumplings)
Difficulty: ●●○○○

Store-bought dumpling wrappers can be used in place of our hot water dough dumpling wrappers. Serve with chili oil, Soy-Vinegar Dipping Sauce (page 23), Chinese black or red vinegar, and/or light, dark, or sweet soy sauce.

- 1 recipe any dumpling filling (page 96)
- 1 recipe Hot Water Dough Dumpling Wrappers (page 95) or 40 store-bought dumpling wrappers
- 2 tablespoons vegetable oil, divided
- 1 cup water, divided

1 Lightly dust 2 parchment paper–lined rimmed baking sheets with flour. Using rubber spatula, mark filling with cross to divide into 4 equal portions. Transfer 1 portion to separate bowl, and refrigerate remaining filling.

2 Working with 1 wrapper at a time (keep remaining wrappers covered), place scant 1 tablespoon filling in center of wrapper. Brush away any flour clinging to surface of wrapper. Shape dumpling following Half-Moon Fold, Two-Pleat Fold, or Triangle Fold (pages 98–101) and transfer to prepared sheet. Repeat with additional 9 wrappers and filling in bowl. Repeat dumpling-making process with remaining wrappers and remaining 3 portions filling. (Dumplings can be refrigerated for up to 24 hours or frozen on sheet until solid, then transferred to zipper-lock bag and stored in freezer for up to 1 month. Do not thaw frozen dumplings before cooking. Follow cooking instructions at right for Cooking Fresh and Frozen Pot Stickers.)

3 Brush 12-inch nonstick skillet with 1 tablespoon oil. Evenly space 16 dumplings flat sides down around edge of skillet and place 4 in center. Cook over medium heat until bottoms begin to turn spotty brown, 3 to 4 minutes. Off heat, carefully add ½ cup water (water will sputter). Return skillet to medium heat and bring water to boil. Cover and reduce heat to medium-low. Cook for 6 minutes.

4 Uncover, increase heat to medium-high, and cook until water has evaporated and bottoms of pot stickers are crispy and browned, 1 to 3 minutes. Transfer pot stickers to platter. Serve immediately. (Before cooking second batch of pot stickers, let skillet cool for 10 minutes. Rinse skillet under cool water and wipe dry with paper towels. Repeat cooking process with remaining 1 tablespoon oil and remaining ½ cup water.)

Cooking Fresh and Frozen Pot Stickers

Here's a handy guide to cooking pot stickers in various amounts. When cooking frozen pot stickers, increase the covered cook time in step 3 to 8 minutes.

Dumplings	Skillet Size	Oil	Water
20 fresh	12" skillet	1 tablespoon oil	½ cup water
20 frozen	12" skillet	1 tablespoon oil	⅔ cup water
10 fresh	10" skillet	2 teaspoons oil	⅓ cup water
10 frozen	10" skillet	2 teaspoons oil	½ cup water

more cooking methods on next page

Shuǐjiǎo 水餃
Boiled Dumplings

Makes: 40 dumplings
Total Time: 1 hour (30 minutes with preshaped dumplings)
Difficulty: ●○○○

Again: Store-bought dumpling wrappers can be used in place of our hot water dough dumpling wrappers. Serve with chili oil, Soy-Vinegar Dipping Sauce (page 23), Chinese black or red vinegar, and/or light, dark, or sweet soy sauce.

> 1 recipe any dumpling filling (page 96)
> 1 recipe Hot Water Dough Dumpling Wrappers
>   (page 95) or 40 store-bought dumpling wrappers

1 Lightly dust 2 parchment paper–lined rimmed baking sheets with flour. Using rubber spatula, mark filling with cross to divide into 4 equal portions. Transfer 1 portion to separate bowl, and refrigerate remaining filling.

2 Working with 1 wrapper at a time (keep remaining wrappers covered), place scant 1 tablespoon filling in center of wrapper. Brush away any flour clinging to surface of wrapper. Shape dumpling following Half-Moon Fold, Two-Pleat Fold, or Gold-Bullion Fold (pages 98–100) and transfer to prepared sheet. Repeat with additional 9 wrappers and filling in bowl. Repeat dumpling-making process with remaining wrappers and remaining 3 portions filling. (Dumplings can be refrigerated for up to 24 hours or frozen on sheet until solid, then transferred to zipper-lock bag and stored in freezer for up to 1 month. Do not thaw frozen dumplings before cooking; the cook time range is the same as for fresh.)

3 Meanwhile, bring 4 quarts water to boil in large Dutch oven over high heat. Add 20 dumplings, a few at a time, stirring gently to prevent sticking. Return to simmer, adjusting heat as necessary to maintain simmer. Cook dumplings until dough is tender and filling is cooked through, 5 to 8 minutes. Using slotted spoon or spider skimmer, transfer dumplings to platter. Serve immediately. (Before cooking second batch of dumplings, return water to boil.)

Zhēngjiǎo 蒸餃
Steamed Dumplings

Makes: 40 dumplings
Total Time: 1¼ hours (20 minutes with preshaped dumplings)
Difficulty: ●○○○

Once more: Store-bought dumpling wrappers can be used in place of our hot water dough dumpling wrappers. Serve with chili oil, Soy-Vinegar Dipping Sauce (page 23), Chinese black or red vinegar, and/or light, dark, or sweet soy sauce.

> 1 recipe any dumpling filling (page 96)
> 1 recipe Hot Water Dough Dumpling Wrappers
>   (page 95) or 40 store-bought dumpling wrappers

1 Lightly dust 2 parchment paper–lined rimmed baking sheets with flour. Using rubber spatula, mark filling with cross to divide into 4 equal portions. Transfer 1 portion to separate bowl, and refrigerate remaining filling.

2 Working with 1 wrapper at a time (keep remaining wrappers covered), place scant 1 tablespoon filling in center of wrapper. Brush away any flour clinging to surface of wrapper. Shape dumpling following Half-Moon Fold, Two-Pleat Fold, Gold-Bullion Fold, or Triangle Fold (pages 98–101) and transfer to prepared sheet. Repeat with additional 9 wrappers and filling in bowl. Repeat dumpling-making process with remaining wrappers and remaining 3 portions filling. (Dumplings can be refrigerated for up to 24 hours or frozen on sheet until solid, then transferred to zipper-lock bag and stored in freezer for up to 1 month. Do not thaw frozen dumplings before cooking; increase steaming time by 2 minutes.)

3 Bring 4 cups water to boil in 14-inch flat-bottomed wok. Poke about 20 small holes in two 9-inch parchment rounds and lightly coat with vegetable oil spray. Place rounds in two 10-inch bamboo steamer baskets. Arrange 10 dumplings evenly in each prepared basket leaving at least ½-inch space between each dumpling; stack baskets and cover. Reduce heat to maintain vigorous simmer and set steamer in wok. Steam until dumpling wrappers have translucent, glossy sheen, 8 to 10 minutes. Serve immediately. (Before cooking second batch of dumplings, replenish water in wok and line steamer baskets with fresh parchment rounds.)

Shāomài 燒賣
Shu Mai

Makes: 40 dumplings — **Total Time:** 1½ hours — **Difficulty:** ●●●○

True story: I once ate 24 shu mais in one sitting, though it's not something I'm proud of sharing. (Much like the time I took the 64-ounce porterhouse challenge—eat the whole steak in an hour and get it for free. I lost.) But it does reveal my infatuation with this Chinese dim sum staple, in my opinion the world heavyweight champion of dumplings.

Allow me to set the scene: a pork-and-shrimp filling studded with mushrooms and water chestnuts, pressed inside a yellow egg dough wrapper with the top of the filling exposed, and steamed and served four to a bamboo basket. The texture is toothsome but tender, and the flavor bursts with rich, meaty savoriness. I dab some chili oil on my shu mai. Writing this paragraph, I'm daydreaming of 24 more.

When we launched *Hunger Pangs*, this recipe—meticulously developed by *Cook's Country* editor Bryan Roof—was the one we decided to film for episode one. Why? It's the first dish I always order at a dim sum parlor. And it's the dish I use to judge the competency of the chefs. Follow this recipe, and the resulting dumplings will cause others to deem you extremely competent.   — Kevin

Do not trim the excess fat from the ribs; it contributes flavor and moisture. For even richer, juicier shu mai, substitute 1 pound skinless pork belly for the ribs. Hong Kong–style dumpling wrappers (containing egg) are preferred here; however, white wheat dumpling wrappers will also work. Serve with chili oil.

1 Combine soy sauce and gelatin in small bowl. Set aside to allow gelatin to bloom, about 5 minutes. Microwave 1 cup water and mushrooms in covered bowl until steaming, about 1 minute. Let sit until softened, about 5 minutes. Lift mushrooms from bowl with fork and discard liquid. Squeeze mushrooms dry, remove stems, and chop.

2 Meanwhile, place half of pork in food processor and pulse until coarsely ground into approximate ⅛-inch pieces, about ten 1-second pulses; transfer to large bowl. Add shrimp and remaining pork to food processor and pulse until coarsely chopped into approximate ¼-inch pieces, about five 1-second pulses. Transfer to bowl with more finely ground pork. Stir in soy sauce mixture, mushrooms, water chestnuts, cornstarch, cilantro, sesame oil, Shaoxing wine, vinegar, sugar, ginger, salt, and pepper.

---

2 tablespoons soy sauce

½ teaspoon unflavored gelatin

¾ ounce dried shiitake mushrooms, rinsed

1 pound boneless country-style pork ribs, cut into 1-inch pieces

8 ounces shrimp (any size), peeled, deveined, and tails removed

¼ cup water chestnuts, chopped

2 tablespoons cornstarch

2 tablespoons minced fresh cilantro

1 tablespoon toasted sesame oil

1 tablespoon Shaoxing wine

1 tablespoon Chinese white rice vinegar

2 teaspoons sugar

2 teaspoons grated fresh ginger

½ teaspoon table salt

¼ teaspoon white pepper

1 (1-pound) package 3½-inch round dumpling wrappers

2 tablespoons tobiko (optional)

recipe continues on next page

3 Lightly dust 2 parchment paper–lined rimmed baking sheets with flour. Working with 6 wrappers at a time, brush edges of each round lightly with water. Place heaping tablespoon of filling into center of each round. Form dumplings, crimping wrapper around sides of filling and leaving top exposed, following one of the methods on page 109. Transfer to prepared sheet, cover with damp dish towel, and repeat in batches of 6 with remaining wrappers and filling. (Shu mai can be refrigerated for up to 24 hours or frozen on sheet until solid, then transferred to zipper-lock bag and stored in freezer for up to 1 month. Do not thaw shu mai before cooking; increase steaming time by 5 minutes.)

4 Bring 4 cups water to boil in 14-inch flat-bottomed wok. Poke about 20 small holes in two 9-inch parchment rounds and lightly coat with vegetable oil spray. Place rounds in two 10-inch bamboo steamer baskets. Arrange 10 dumplings evenly in each prepared basket, leaving at least ½-inch space between each dumpling; stack baskets and cover. Reduce heat to maintain vigorous simmer and set steamer in wok. Steam until filling is no longer pink and dumpling wrappers have translucent, glossy sheen, 8 to 10 minutes. Top dumplings with tobiko, if using. Serve immediately. (Before cooking second batch of dumplings, replenish water in wok and line steamer baskets with fresh parchment rounds.)

Why Our Shu Mais Are So Juicy

For shu mai filling that is extra-tender and juicy we turn to a favorite ATK trick for avoiding dry meat—adding unflavored gelatin. Gelatin can hold up to 10 times its weight in water, and when added to meat it suspends the juices in a mesh-like, semisolid state that prevents them from leaching out. This translates to a moist shu mai with a luxuriant texture.

Basic Shaping Method

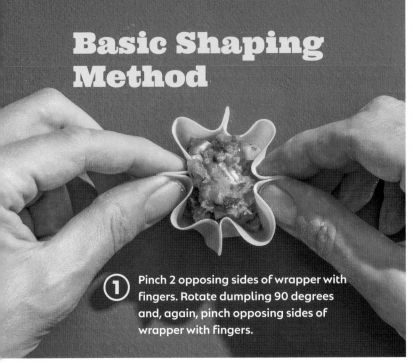

① Pinch 2 opposing sides of wrapper with fingers. Rotate dumpling 90 degrees and, again, pinch opposing sides of wrapper with fingers.

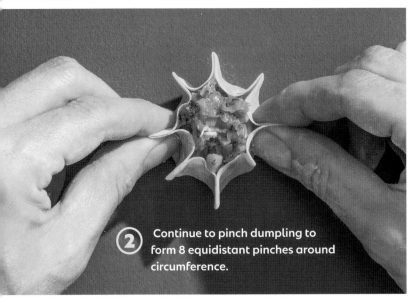

② Continue to pinch dumpling to form 8 equidistant pinches around circumference.

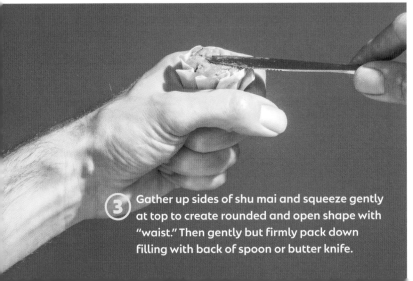

③ Gather up sides of shu mai and squeeze gently at top to create rounded and open shape with "waist." Then gently but firmly pack down filling with back of spoon or butter knife.

Jeffrey's Method

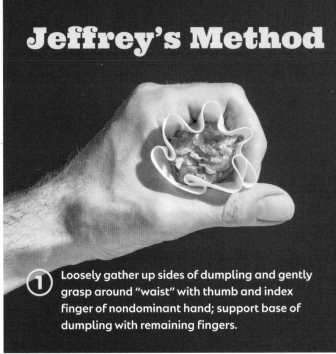

① Loosely gather up sides of dumpling and gently grasp around "waist" with thumb and index finger of nondominant hand; support base of dumpling with remaining fingers.

② Using fingers, slowly rotate dumpling within grasp, allowing friction between wrapper and hand to naturally form pleats around perimeter.

③ While rotating dumpling to form pleats, use thumb of dominant hand to compress filling in center and create smooth top.

I Am the Har Gow Captain Now

A semisheer wrapper allows a hazy glimpse of the blush-pink mixture inside. Its tacky surface clings lightly to the bamboo steamer and your chopsticks, momentarily prolonging the anticipation. Then you pop it in your mouth: At first, the dumpling resists your chew, but it soon gives way, baring a pristine, delicately sweet, juicy shrimp filling. This is har gow.

My approach deviates slightly from tradition to make it easier for anyone to embrace the challenge and experience the pleasure of making the dumplings at home.

This starts with the wrapper, a springy, translucent dough made from wheat and tapioca starches. Dim sum chefs make it by slowly stirring boiling water (and then melted lard) into the starches and then kneading; getting it right is a skill. For consistent results, I use a food processor, adding water and letting the starches gel for 5 seconds before drizzling in melted lard and whizzing the mixture into a dough that is easy to flatten and pliable enough to pleat around a filling.

Har gow filling is a master class in spotlighting one ingredient. Traditionally, shrimp are brined, chopped, and vigorously mixed with seasonings. The brine helps draw out myosin during mixing for postcooking resilience and juiciness. Bamboo shoots or water chestnuts add crunch, and fat injects the lean mixture with richness.

Here again, using a food processor offers benefits. One is that finely ground shrimp is easier to veil in the thin wrapper. The other is that the whirring blade extracts myosin so efficiently that brining the shrimp becomes unnecessary.

Unlike other dumpling doughs, har gow dough is not rolled. Instead, chefs smear pieces of dough into wafer-thin wrappers using the side of a cleaver. For those who aren't so adept, in *The Wisdom of the Chinese Kitchen* award-winning author Grace Young suggests using a tortilla press. It ended up being my go-to tool.

Finally I shape the har gow in a purse form that flaunts pleats across the top. A generous number of pleats are signs of mastery, and it takes practice. My early efforts produced four or five pleats, but after a while I could form eight. To finish the shape, I follow the common process of gently tugging off excess dough with my fingers. Cook the dumplings in a bamboo steamer, and then it's time to eat.

— Lan Lam
Senior Editor, *Cook's Illustrated*

Xiājiǎo 蝦餃
Har Gow

Makes: 24 dumplings — **Total Time:** 1¼ hours, plus 30 minutes chilling and resting — **Difficulty:** ● ● ● ●

Dough

- 1 cup plus 2 tablespoons (5¼ ounces) wheat starch
- ¼ cup plus 3 tablespoons (1¾ ounces) tapioca starch
- Pinch table salt
- ½ cup plus 1 tablespoon boiling water
- 4 teaspoons lard, melted

Filling

- 6 ounces shrimp (any size), peeled, deveined, and tails removed
- 2 tablespoons finely chopped canned bamboo shoots
- 1 tablespoon lard, melted and cooled
- 1 teaspoon Shaoxing wine
- ½ teaspoon grated fresh ginger
- ½ teaspoon minced garlic
- ¼ teaspoon sugar
- ¼ teaspoon table salt
- ¼ teaspoon white pepper
- ¼ teaspoon soy sauce

Known to some as crystal shrimp dumplings, these delicate purses of crunchy prawns are a true Cantonese classic, found in virtually every dim sum house around the globe. Har gow's defining feature is its wrapper, which takes on both a tacky and a slippery luscious quality when steamed. It must not be too thick or too thin; the margin of error is unyieldingly low.

We Chinese will admire a first-rate har gow when we taste one, because it's hard to mask a subpar version. For one thing, these dumplings really can't be made ahead of time, as the dough is rather particular. For another, restaurants don't want to be caught using anything but the freshest shrimp, since the ingredient plays front and center and will quickly lose its toothsome texture.

If you're opening up a dim sum restaurant and plan on sticking around, you'd best nail down your har gow recipe. We won't be opening a restaurant, but we were lucky to learn to make them from our colleague Lan Lam, who through months of recipe development earned her har gow doctorate.   — Kevin + Jeffrey

We strongly recommend weighing the starches. You can substitute vegetable oil for the lard. Canned water chestnuts can be substituted for the bamboo shoots. Serve with chili oil.

1 **For the dough:** Process wheat starch, tapioca starch, and salt in food processor until combined, about 3 seconds. Add boiling water and let rest for 5 seconds. Pulse once. Add lard and process until dough forms ball that clears sides of processor bowl, about 1 minute (if dough does not come together, add up to 2 teaspoons hot water, ½ teaspoon at a time, processing for 10 seconds between additions, until dough ball forms). Transfer to lightly greased counter and knead for 1 minute. Dough should be slightly tacky. Shape dough into ball, and cover with plastic wrap.

2 **For the filling:** In clean, dry workbowl, pulse all ingredients until shrimp is finely ground, 10 to 20 pulses. Transfer to bowl, cover, and refrigerate until filling is well chilled, about 20 minutes.

3 Divide dough into 4 equal portions. On lightly greased counter, roll 1 portion of dough into 6-inch rope. Divide rope into 6 equal pieces. Cover all pieces with plastic. Using lightly oiled tortilla press or pie plate, press 1 piece of dough into 3¼-inch round.

4   Place dough round on fingers of nondominant hand. Place heaping ½ tablespoon filling in center of dough. To create first pleat, use thumb and index finger of dominant hand to pinch dough that is above pinky and lift pleat toward top of filling.

5   Using index finger of hand holding dumpling, push dough toward pinched portion to begin forming second pleat. Use index finger of dominant hand to position second pleat against first pleat. Repeat pleating motion, rotating dough with each pleat, until all of dough is pleated and dumpling has rounded shape.

6   Holding dumpling pleated side up, use thumb and index finger to press pleats together just above filling to seal dumpling. Gently tear excess dough from dumpling. Place dumpling pleated side up on counter and cover with plastic. Repeat with remaining dough and filling, lightly oiling tortilla press and counter as needed.

7   Bring 4 cups water to boil in 14-inch flat-bottomed wok. Poke about 20 small holes in two 9-inch parchment rounds and lightly coat with vegetable oil spray. Place rounds in two 10-inch bamboo steamer baskets. Arrange 12 dumplings in each prepared basket so that they are not touching; stack baskets and cover. Reduce heat to maintain vigorous simmer and set steamer in wok. Steam until har gow wrappers are translucent, about 8 minutes. Off heat, remove steamer from wok and let rest, covered, for 10 minutes. Serve immediately.

turn to see how to shape har gow

Making Har Gow

① To create first pleat, use thumb and index finger to pinch dough.

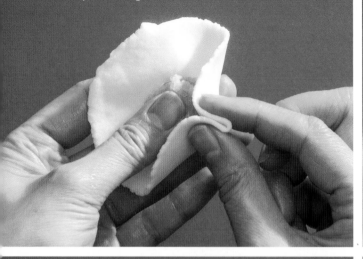

② Use index finger of other hand to push dough to begin second pleat.

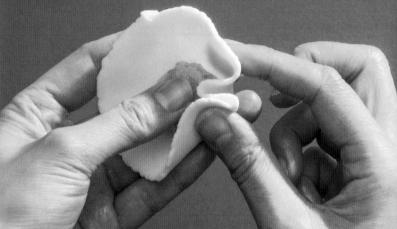

③ Use index finger of pleating hand to position second pleat against first pleat.

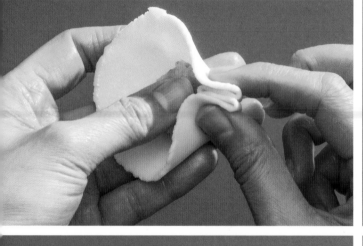

④ Repeat, rotating with each pleat, until all of dough is pleated and dumpling has rounded shape.

⑤ Press pleats above filling to seal.

⑥ Gently tear off excess dough.

for tips on how
to eat these,
see page 119

Xiǎolóngbāo 小籠包
Shanghai Soup Dumplings

Makes: 40 dumplings — **Total Time:** 7 hours, plus 5 hours resting and cooling — **Difficulty:**

It's thrilling to watch people try their first xiao long bao. They gingerly pick up their dumpling with chopsticks, carefully transferring it to a soup spoon. They dab a few drops of Chinese vinegar on it. They're warned about the molten temperature inside. Then dumpling approaches mouth, enters whole, and lips form a seal.

And then: the magic moment. Eyes bulge. The nondominant hand reflexively reaches for the mouth, ready to catch any escaping liquid. Then they laugh, not because it's funny, but from the surprise and joy of what they just experienced: a satisfying burst of savory soup inside their mouths. The tender steamed wrapper surrounding the luscious pork filling is just the figurative icing.

We couldn't write a Chinese cookbook without including the almighty xiao long bao, so we leaned on the cook renowned for tackling the mightiest of recipes: Joe Gitter. To get it right, Joe cooked and ate his way through so many batches of soup dumplings that the Chinese granted him honorary citizenship.

Said Joe: "There's a craft to forming these dumplings that comes with time, but by tackling each component—broth, filling, wrapper—success can be achieved."

Broth: To get the broth inside the dumplings, it needs to be jellified. Chicken wings, with all that skin, give us a collagen-rich broth, which we reduce to concentrate the gelatin. Bolstered with dried shiitakes, the broth has a rich but neutral flavor.

Filling: For tender and bouncy filling, you want a fatty, coarsely ground meat, which is typically sold at the butcher's counter. Vigorously agitating the meat with a stand mixer develops sticky myosin proteins that trap juices during cooking. The stand mixer easily incorporates the jellified stock into the filling.

The wrapper: It's important to make dough rounds with a slightly thicker center, so the filling doesn't leak, and a thinner border, so the tops don't get too doughy. Once you have a 3-inch round, start rolling toward you from just below the dough's center to taper the edges, rotating the circle as you go. We add a teaspoon of oil to our dough to make it a bit easier to roll. To allow for practice, this recipe yields extra dough and filling.

Notes on flour: Weigh your flour to be sure your dough has the right hydration. And use minimal flour when kneading, rolling, and shaping so the dough remains slightly tacky. A short, narrow rolling pin will make the job easiest. Lastly: Wet fingers can hamper shaping. We chill balls of filling in the freezer to minimize this, but dry your fingers periodically with paper towels if need be.

— Kevin + Jeffrey (+ Joe)

recipe continues on next page

Soup

- 3 pounds chicken wings
- 6 cups water
- 1 (2-inch) piece ginger, sliced into ¼-inch-thick rounds
- 3 scallions, cut into 2-inch lengths
- ¼ ounce dried shiitake mushrooms, rinsed

Dough

- 2 cups (10 ounces) all-purpose flour
- ¾ cup boiling water, plus extra as needed
- 1 teaspoon vegetable oil

Filling

- 1 pound ground pork
- 1 tablespoon Shaoxing wine
- 1 tablespoon soy sauce
- 1 scallion, minced
- 2 teaspoons toasted sesame oil
- 1 teaspoon grated fresh ginger
- 1 teaspoon sugar
- ½ teaspoon table salt
- ⅛ teaspoon white pepper

For Serving

- Chinese black vinegar
- Fresh ginger, peeled and cut into thin matchsticks

1 **For the soup:** Bring chicken and water to boil in large saucepan over medium-high heat, skimming off any scum that comes to surface. Reduce heat to low, partially cover, and simmer gently for 1 hour.

2 Add ginger, scallions, and mushrooms and continue to simmer for 2 hours. Strain soup through fine-mesh strainer into large bowl or container; discard solids. Let soup settle for about 5 minutes, then, using wide, shallow spoon, skim excess fat from surface. Wipe pot clean with paper towels.

3 Return soup to now-empty pot. Bring to simmer over medium-high heat and cook until reduced to 2 cups, 10 to 15 minutes. Transfer soup to 13 by 9-inch baking dish and let cool for 30 minutes. Cover and refrigerate until fully gelatinized, about 4 hours. Scrape any hardened fat from top of soup. (Jellied soup can be refrigerated for up to 5 days.) Using fork, mash jellied soup into ⅛-inch pieces.

4 **For the dough:** Place flour in bowl of stand mixer and fit mixer with paddle. With mixer on medium-low speed, slowly add boiling water and oil until dough forms ball and clears sides of bowl, 2 to 4 minutes. If dough ball does not form, add extra boiling water 1 teaspoon at a time until dough ball forms. Transfer dough to counter and gently knead until mostly smooth, 2 to 3 minutes. Wrap dough in plastic wrap and let rest for at least 30 minutes or up to 4 hours.

5 **For the filling:** Using clean, dry stand mixer fitted with paddle, beat all ingredients on medium speed until well combined, mixture has stiffened and started to pull away from sides of bowl, and pork has slightly lightened in color, about 2 minutes. Scrape down sides of bowl, add jellied soup, and mix on medium-low speed until incorporated, about 1 minute. Divide filling into 1-tablespoon portions (you should have at least 40 portions). Using wet hands, roll each portion into ball and arrange on parchment paper–lined rimmed baking sheet. Freeze until firm, about 15 minutes, then store in refrigerator until needed.

6 Roll dough into 12-inch cylinder on counter, then cut cylinder into 4 equal pieces. Set 3 pieces aside and cover with plastic. Roll remaining piece into 8-inch cylinder. Cut cylinder in half and cut each half into 7 equal pieces (each piece should weigh about ¼ ounce, or 8 grams). Roll each piece into ball. Place dough balls on lightly floured counter and lightly dust with flour. Using pie plate or palm of your hand, press each ball into 2-inch disk. Cover disks with damp dish towel.

7 Working with 1 disk at a time, roll into 3-inch round. Continue rolling outer 1-inch edge of dough to create 4-inch round wrapper with tapered edges. As you roll, hold center of wrapper with nondominant hand and rotate dough slightly after each roll to maintain uniform shape. Re-cover wrapper with damp dish towel; do not overlap wrappers. Line additional 2 rimmed baking sheets with parchment paper and lightly dust with flour.

8   Place wrapper on fingers of nondominant hand and brush away any flour clinging to surface. Place 1 ball of filling in center of round. Steady dough by lightly pinching outer edge with thumb and index finger of nondominant hand. Using thumb and index finger of dominant hand, push edge of dough toward pinched portion to create first ¼-inch pleat on exterior of dumpling. Pinch pleat with fingers of nondominant hand to seal, and continue pinching to secure dough while creating next pleat. Continue with pleating and pinching motion, pinching each pleat to edge of previous pleat to create round purse-shape dumpling. Rotate dumpling as you pleat, and support dumpling base with palm of hand. As opening in top of dumpling narrows, you may need to gently push filling into dumpling and use very tips of fingers to create final pleats.

9   Pinch top of gathered dough edges together to seal dumpling. Gently twist off any excess dough from dumpling, leaving small point on top. Place dumpling pleated side up on prepared sheet and cover with plastic. Repeat with remaining dough and filling. (Dumplings can be refrigerated for up to 1 hour or frozen on sheet until solid, then transferred to zipper-lock bag and stored in freezer for up to 1 month. Do not thaw dumplings before cooking; increase steaming time to about 10 minutes.)

10   Bring 4 cups water to boil in 14-inch flat-bottomed wok. Poke about 20 small holes in two 9-inch parchment rounds and lightly coat with vegetable oil spray. (Use leaves of napa cabbage in place of parchment if desired.) Place rounds in two 10-inch bamboo steamer baskets. Arrange 10 dumplings in each prepared basket so that they are not touching; stack baskets and cover. Reduce heat to maintain vigorous simmer and set steamer in wok. Steam until dumpling wrappers have translucent, glossy sheen, about 8 minutes. Serve immediately with vinegar and ginger. (Before cooking second batch of dumplings, replenish water in wok and line steamer baskets with fresh parchment rounds.)

How to Eat Soup Dumplings

- If you eat a xiao long bao the moment the steamer basket is uncovered, you will scald the inside of your mouth and hate yourself. Give it at least 2 minutes to cool.

- Next, add vinegar and a ginger sliver to the soup spoon.

- The xiao long bao is folded with a nub at the tip of the dumpling. Carefully grab this with chopsticks, slowly lifting it from the basket to ensure the bottom doesn't puncture. Transfer onto the spoon. If you like, bite off a bit of wrapper to expedite interior cooling. You can even suck out the soup.

- Slurp the dumpling directly from the spoon in one go. No regrets.

turn to see how to shape soup dumplings

Shaping Shanghai Soup Dumplings

① Roll outer edge of 3-inch round, starting from perimeter and rolling inward, to create tapered edges.

② To create first pleat, lightly pinch outer edge of wrapper with thumb and index finger of nondominant hand. Using thumb and index finger of dominant hand, push edge of dough toward pinched portion.

③ Pinch pleat with fingers of nondominant hand to seal, and continue pinching to secure dough while creating next pleat.

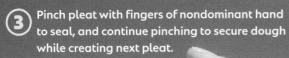

④ Continue with pleating and pinching motion, pinching each pleat to edge of previous pleat to create round purse-shape dumpling.

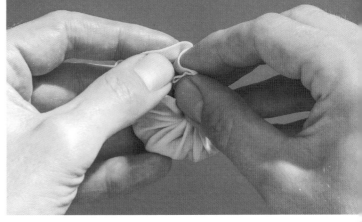

⑤ Pinch top of gathered dough edges together to seal dumpling.

⑥ Gently twist off any excess dough from dumpling, leaving small point on top.

Shanghai Pan-Fried Pork Buns

Makes: 20 buns — **Total Time:** 6 hours, plus 5¾ hours resting, cooling, and rising — **Difficulty:** ●●●●

I grew up across the street from my wife, Catherine, so we've known each other since we were kids. Her family came to Hong Kong from Shanghai, and they missed the food of their hometown terribly. She told me how her father would walk 30 minutes each way to a tiny stall that sold only Shanghai pan-fried buns, her favorite food. This place was so small—it was at the base of government housing—it didn't even have a name.

Her father would return with a paper bag filled with these extraordinary pork-filled buns, the exteriors golden and crisp, the yeasted-dough interior savory and juicy.

When our family immigrated to North America in the 1980s, it was hard to find a decent version. I knew how much Catherine missed eating those pan-fried buns. This recipe, which I worked on with recipe developer Camila Chaparro, results in buns that taste exactly like the ones from our memory.

We Chinese aren't particularly emotive, especially in verbalizing our affection. Instead, we express it with food—and this isn't an exaggeration. We'd walk an hour to buy our daughter a special treat. We'd spend years perfecting a recipe to re-create the food our spouse grew up eating. We'd make YouTube cooking shows with our children. We love food, but food is also love.   — Jeffrey

---

This recipe uses a similar filling and shaping method as Shanghai Soup Dumplings and many of the same tips apply here. Partially freezing portions of filling helps to keep it in place while shaping and sealing the dumplings. Look for freshly ground pork at the butcher's counter, which has more fat and a coarser texture than prepackaged pork. We strongly recommend weighing the flour. We had the best success using a short, narrow rolling pin for rolling the wrappers; however, a traditional rolling pin will also work. Use minimal flour if the dough begins to stick when kneading, rolling, and shaping so that it stays slightly tacky. The more you practice making pork buns, the more dexterous you will become; to allow for practice, the recipe yields extra dough and filling. You will need a 12-inch nonstick skillet with a tight-fitting lid.

---

1 For the soup: Bring chicken and water to boil in large saucepan over medium-high heat, skimming off any scum that comes to surface. Reduce heat to low, partially cover, and simmer gently for 1 hour.

recipe continues on next page

Soup

- 1½ pounds chicken wings
- 5 cups water
- 1 (2-inch) piece ginger, sliced into ¼-inch-thick rounds
- 3 scallions, cut into 2-inch lengths
- ¼ ounce dried shiitake mushrooms, rinsed

Dough

- 3½ cups (17½ ounces) all-purpose flour
- 3½ tablespoons cornstarch
- 1¾ teaspoons instant or rapid-rise yeast
- 1 teaspoon sugar
- ¼ teaspoon table salt
- 1½ cups water, room temperature

Filling

- 12 ounces ground pork
- 1 scallion, minced
- 2 teaspoons Shaoxing wine
- 2 teaspoons soy sauce
- 1½ teaspoons dark soy sauce
- 1½ teaspoons toasted sesame oil
- 1 teaspoon sugar
- 1 teaspoon grated fresh ginger
- ⅛ teaspoon table salt
- ⅛ teaspoon white pepper

- 4 teaspoons vegetable oil
- ⅓ cup water
- 1 scallion, sliced thin
- 1 teaspoon black sesame seeds, toasted

2 Add ginger, scallions, and mushrooms; continue to simmer for 2 hours. Strain soup through fine-mesh strainer into large bowl or container; discard solids. Let settle for about 5 minutes. Using wide, shallow spoon, skim excess fat from surface.

3 Return soup to now-empty pot. Bring to simmer over medium-high heat and cook until reduced to 1 cup, 5 to 10 minutes. Transfer soup to 9-inch round baking pan and let cool for 30 minutes. Cover and refrigerate until fully gelatinized, about 4 hours. Scrape any hardened fat from top of soup. (Jellied soup can be refrigerated for up to 5 days.) Using fork, mash jellied soup into ⅛-inch pieces.

4 **For the dough:** Whisk flour, cornstarch, yeast, sugar, and salt together in bowl of stand mixer. Using dough hook on low speed, slowly add water to flour mixture and mix until cohesive dough starts to form and no dry flour remains, about 2 minutes, scraping down sides of bowl as needed. Increase speed to medium-low and knead until dough is smooth and elastic, about 10 minutes. Transfer dough to clean counter and knead by hand to form smooth, round ball, about 30 seconds. Place dough seam side down in lightly greased large bowl or container, cover tightly with plastic wrap, and let rise at room temperature until slightly puffy, about 30 minutes.

5 **For the filling:** Using clean stand mixer fitted with paddle, beat pork, scallion, Shaoxing wine, soy sauce, dark soy sauce, sesame oil, sugar, ginger, salt, and pepper on medium speed until well combined, mixture has started to pull away from sides of bowl, and pork has slightly lightened in color, about 2 minutes. Scrape down sides of bowl, add jellied soup, and mix on medium-low speed until incorporated, about 1 minute. Divide filling into heaping 1-tablespoon portions (you should have at least 20 portions). Using wet hands, roll each portion into ball and arrange on parchment paper–lined rimmed baking sheet. Freeze until firm, about 15 minutes, then refrigerate until needed.

6 Brush 12-inch nonstick skillet with vegetable oil. Press down on dough to deflate. Transfer dough to clean counter and divide in half; set 1 piece aside and cover with plastic. Roll remaining half into even 12-inch cylinder. Cut cylinder into 12 equal pieces (each piece should weigh about 1¼ ounces, or 35 grams). Roll each piece into ball. Place balls on lightly floured counter and lightly dust with flour. Using pie plate or palm of hand, press each ball into 2-inch disk. Cover disks with damp dish towel.

7 Working with 1 disk at a time, roll into 3-inch round. Continue rolling outer 1-inch edge of dough to create 4-inch round wrapper with tapered edges. As you roll, hold center of wrapper with nondominant hand and rotate dough slightly after each roll to maintain uniform shape. Re-cover wrapper with damp dish towel; do not overlap wrappers.

8 Place wrapper on fingers of nondominant hand and brush away any flour clinging to surface. Place 1 ball of filling in center of round. Steady dough by lightly pinching outer edge with thumb and index finger of nondominant hand. Using thumb and index finger of dominant hand, push edge of dough toward pinched portion to create first ¼-inch pleat on exterior of dumpling. Pinch pleat with fingers of nondominant hand to seal, and continue pinching to secure dough while creating next pleat. Continue with pleating and pinching motion, pinching each pleat to edge of previous pleat to create round purse-shape dumpling. Rotate dumpling as you pleat, and support dumpling base with palm of hand. As opening in top of dumpling narrows, you may need to gently push filling into dumpling and use very tips of fingers to create final pleats.

9 Pinch top of gathered dough edges together to seal dumpling. Gently twist off any excess dough from dumpling, leaving small point on top. Place bun pleated side down in center of prepared skillet and loosely cover with greased plastic. Repeat with remaining dough wrappers and filling to create 9 more buns; you will not need all of dough. Evenly space buns in 2 concentric circles around center dumpling.

10 Transfer reserved dough to clean counter and press to deflate. Repeat portioning, rolling, and filling to make 10 more buns. Evenly space buns in skillet, cover loosely with greased plastic, and let rise until buns are puffy and just touching one another, about 30 minutes.

11 Discard plastic. Cover skillet and place over medium heat. Cook until bottoms of buns are golden brown, 6 to 8 minutes. Reduce heat to medium-low, carefully add water around perimeter of skillet (water will spatter and create steam), and continue to cook, covered, until water is fully absorbed and buns begin to sizzle and are crispy on bottom, about 7 minutes. Sprinkle buns with scallion and sesame seeds. Serve immediately.

RICE AND NOODLE DISHES

♫ Rice cakes and ho fun and sesame noodles

We'll teach it all, the whole kit and caboodle

Dishes from Taiwan, Hong Kong, and Beijing

Starches and carbs are our favorite things ♪

Báifàn 白飯
100% Perfect Rice

Serves: 4 to 6 — **Total Time:** 45 minutes — **Difficulty:** none whatsoever

Here lies the single most important recipe in this cookbook—dare I say in any Chinese cookbook published since time immemorial. This is the Cantonese secret for making 100 percent perfect rice, because 99.9 percent won't do.

Ready?

Buy a $250 Zojirushi rice cooker. This rice cooker is every Cantonese family's secret for perfect rice. The end.

1 Add rice to interior rice cooker bowl. Wash rice until water is clear.

2 Fill with water to "2 cups" line.

3 Press start.

2 plastic cups (use the one that comes with the rice cooker) jasmine rice

1 $250 Zojirushi rice cooker

Rinse Your Rice

Rinsing rice before cooking washes away excess starch that would absorb water, causing grains to clump. To rinse rice directly in a rice cooker insert or bowl, cover with cool water and gently agitate with your fingers, then pour off the water; repeat this until the water runs clear. You can also rinse rice in a fine-mesh strainer under cool water until the water runs clear, stirring occasionally. Let the grains drain briefly.

No Rice Cooker? Use the Stovetop or Microwave

Okay, fine, not everyone wants to shell out for a $250 rice cooker because you don't eat rice nightly. You can still achieve excellent rice on the stovetop, though it'll require a touch more management and supervision. Easier yet? The microwave makes surprisingly good rice.

Stovetop Steamed Long- or Medium-Grain Rice

Serves: 4 to 6
Total Time: 35 minutes

This recipe works with a variety of rices, including jasmine and Calrose. Do not stir the rice as it cooks. To halve this recipe, decrease the water to 2 cups. To double this recipe, use a Dutch oven and increase the water to 5 cups.

- 3 cups water
- 2 cups long-grain or medium-grain rice, rinsed

Bring water and rice to boil in large saucepan over medium-high heat. Cook, uncovered, until water level drops below surface of rice and small holes form, about 5 minutes. Reduce heat to low, cover, and cook until rice is tender and water is fully absorbed, about 15 minutes. Serve.

Stovetop Steamed Short-Grain Rice

Serves: 4 to 6
Total Time: 50 minutes

Short-grain rice varieties (except for glutinous rice) such as sushi rice work well here. Do not stir the rice as it cooks. To halve the recipe, decrease the water to 1¼ cups. To double this recipe, use a Dutch oven and increase the water to 4¼ cups.

- 2¼ cups water
- 2 cups short-grain white rice, rinsed

Bring water and rice to boil in large saucepan over medium-high heat. Reduce heat to low, cover, and cook until rice is tender and water is fully absorbed, about 20 minutes. Remove from heat and let sit for 15 minutes to finish cooking. Serve.

Microwave-Steamed Rice

Yes, you can in fact microwave rice with consistent results. This works with long-, medium-, and short-grain rice. Using the ratio of water to rice listed in the stovetop methods, microwave the water and rice in a large microwave-safe covered bowl on full power for 5 minutes. Continue to microwave on 50 percent power for 15 minutes. Carefully remove the bowl from the microwave and let sit covered for 5 minutes to finish cooking. Serve.

Faux Leftover Rice

Makes: 4 cups
Total Time: 1¼ hours

*What do you do when you want great fried rice but don't
have leftover rice? Chilled day-old rice undergoes a
process in which the starches harden up enough for the
rice to withstand a second round of cooking. There's no
reliable way to speed up the process (believe us, we've tried
everything), but we found a workaround that produces
comparably dry, firm rice in less than an hour. It involves
coating the rice with oil before cooking to prevent grains
from clumping, using less water to achieve more rigid
grains, and instituting a brief rest and chill to ensure the
rice is dry and firm—perfect for fried rice.*

  4 teaspoons vegetable oil
  1⅓ cups long-grain rice, rinsed
  1¾ cups water

1 Heat oil in large saucepan over medium-high heat
until shimmering. Add rice and stir to coat grains with oil,
about 30 seconds. Add water and bring to boil. Reduce
heat to low, cover, and cook until water has been fully
absorbed, about 18 minutes.

2 Off heat, lay clean dish towel underneath lid and let
sit until rice is just tender, about 8 minutes. Spread cooked
rice onto rimmed baking sheet and let cool on wire rack for
10 minutes. Transfer sheet to refrigerator and let rice chill
for 20 minutes. (Rice can be refrigerated for up to 3 days.
Bring to room temperature before using.)

Jiǎnyì Chǎofàn 簡易炒飯
Simple Fried Rice

Serves: 4 — **Total Time:** 30 minutes — **Difficulty:** ●○○○

The two versions of fried rice presented in this chapter aren't so much recipes as they are itineraries. Think of how an itinerary works: It's a schedule of events. This really is what separates great fried rice from merely good versions—it's about timing and sequence, learning when to add the various components.

The reason you don't want to throw everything into a wok arbitrarily and hope for the best: This is the surest way to achieve a sticky, clumpy mess of a fried rice. What proper timing yields are slick and individual rice granules, eggs that remain fluffy, vegetables that don't get mushy. (In the pages that follow, we'll talk more about the timing of ingredients and give our favorite tips for exemplary fried rice.)

This level-one recipe is easy but exquisite. Day-old jasmine rice works best for this version; the varietal is loaded with a popcorn-y aromatic compound that perfumes the fried rice with gorgeous fragrance, and, when stir-fried, the hard, dry clumps relax into tender-firm, distinct grains.   — Kevin + Jeffrey

While we prefer jasmine rice, any long- or medium-grain rice will work. Day-old rice works best; in a pinch you can use our Faux Leftover Rice (page 131).

1   Beat eggs and ¼ teaspoon salt in bowl until well combined. Heat empty 14-inch flat-bottomed wok over high heat until just beginning to smoke. Reduce heat to medium-high, drizzle 2 teaspoons oil around perimeter of wok, and heat until just smoking. Add eggs and cook, stirring constantly, until very little liquid egg remains, 30 to 60 seconds. Transfer to large plate.

2   Add 1 teaspoon oil to now-empty wok and reduce heat to medium. Add carrot and ¼ teaspoon salt and cook, tossing slowly but constantly, until carrot is just beginning to brown, 2 to 4 minutes. Add ham and cook, stirring constantly, until ham is warmed through, 1 to 2 minutes. Transfer to plate with eggs.

3   Add scallion whites and remaining 1 tablespoon oil to now-empty wok. Cook, stirring constantly, until fragrant, about 1 minute. Sprinkle rice over scallion whites and stir until combined. Spread into even layer. Sprinkle pepper and remaining 1 teaspoon salt evenly over rice. Continue to cook, stirring frequently and pressing on rice with spatula to break up clumps, until grains are separate and heated through, 2 to 5 minutes. Add peas, egg mixture, and scallion greens and cook, stirring constantly and using edge of spatula to break eggs into small pieces, until peas are warmed through, about 2 minutes. Serve.

3 large eggs

1½ teaspoons kosher salt, divided

2 tablespoons vegetable oil, divided

1 carrot, peeled and cut into ¼-inch pieces

4 ounces ham steak, cut into ½-inch pieces (¾ cup)

4 scallions, white and green parts separated and sliced thin

4 cups cooked jasmine rice, room temperature, large clumps broken up with fingers

¼ teaspoon pepper

½ cup frozen peas

That's So Retrograde

- Few dishes are made better using leftover ingredients, and fried rice is one of them. The starch molecules in cooked rice crystallize during chilling (a process called retrogradation), hardening into grains that can be fully coated in oil, ready for stir-frying.

- If you're working with fridge-cold rice, let it sit out while you prep the other ingredients so the clumps soften and become easier to break apart. Or microwave at 50 percent power for two minutes.

Customizing Fried Rice Mix-Ins

Fried rice is deliciously versatile because it's a canvas on which you can use any tool to paint any object in any color. You can change up fried rice with almost anything found in your pantry. (One of our most memorable fried rices came from a Mexican friend who used leftover "al pastor" pork and escabeche!) Here are a few starter ideas, grouped by how much cooking they need. Plan on using a total of 1½ cups of mix-ins.

Cook Time	Ingredient	Preparation
Stir-fry separately until tender (2 to 4 minutes), then stir-fry with hot rice to finish cooking (about 2 minutes)	Broccoli	½-inch pieces
	Mushrooms	¾-inch pieces
	Shallot/onion	½-inch pieces
Stir-fry separately until warmed through (1 to 2 minutes), then stir-fry with hot rice to finish cooking (about 2 minutes)	Bell pepper	¼-inch pieces
	Bok choy	¼-inch slices
	Char siu	½-inch pieces
	Roast chicken	½-inch pieces
	Spam	½-inch pieces
	Sugar snap peas	¼-inch slices
Stir into hot rice and stir-fry until warmed through (1 to 2 minutes)	Bean sprouts	as is
	Napa cabbage	finely shredded
	Yacai (pickled mustard greens)	as is

4 Pointers for Exquisite Fried Rice

Like some ancient philosopher probably said, there is no one path to greatness. The same goes for fried rice. Different cooks have different strategies; these happen to be our favorites.

1 Pour eggs into oil that's just beginning to smoke, not just shimmering. The water in the eggs rapidly turns to steam and their proteins set, helping to make the eggs fluffy.

2 Cook the vegetables and protein separate from the eggs and rice to ensure the wok isn't overcrowded, thereby retaining its high heat for proper cooking.

3 Crumble and sprinkle rice into the wok to break up large clumps and separate rice grains. Visualize a rice snowstorm.

4 While stir-frying the rice, continue to break up any remaining clumps with a spatula so that they separate into fluffy, distinct grains that will easily merge with the mix-ins.

Shrimp and Pork Fried Rice

Serves: 4 to 6 — **Total Time:** 30 minutes — **Difficulty:** ●●○○

½ ounce dried shiitake mushrooms, rinsed

¼ cup oyster sauce

1 tablespoon soy sauce

2 large eggs

3 tablespoons vegetable oil, divided

8 ounces small shrimp (51 to 60 per pound), peeled, deveined, and tails removed

4 scallions, white and green parts separated and sliced thin

2 garlic cloves, minced

1 cup frozen peas

8 ounces char siu (Chinese barbecue pork) or lap cheong (Chinese sausage), cut into ½-inch pieces

4 cups cooked jasmine rice, room temperature, large clumps broken up with fingers

2 ounces (1 cup) bean sprouts

Meat Me Halfway

Char siu and lap cheong aren't the easiest to find. You know what else is good? Spam luncheon meat. The teriyaki and tocino versions are especially tasty.

If you've mastered our Simple Fried Rice, this level-two version improves upon the dish in several delicious ways. First, we incorporate shrimp and dried shiitake mushrooms, and replace ham with char siu, the Cantonese barbecued pork (get takeout if you live near a Chinatown, or make the recipe on page 321). You can also use lap cheong, the dried Chinese sausage that adds a lovely sweetness. We then finish the fried rice with oyster sauce, which bumps up the savoriness to new heights. This dish is our most popular episode of *Hunger Pangs* by a country mile.
— Kevin + Jeffrey

While we prefer jasmine rice, any long- or medium-grain rice will work. Day-old rice works best; in a pinch you can use our Faux Leftover Rice (page 131).

1 Microwave 1 cup water and mushrooms in covered bowl until steaming, about 1 minute. Let sit until softened, about 5 minutes. Lift mushrooms from bowl with fork and discard liquid. Squeeze mushrooms dry, remove stems, and slice into ¼-inch-thick strips; set aside. Combine oyster sauce and soy sauce in small bowl; set aside.

2 Beat eggs in separate bowl until well combined. Heat empty 14-inch flat-bottomed wok over high heat until just beginning to smoke. Reduce heat to medium-high, drizzle 2 teaspoons oil around perimeter of wok, and heat until just smoking. Add eggs and cook, stirring constantly, until very little liquid egg remains, 30 to 60 seconds. Transfer to large plate.

3 Add 1 teaspoon oil to now-empty wok and reduce heat to medium. Add shrimp and cook, stirring constantly, until opaque and just cooked through, about 30 seconds. Transfer to plate with eggs.

4 Add remaining 2 tablespoons oil to now-empty wok and increase heat to high. Add scallion whites and garlic and cook, stirring constantly, until fragrant, 15 to 30 seconds. Add peas, mushrooms, and char siu and cook, stirring constantly, until ingredients are warmed through, about 1 minute. Sprinkle rice over char siu and vegetables and stir until combined. Spread into even layer. Cook, stirring and pressing on rice with spatula to break up clumps, until grains are separate and heated through, 2 to 5 minutes. Add oyster sauce mixture, eggs, shrimp, bean sprouts, and scallion greens and cook, stirring constantly and using edge of spatula to break eggs into small pieces, until warmed through, about 2 minutes. Serve.

Chǎo Niángāo 炒年糕
Stir-Fried Rice Cakes

Serves: 4 to 6 — **Total Time:** 1 hour, plus 20 minutes marinating — **Difficulty:** ●○○○

1 (8-ounce) boneless pork chop, ¾ to 1 inch thick, trimmed

3 tablespoons plus 1 teaspoon vegetable oil, divided

5 teaspoons soy sauce, divided

1 tablespoon water

1 tablespoon Shaoxing wine

1 teaspoon cornstarch

1 teaspoon toasted sesame oil, divided

¼ teaspoon white pepper

2 teaspoons oyster sauce

1½ teaspoons dark soy sauce

2 garlic cloves, minced

2 ounces shiitake mushrooms, stemmed and sliced thin

1 carrot, peeled and sliced thin on bias

1 pound refrigerated or frozen sliced rice cakes, thawed if necessary and rinsed

½ cup chicken broth

4 ounces snow peas, strings removed and halved crosswise

Test Kitchen Tip

Recipe developer Faye Yang notes: "After adding the sauce, it's important to keep the rice cakes moving in the wok to prevent sticking. Frequent stirring will yield whole coins of glossy rice cakes."

Rice cakes, you won't be surprised to hear, are made from rice (pounded into a powder, mixed with water, formed into logs, sliced into ovals). What's delightful to the rice cake–uninitiated is its gummy texture—like a chewier gnocchi, with enough surface area to cling to whatever sauce you toss its way. Rice cakes are sold dried (you'll need to rehydrate), fresh, or frozen. Increasingly, you'll find them at non-Asian grocers; we recently bought some (labeled as sliced Korean rice cakes) from Trader Joe's. As for this dish, think of it as halfway between fried rice and fried noodles, with all the familiar weeknight stir-fry elements. — Kevin + Jeffrey

Don't thaw frozen rice cakes in the microwave; let them sit in the refrigerator overnight or on the counter for 4 to 5 hours.

1 Transfer pork to plate and freeze until firm, about 15 minutes. Slice pork crosswise ¼ inch thick on bias. Cut each slice lengthwise into ¼-inch strips.

2 Combine 1 teaspoon vegetable oil, 2 teaspoons soy sauce, water, Shaoxing wine, cornstarch, ½ teaspoon sesame oil, and pepper in medium bowl; add pork and stir to break up clumps. Cover and refrigerate for at least 15 minutes or up to 1 hour.

3 Whisk oyster sauce, remaining 1 tablespoon soy sauce, dark soy sauce, and remaining ½ teaspoon sesame oil together in small bowl; set aside.

4 Heat empty 14-inch flat-bottomed wok over high heat until just beginning to smoke. Drizzle remaining 3 tablespoons vegetable oil around perimeter of hot wok and heat until just smoking. Add pork mixture and garlic and cook, tossing slowly but constantly, until pork is no longer pink, about 1 minute. Add mushrooms and cook, tossing slowly but constantly, until beginning to soften, about 1 minute. Add carrot and cook, tossing slowly but constantly, until crisp-tender, about 1 minute.

5 Push pork and vegetables to center of wok and place rice cakes on top. Add broth, cover, and cook until rice cakes are softened, about 2 minutes. Stir in snow peas and reserved sauce and cook uncovered, stirring frequently, until sauce is thick-ened and coats rice cakes, and snow peas are crisp tender, about 1 minute. Serve.

Huájī Bāozǎifàn 滑雞煲仔飯
Clay Pot Chicken Rice

Serves: 4 to 6 — **Total Time:** 1¾ hours, plus 45 minutes soaking and marinating — **Difficulty:** ●●○○

Clay pots aren't just steady cooking vessels that look ornate on the dining table. They imbue food with an inimitable flavor, like wood fire does to a tomahawk steak. In China you'll often find clay pots cooked over live charcoal. Because of the pot's porous nature, the smoky flavors seep into what's cooked inside.

In the case of chicken rice, an exquisite one-pot dish of Guangdong Province, the heated clay surface comes in contact with the rice, caramelizing the grains into a crunchy sheet of toasty goodness. It's immensely satisfying to scrape the bottom of a clay pot chicken rice to reveal how much of this golden crust—飯焦 or fan zui, meaning "scorched rice" in Cantonese—the cooking produces. We haven't even mentioned the rest of the dish, a classic Cantonese combination of ingredients: savory marinated dark-meat chicken, dried shiitake mushrooms, and sweet lap cheong sausage (we call it optional, but we highly recommend its inclusion).

Some folks liken clay pot chicken rice to a casserole. We can see that connection. You dump ingredients into a dish, give it a good mix, and let heat and time meld flavors into something comforting and wondrous. This version, which we worked on for weeks with recipe developer Carmen Dongo, achieves just that.

If you want the unadulterated Chinese experience, use a cleaver to split the chicken thighs straight through the bone (please, do not ruin your pricey chef's knife). We derive much tactile pleasure from gnawing on chicken and spitting out the bones. Otherwise, debone the chicken thighs and cut into 1-inch pieces, leaving the skin intact. — Kevin + Jeffrey

---

This dish is traditionally made in a glazed ceramic or earthenware pot with lid; however, a cast-iron Dutch oven with a tight-fitting lid will also work.

---

1 Combine scallion whites, garlic, soy sauce, Shaoxing wine, oyster sauce, dark soy sauce, ginger, sugar, and pepper in large bowl. Transfer 3 tablespoons sauce to small bowl; set aside. Whisk cornstarch into remaining marinade.

2 Working with 1 thigh at a time, position cleaver at middle of thigh, perpendicular to bone. Slice through meat so bone is exposed. Hold knife steady, with base of blade resting on top of bone, and use nondominant hand to push down on spine of knife to split thigh into 2 pieces. Transfer thigh pieces to bowl with marinade and toss to coat. Cover and refrigerate for 30 minutes.

recipe continues on next page

- 3 **scallions, white and green parts** separated and sliced thin
- 4 **garlic cloves, minced**
- 2 **tablespoons soy sauce**
- 2 **tablespoons Shaoxing wine**
- 4 **teaspoons oyster sauce**
- 2 **teaspoons dark soy sauce**
- 2 **teaspoons grated fresh ginger**
- 2 **teaspoons sugar**
- ½ **teaspoon white pepper**
- 1 **tablespoon cornstarch**
- 4 **(5- to 7-ounce) bone-in chicken thighs, trimmed**
- 2 **ounces dried shiitake mushrooms, rinsed**
- 1½ **cups jasmine rice, rinsed**
- 1 **teaspoon table salt, plus** 2 **teaspoons salt for soaking rice**
- 2 **tablespoons vegetable oil**
- 1 **cup chicken broth**
- 2 **ounces lap cheong (Chinese sausage), sliced thin (optional)**

3   Meanwhile, microwave 4 cups water and mushrooms in covered bowl until steaming, about 10 minutes, stirring halfway through microwaving. Let sit until softened, about 30 minutes. Lift mushrooms from bowl with fork and transfer to cutting board. Squeeze mushrooms dry, stem, and slice ¼ inch thick. Measure out and reserve ¼ cup mushroom soaking liquid; discard remaining liquid.

4   Place rice and 2 teaspoons salt in medium bowl and cover with 4 cups hot tap water. Stir gently to dissolve salt; let sit for 15 minutes, then drain rice.

5   Heat oil in 4½- to 7-quart glazed ceramic or earthenware pot over medium-low heat until shimmering. Arrange chicken skin side down in single layer in pot and cook until fat begins to render, 5 to 7 minutes; return chicken to bowl. Add broth and reserved mushroom liquid to fat left in pot, scraping up any browned bits. Stir in rice and 1 teaspoon salt and bring to boil over medium-high heat. Reduce heat to medium-low and simmer until no water is visible above rice, about 5 minutes.

6   Arrange chicken skin side up on top of rice and add any accumulated juices. Top with mushrooms and lap cheong, if using. Cover and continue to cook until chicken registers at least 175 degrees, rice is tender, and deep golden crust has formed on bottom of pot, 25 to 35 minutes, rotating pot halfway through cooking. Off heat, drape clean dish towel underneath lid and let sit for 10 minutes. Drizzle reserved sauce over chicken and sprinkle with scallion greens. Serve.

No Clay Pot? No Problem.

Diànguō Huájī Fàn 電鍋滑雞飯
Rice Cooker Chicken Rice

Serves: 4 to 6
Total Time: 1 hour, plus 30 minutes soaking
Difficulty: ●○○○

Achieve 95 percent deliciousness of the clay pot version with 20 percent of the effort. How? You will need an electric rice cooker with a 5½- to 6-cup capacity. If you have semidecent aim dumping ingredients into a bowl, you can make this.

- 3 scallions, white and green parts separated and sliced thin
- 4 garlic cloves, minced
- 2 tablespoons soy sauce
- 2 tablespoons Shaoxing wine
- 4 teaspoons oyster sauce
- 2 teaspoons dark soy sauce
- 2 teaspoons grated fresh ginger
- 2 teaspoons sugar
- ½ teaspoon white pepper
- 1 tablespoon cornstarch
- 1¼ pounds boneless, skinless chicken thighs, trimmed and halved crosswise
- 2 ounces dried shiitake mushrooms, rinsed
- 1½ cups jasmine rice, rinsed
- 1 teaspoon table salt, plus 2 teaspoons salt for soaking rice
- 1 cup chicken broth
- 2 tablespoons vegetable oil
- 2½ ounces lap cheong (Chinese sausage), sliced thin (optional)

1 Combine scallion whites, garlic, soy sauce, Shaoxing wine, oyster sauce, dark soy sauce, ginger, sugar, and pepper in large bowl. Transfer 3 tablespoons sauce to small bowl; set aside. Whisk cornstarch into remaining marinade and add chicken and toss to coat. Cover and marinate for 30 minutes.

2 Meanwhile, microwave 4 cups water and mushrooms in covered bowl until steaming, about 10 minutes, stirring halfway through microwaving. Let sit until softened, about 30 minutes. Lift mushrooms from bowl with fork and transfer to cutting board. Squeeze mushrooms dry, stem, and slice ¼ inch thick. Measure out and reserve ¼ cup mushroom soaking liquid; discard remaining liquid.

3 Place rice and 2 teaspoons salt in medium bowl and cover with 4 cups hot water. Stir gently to dissolve salt; let sit for 15 minutes, then drain rice.

4 Combine broth, reserved mushroom liquid, rice, oil, and 1 teaspoon salt in cooking chamber of electric rice cooker. Arrange chicken on top of rice and top with mushrooms and lap cheong, if using. Cover and cook on standard rice setting according to manufacturer's directions. Machine will automatically shut off when cooking is completed. Drizzle reserved sauce over chicken and sprinkle with scallion greens. Serve.

Májiàng Bànmiàn 麻醬拌麵

Sesame Noodles

Serves: 4 to 6 — **Total Time:** 30 minutes — **Difficulty:** ●○○○

- 5 tablespoons soy sauce
- ¼ cup Chinese sesame paste
- 2 tablespoons sugar
- 4 teaspoons Chinese black vinegar
- 1 tablespoon chili oil
- 2 garlic cloves, minced
- 2 teaspoons grated fresh ginger
- 1 pound fresh thin white wheat noodles
- ½ English cucumber, cut into 3-inch-long matchsticks
- ¼ cup fresh cilantro leaves
- 2 scallions, green parts only, sliced thin
- 1 tablespoon sesame seeds, toasted

Endless Pasta-bilities

This dish is wholly satisfying as written, but you can add any topping. Poached chicken is a natural pairing. In Hong Kong you'll find deli ham, red bell peppers, and sliced egg omelet on cold noodles.

Kevin went to college in Southern California, and every time he returned home to Seattle, I would pick him up from the airport. Ten times out of ten, he would request I meet him at the airport with cold sesame noodles from Green Village.

Green Village is a family-run Chinese restaurant in Kent, Washington, where we lived. Kevin was in love with their version of sesame noodles, which was served with cold poached chicken. Sometimes at the airport he'd jump in the car and, without a word, immediately start eating, greeting me hello only after a few bites! What an ungrateful kid.

Cold sesame noodles is a classic street food found throughout China. It's easy to understand why it's a favorite: It's inexpensive, filling, and supremely delicious. I suggest you make a jar of this rich, nutty, tingly sauce ahead of time, and you'll have this magnificent dish ready anytime—like when your kid comes home to visit.
— Jeffrey

If fresh thin white wheat noodles are unavailable, substitute fresh lo mein or 12 ounces dried wheat noodles. In a desperate pinch, spaghetti will work.

1 Process soy sauce, sesame paste, sugar, vinegar, 1 tablespoon water, chili oil, garlic, and ginger in blender until smooth, about 30 seconds, scraping down sides of blender jar as needed; transfer to large bowl.

2 Meanwhile, bring 4 quarts water to boil in large pot. Add noodles and cook, stirring often, until just tender. Drain noodles and rinse under cold running water until chilled; drain well.

3 Transfer noodles to bowl with dressing and toss to combine. Adjust consistency with extra water as needed until sauce smoothly coats noodles. Transfer noodles to shallow serving bowl and top with cucumber, cilantro, scallions, and sesame seeds. Serve.

Cōngyóu Bànmiàn 葱油拌麵

Scallion Oil Noodles

Serves: 4 to 6 — **Total Time:** 1 hour — **Difficulty:** ●●○○

My first stop after arriving in Shanghai is a soup dumpling restaurant. There's no negotiating on that. My second stop is a restaurant called Taihuang Chicken. There they specialize in a Shanghainese version of poached chicken that's out of this world. You'll never taste a more succulent and juicy bird.

But what they serve alongside the chicken is just as memorable: a bowl of scallion oil noodles. The key is infusing the oil with the flavor of slow-caramelized scallions, which release a sweet-onion perfume as they fry. At Taihuang Chicken the chefs toss this fragrant oil in a tangle of fresh, springy noodles. The simplicity of making this Shanghainese favorite belies its profound tastiness. — Jeffrey

If fresh thin white wheat noodles are unavailable, substitute 12 ounces dried wheat noodles. Japanese yakisoba noodles are also a good stand-in with their toothsome texture. Before serving, individual bowls can be topped with blanched pea greens (sometimes called pea tendrils or mature pea shoots) or fresh cucumber sliced into matchsticks.

¼ cup soy sauce

2 tablespoons dark soy sauce

5 teaspoons sugar

10 scallions (6 ounces), white and green parts separated

1 pound fresh thin white wheat noodles

⅔ cup peanut or vegetable oil

⅛ teaspoon table salt

1 shallot, halved and sliced thin

1 (1-inch) piece ginger, peeled and cut into thin matchsticks

1 Combine soy sauce, dark soy sauce, and sugar in small bowl; set aside. Halve scallion whites lengthwise, then slice white and green parts into 1½-inch segments; reserve white and green parts separately.

2 Bring 4 quarts water to boil in large pot. Add noodles and cook, stirring often, until just tender. Drain noodles and rinse well; set aside.

3 Meanwhile, add oil and scallion greens to empty 14-inch flat-bottomed wok and cook over medium-high heat, stirring constantly, until most scallions are browned and crisp, 8 to 10 minutes. Using spider skimmer or slotted spoon, transfer scallion greens to separate small bowl; sprinkle with salt and set aside.

4 Reduce heat to medium-low and add scallion whites, shallot, and ginger to oil in wok. Cook, stirring often, until scallions and shallot are golden and wilted, 11 to 13 minutes.

5 Add reserved soy sauce mixture and cook, stirring constantly, until sugar is dissolved and sauce is rapidly bubbling, 1 to 2 minutes. Add noodles and cook, tossing slowly but constantly until well coated and heated through, 2 to 3 minutes. Sprinkle with reserved scallion greens and serve.

Sweet and Lowdown

Patience is key when flavoring the oil for this recipe. Too high a heat and the scallions, shallot, and ginger will brown too quickly, turning the oil acrid. When in doubt, lower the heat a tad.

Dan Dan Mian
(page 150)

Dàndànmiàn 擔擔麵

Dan Dan Mian

Serves: 4 — **Total Time:** 1¼ hours — **Difficulty:** ●●○○

Sauce

- ¼ cup vegetable oil
- 1 tablespoon Sichuan chili flakes
- 2 teaspoons Sichuan peppercorns, ground fine
- ¼ teaspoon ground cinnamon
- 2 tablespoons soy sauce
- 2 teaspoons Chinese black vinegar
- 2 teaspoons tianmianjiang (sweet wheat paste)
- 1½ teaspoons Chinese sesame paste

Noodles

- 8 ounces ground pork
- 2 teaspoons Shaoxing wine
- 1 teaspoon soy sauce
- 2 small heads baby bok choy (about 3 ounces each)
- 1 tablespoon vegetable oil, divided
- 3 garlic cloves, minced
- 2 teaspoons grated fresh ginger
- 1 pound fresh thick white wheat noodles
- ⅓ cup yacai
- 2 scallions, sliced thin

The food of Sichuan is one of the world's most sophisticated, unapologetically bold, full-flavored gastronomic traditions. I learned about the cuisine through the book *Land of Plenty* by the food writer Fuchsia Dunlop, who studied at the renowned Sichuan Institute of Higher Cuisine. That cookbook was my Harry Potter, whisking me off to a magical world where peppers numbed and chiles scorched palates, a province that has birthed some 5,000-plus dishes. One of those is dan dan mian, the most famous dish in the street-food-mad capital city of Chengdu. Contained in one bowl is Sichuan's culinary sophistication in vibrant display:

- A fiery, complex chili oil sauce, spiced with Sichuan peppercorns and cinnamon, with the sweet-heady depth of black vinegar, sesame, and sweet wheat paste.

- Deeply savory bits of pork, fried crispy with garlic and ginger.

- Juicy lengths of baby bok choy, and the crunchy sour bite of pickled mustard.

All this is layered in a bowl along with freshly boiled wheat noodles. The pleasure comes in mixing the components yourself and watching the bowl turn a fervid red: Tactilely, it's as satisfying as bursting the yolk of a just-fried egg.   — Kevin

---

If fresh thick white wheat noodles are unavailable, substitute fresh lo mein or 8 ounces dried lo mein noodles. If tianmianjiang is unavailable, substitute hoisin. Yacai, a type of pickled mustard, is sometimes labeled suimiyacai. We do not recommend substituting other varieties of pickled mustard.

---

1   For the sauce: Heat oil, chili flakes, peppercorns, and cinnamon in 14-inch flat-bottomed wok over low heat for 10 minutes. Using rubber spatula, transfer oil mixture to bowl (do not wash wok). Whisk soy sauce, vinegar, tianmianjiang, and sesame paste into oil mixture. Divide evenly among 4 shallow bowls.

2   For the noodles: Combine pork, Shaoxing wine, and soy sauce in medium bowl and toss with your hands until well combined; set aside. Working with 1 head bok choy at a time, trim base (larger leaves will fall off) and halve lengthwise through core; rinse well.

3   Heat 2 teaspoons oil in now-empty wok over medium-high heat until shimmering. Add reserved pork mixture and use rubber spatula to smear into thin layer across surface of wok. Break up meat into ¼-inch chunks with edge of spatula and cook, stirring frequently, until pork is firm and well browned, about 5 minutes. Push pork mixture to far side of wok and add garlic, ginger, and remaining 1 teaspoon oil to cleared space. Cook, stirring constantly, until garlic mixture begins to brown, about 1 minute. Stir to combine pork mixture with garlic mixture. Off heat, cover to keep warm.

4   Meanwhile, bring 4 quarts water to boil in large pot. Add bok choy and cook until leaves are vibrant green and stems are crisp-tender, about 1 minute. Using spider skimmer or slotted spoon, transfer bok choy to plate; set aside. Return water to boil. Add noodles and cook, stirring often, until almost tender (center should still be firm with slightly opaque dot). Drain noodles. Rinse under hot running water, tossing with tongs, for 1 minute; drain well.

5   Divide noodles evenly among prepared bowls. Return wok with pork mixture to medium heat. Add yacai and cook, stirring frequently, until warmed through, about 2 minutes. Spoon pork mixture over noodles. Divide bok choy evenly among bowls, shaking to remove excess moisture as you portion. Top with scallions. Serve warm or at room temperature.

Bring on the Funk

A big scoop of the Sichuan pickle yacai is a key component to this noodle bowl. Made by fermenting stalks of a Chinese mustard plant, it adds tangy, complex, subtly spicy funk. There's nothing quite like it (even in Sichuan, where fermented foods are a particular specialty), and since it's shelf-stable, you may as well stock up on it for future dan dan mian.

Crispy, Savory Pork Topping

Tender, juicy meat is not the goal here. What you want is a crispy, umami-rich seasoning that clings to the noodles. To get it really fine-textured and brown, smear the ground pork into a thin layer across the wok with a rubber spatula, jab at it with the tool's edge to break it up into bits, and sear it hard—really hard. The end result is fine bits of pork with crispy edges.

Ròusī Chǎomiàn 肉絲炒麵
Pork Stir-Fried Noodles

Serves: 4 to 6 — **Total Time:** 1¼ hours — **Difficulty:** ●●○○

1 pound boneless country-style pork ribs, trimmed

3 tablespoons soy sauce

2 tablespoons oyster sauce

2 tablespoons hoisin sauce

1 tablespoon toasted sesame oil

¼ teaspoon liquid smoke

¼ teaspoon five-spice powder

½ cup chicken broth

1 tablespoon chili-garlic sauce

1 teaspoon cornstarch

5 teaspoons vegetable oil, divided

¼ cup Shaoxing wine, divided

8 ounces shiitake mushrooms, stemmed and halved if small or quartered if large

½ small head napa cabbage, halved, cored, and sliced crosswise into ½-inch strips (4 cups)

10 scallions, white parts sliced thin, green parts cut into 1-inch pieces

2 garlic cloves, minced

2 teaspoons grated fresh ginger

12 ounces fresh lo mein noodles

Not everyone is fortunate enough to live 10 minutes from a Chinese barbecue shop, much less near any Chinatown at all (maybe real estate companies should list proximity to roast goose?). What we love about living so close to a Chinese barbecue is the ready availability of fresh char siu. Sweet roast pork is a versatile ingredient, equally delicious in both Chinese (stir-fries, on top of white rice) and non-Chinese (it makes terrific taco filling) applications. It's the Chinese equivalent of supermarket rotisserie chicken.

This dish approximates char siu when char siu isn't available. The pork gets marinated in a host of savory flavors, including hoisin sauce, five-spice powder, and liquid smoke, lending the pork a sweet, smoky edge. — Kevin + Jeffrey

---

If fresh lo mein noodles are unavailable, you can substitute 8 ounces dried lo mein noodles.

---

1 Transfer pork to plate and freeze until firm, about 15 minutes. Slice pork crosswise ⅛ inch thick on bias. Whisk soy sauce, oyster sauce, hoisin, sesame oil, liquid smoke, and five-spice powder together in bowl. Transfer 3 tablespoons soy sauce mixture to medium bowl; add pork and stir to break up clumps. Cover and refrigerate for at least 15 minutes or up to 1 hour.

2 Whisk broth, chili-garlic sauce, and cornstarch into remaining soy sauce mixture; set aside.

3 Heat empty 14-inch flat-bottomed wok over high heat until just beginning to smoke. Drizzle 1 teaspoon vegetable oil around perimeter of wok and heat until just smoking. Add half of pork mixture and cook, tossing slowly but constantly, until pork is lightly browned, 2 to 3 minutes. Add 2 tablespoons Shaoxing wine and cook, stirring constantly, until liquid is reduced and pork is well coated, 30 to 60 seconds. Transfer pork mixture to clean medium bowl and repeat with 1 teaspoon oil, remaining pork mixture, and remaining 2 tablespoons Shaoxing wine. Wipe wok clean with damp paper towels.

4 Heat now-empty wok over high heat until just beginning to smoke. Drizzle 1 teaspoon vegetable oil around perimeter of wok and heat until just smoking. Add mushrooms and cook, tossing slowly but constantly, until light golden brown, 4 to 6 minutes; transfer to bowl with pork mixture.

All Mixed Up

Use tongs (or a long pair of chopsticks) plus a spatula to toss everything together at the end, folding the vegetables and meat into the noodles.

5 Add 1 teaspoon vegetable oil and cabbage to now-empty wok and cook, tossing slowly but constantly, until spotty brown, 3 to 5 minutes. Push cabbage to 1 side of wok. Add remaining 1 teaspoon oil, scallions, garlic, and ginger to clearing and cook, mashing mixture into wok, until fragrant, about 30 seconds. Stir scallion mixture into cabbage. Add pork mixture and reserved chicken broth mixture and cook, stirring frequently, until sauce is thickened, about 2 minutes.

6 Meanwhile, bring 4 quarts water to boil in large pot. Add noodles and cook, stirring often, until almost tender (center should still be firm with slightly opaque dot). Drain noodles, transfer to wok, and cook over medium-high heat, tossing gently, until noodles are tender and evenly coated with sauce. Serve.

Zha Jiang Mian

Serves: 4 — **Total Time:** 1 hour — **Difficulty:** ●●○○

- 3 tablespoons ganhuangjiang (dry soybean paste)
- 3 tablespoons huangdoujiang (soybean sauce)
- 2 tablespoons Shaoxing wine
- 1 tablespoon tianmianjiang (sweet wheat paste)
- 8 ounces skinless pork belly, top layer of fat trimmed off, meat cut into ½-inch pieces
- 2 tablespoons vegetable oil
- 1 star anise pod
- 6 scallions, white and light-green parts chopped, divided, dark-green parts sliced thin
- 1 tablespoon sugar
- 4 ounces (2 cups) bean sprouts
- 1 pound fresh thin white wheat noodles
- ½ English cucumber, cut into 2-inch-long matchsticks
- 1 carrot, peeled and cut into 2-inch-long matchsticks

Test Kitchen Tip

Recipe developer Faye Yang notes: "It's important to slowly build the sauce by frying each component, adding depth of flavor. Don't be afraid of the sheen of oil that appears as you fry the sauce. The aromatic oil will coat the noodles beautifully."

If you take away the city's namesake roast duck, Beijing's next most popular dish features noodles served with a viscous, subtly sweet, and ultrarich pork sauce. Zha jiang mian translates as "fried sauce noodles"—an apt description, as pork belly and various pastes are fried until reduced to a thick, exceedingly flavor-dense topping. This "fried sauce" gets spooned onto wheat noodles (a little sauce goes a long way), and an assortment of vegetables provides the crunch.

This dish requires some special ingredients: ganhuangjiang (dry soybean paste), which gives the sauce its dark color and savory taste, huangdoujiang (soybean sauce), which contributes a savory bean flavor, and tianmianjiang (sweet wheat paste), which adds a touch of sugar to balance the dish's saltiness. While we strongly suggest you seek out these ingredients, we understand it can be tough to find certain pastes, even in well-stocked Asian grocers. So do as our respective parents say: "Try your best and never give up!" — Kevin + Jeffrey

If fresh thin white wheat noodles are unavailable, substitute 12 ounces dried wheat noodles. Red miso paste can be used in place of ganhuangjiang. For more information on ganhuangjiang, huangdoujiang, and tianmianjiang, see pages 16–18.

1 Whisk ¼ cup water, ganhuangjiang, huangdoujiang, Shaoxing wine, and tianmianjiang together in bowl.

2 Add pork and oil to empty 14-inch flat-bottomed wok. Cook over medium heat, stirring occasionally, until pork begins to brown, 5 to 9 minutes. Add star anise and half of white and light-green scallions and cook until fragrant, about 3 minutes.

3 Carefully stir in half of soybean paste mixture and cook for 1 minute (mixture will bubble and sizzle). Stir in remaining soybean paste mixture and cook for 1 minute. Reduce heat to low and continue to cook, stirring occasionally, until sauce begins to thicken and darken, 5 to 8 minutes.

4 Stir in sugar and remaining white and light-green scallions and cook until softened, 2 to 3 minutes. (Sauce will look separated and oily.) Off heat, discard star anise and cover sauce to keep warm.

5 Meanwhile, bring 4 quarts water to boil in large pot. Add bean sprouts and cook until just softened, about 30 seconds. Using spider skimmer or slotted spoon, transfer to small bowl. Return water to boil. Add noodles and cook, stirring often, until just tender. Drain noodles and immediately divide among 4 serving bowls. Spoon sauce over center of noodles in each bowl. Top with bean sprouts, cucumber, carrot, and sliced scallions. Serve.

Gānchǎo Niúhé 乾炒牛河
Beef Ho Fun

Serves: 4 to 6 — **Total Time:** 30 minutes, plus 30 minutes marinating — **Difficulty:** ●●○○

6 ounces flank steak, trimmed

1 tablespoon water

¼ teaspoon baking soda

5 teaspoons soy sauce, divided

1 tablespoon oyster sauce, divided

1 tablespoon Shaoxing wine, divided

1 teaspoon cornstarch

¼ teaspoon white pepper

2 teaspoons dark soy sauce

12 ounces fresh ho fun noodles

2 tablespoons vegetable oil, divided

6 ounces (3 cups) bean sprouts

½ small onion, sliced ¼ inch thick

2 garlic cloves, minced

1 teaspoon grated fresh ginger

3 scallions, green parts only, cut into 1½-inch pieces

Separating Fresh Ho Fun

Are your ho fun noodles stuck together out of the package? Place them on a plate and cover with a wet paper towel. Microwave at 50 percent power 20 seconds at a time until the noodles pull apart.

When I was a food critic at the *Chicago Tribune*, one of my methods of assessing a chef's acumen was by ordering the most rudimentary dish on the menu, such as a roast chicken. How a chef pulls off those foundational recipes—the ones taught in semester one of cooking school—speaks volumes about the care and execution of everything else at the restaurant.

If I wanted to know if a Cantonese chef was up to snuff, I'd order the beef ho fun. (Not knowing how to make this dish is like not knowing how to boil water.) For such a simple dish of noodles, there are a lot of things to get right: the velveting of the beef, how you balance the sauce, the amount of char applied to the noodles, how you keep all the components from sticking together into a gummy mass. Nail down those details, and you'll be rewarded with one of Hong Kong's finest culinary exports. Beef ho fun is everything you'd want in a stir-fried noodle: savory rice noodles, crunchy veg, and tender wok-fried beef, served up hot and fast.   — Kevin

Fresh ho fun noodles are wide, flat rice noodles and are critical to this dish; do not substitute other types of fresh or dried noodles.

1   Cut beef with grain into 2½- to 3-inch-wide strips. Transfer to plate and freeze until firm, about 15 minutes. Slice strips crosswise against grain ¼ inch thick. Combine water and baking soda in medium bowl. Add beef and toss to coat; let sit for 5 minutes.

2   Whisk 2 teaspoons soy sauce, 1 teaspoon oyster sauce, 1 teaspoon Shaoxing wine, cornstarch, and pepper together in large bowl. Add beef mixture, toss to coat, and let sit at room temperature for 30 minutes.

3   Whisk remaining 1 tablespoon soy sauce, remaining 2 teaspoons oyster sauce, remaining 2 teaspoons Shaoxing wine, and dark soy sauce together in small bowl. Using fingers, unfurl noodles and transfer to rimmed baking sheet; set sauce and noodles aside.

4   Heat empty 14-inch flat-bottomed wok over high heat until just beginning to smoke. Drizzle 1 tablespoon oil around perimeter of wok and heat until just smoking. Add beef mixture and cook, tossing slowly but constantly, until just beginning to brown, about 2 minutes; transfer to clean bowl. Wipe wok clean with damp paper towels.

5 Heat now-empty wok over high heat until just beginning to smoke. Drizzle 1½ teaspoons oil around perimeter of wok and heat until just smoking. Add bean sprouts, onion, garlic, and ginger and cook, tossing slowly but constantly, until vegetables begin to soften and lightly char, about 1 minute; transfer to bowl with beef.

6 Heat now-empty wok over high heat until just beginning to smoke. Drizzle remaining 1½ teaspoons oil around perimeter of wok and heat until just smoking. Add noodles and cook, tossing gently but constantly, until beginning to char, about 1 minute. Add beef mixture and scallions and gently toss to combine. Drizzle reserved soy sauce mixture around perimeter of hot wok and cook, tossing gently to coat noodles, about 30 seconds. Serve.

Singapore Noodles

Serves: 4 to 6 — **Total Time:** 1 hour — **Difficulty:** ●●○○

- 6 ounces mei fun (dried rice vermicelli)
- 12 ounces large shrimp (26 to 30 per pound), peeled, deveined, and tails removed
- ½ teaspoon table salt, divided
- 6 tablespoons vegetable oil, divided
- 6 ounces char siu (Chinese barbecue pork), sliced thin
- 4 large eggs
- 2 large shallots, halved and sliced thin
- 1 red or green bell pepper, stemmed, seeded, and sliced thin
- 3 garlic cloves, minced
- 1 teaspoon grated fresh ginger
- 2 tablespoons curry powder
- ⅛ teaspoon cayenne pepper
- 2 tablespoons soy sauce
- 1 teaspoon sugar
- 4 ounces (2 cups) bean sprouts
- 4 scallions, sliced thin

Test Kitchen Tip

Recipe developer Hannah Fenton notes: "Blooming and softening the spices in warm oil help to reduce any gritty texture, so be sure to stir the spices for the full 2 minutes. There won't be much of a visual change, but you will be rewarded later on for your patience."

Just as every pub in London is obligated to serve fish and chips, every Cantonese restaurant must offer Singapore Noodles. It's a knockout of a dish: slick rice noodles coated yellow with aromatic curry powder, dry stir-fried with shrimp, char siu, crunchy bean sprouts, and bell pepper. (Dry stir-frying is a method of cooking with minimal oil and without sauce.) If we could pick only one recipe in this book to impress dinner guests, Singapore Noodles would be in contention.

Please know you're as likely to find Singapore Noodles in Singapore as you would Mongolian Beef in Mongolia, which is to say, not very likely. This dish is a pride and joy of Hong Kong through and through; we're just glad our friendly Singaporean neighbors let us borrow the name. — Kevin + Jeffrey

Mei fun are often labeled rice vermicelli. When shopping, make sure to buy a Chinese brand. Other kinds of rice vermicelli may be too thin and may stick together after soaking. If char siu is not available you can make your own (page 321) or make our approximated version (page 152).

1 Bring 4 quarts water to boil in large pot. Off heat, add noodles and let sit until just tender, about 3 minutes, stirring once halfway through soaking. Drain noodles and transfer to greased wire rack set in rimmed baking sheet; set aside.

2 Cut shrimp in half lengthwise, pat dry with paper towels, and sprinkle with ¼ teaspoon salt. Heat empty 14-inch flat-bottomed wok over high heat until just beginning to smoke. Drizzle 1 tablespoon oil around perimeter of wok and heat until just smoking. Add shrimp and cook, tossing slowly but constantly, until opaque throughout, about 2 minutes. Add char siu and cook, stirring frequently, until heated through, about 1 minute; transfer to bowl.

3 Beat eggs and remaining ¼ teaspoon salt in separate bowl until well combined. Heat now-empty wok over high heat until just smoking. Drizzle 2 teaspoons oil around perimeter of wok and heat until just smoking. Add eggs and cook, stirring constantly, until very little liquid egg remains, 30 to 60 seconds; transfer to bowl with shrimp mixture.

4 Drizzle 1 tablespoon oil around perimeter of now-empty wok and heat over medium-high heat until just smoking. Add shallots and bell pepper and cook, tossing slowly but constantly, until crisp-tender, about 2 minutes.

Push vegetables to 1 side of wok and add 1 teaspoon oil, garlic, and ginger to clearing. Cook, mashing mixture into wok, until fragrant, about 30 seconds. Stir garlic-ginger mixture into vegetables, then transfer to bowl with shrimp, char siu, and eggs.

5   Drizzle remaining 3 tablespoons oil around perimeter of now-empty wok and heat over medium heat until just smoking. Off heat, add curry powder and cayenne. Cook, stirring constantly, until fragrant and darkened in color, about 2 minutes. Stir in ¼ cup water, soy sauce, and sugar until sugar has dissolved.

6   Return wok to medium heat, add noodles, and toss gently until well coated. Add shrimp mixture and bean sprouts and cook, tossing gently, until heated through, about 1 minute. Sprinkle with scallions and serve.

Biángbiáng Miàn 奤奤麵
Flat Hand-Pulled Noodles

Serves: 4 — **Total Time:** 1¼ hours, plus 12-hour rest — **Difficulty:** ●●●●

Great moments in "Chinese Food on TV" history: 1) That episode of *Seinfeld* at the Chinese restaurant; 2) Martin Yan, the forever king; 3) The time Anthony Bourdain visited Xi'an Famous Foods in Flushing, New York. When that episode of *Anthony Bourdain: No Reservations* aired in 2009, it was a huge deal for us Chinese folks.

For those not paying attention to the historical representation of Sino-cookery in America (I do), know that for many decades Chinese restaurants were categorized as either Cantonese or Mandarin—whatever that meant. Only in the past 30 years has Sichuan cuisine broken through the pop culture threshold, entering the mainstream and gaining popularity beyond Chinese folks. Then the Bourdain segment aired. It propelled a small family business serving the relatively unknown food of Shaanxi province into a thriving restaurant empire across New York City. Now more than ever, Americans know that saying "Chinese food" is as ambiguous as saying "European food"—the cooking of Xinjiang bears little resemblance to that of Fujian.

This is a long-winded way of explaining the important role Xi'an Famous Foods (by way of Anthony Bourdain) played in introducing biang biang mian to a Western audience. The dish is appealingly demonstrable, especially on TV: The hand-pulled noodles get *thwap-thwap-thwapped* against the counter, stretching the dough into pappardelle-like bands. (Thwap Thwap Noodles would've been a more accurate onomatopoeia, methinks.) The fresh noodles get dropped in boiling water, quickly turning luscious and pleasantly chewy, and then they're tossed in a piquant chili oil vinaigrette. For cultural reasons, for historical reasons, for delicious reasons, the world is better off knowing about these superb noodles.   — Kevin

---

It is critical to rest the dough for at least 12 hours (and up to 48 hours). During this period, the gluten network becomes more extensible, making it easier to pull long, flat noodles by hand. Note that after 24 hours the dough's surface may develop black speckles. This is a result of oxidation and has no impact on flavor or safety.

---

1 For the dough: Whisk flour and salt together in bowl of stand mixer. Add water and oil. Fit stand mixer with dough hook and mix on low speed until all flour is moistened, 1 to 2 minutes. Increase speed to medium and knead until dough is smooth and satiny, 10 to 12 minutes. Transfer dough to counter, knead for 30 seconds, and shape into 9-inch log. Wrap log in plastic wrap and refrigerate for at least 12 hours or up to 48 hours.

Dough

2⅓ cups (12¾ ounces) bread flour

¾ teaspoon table salt

1 cup (8 ounces) water

1 tablespoon vegetable oil

Chili Oil Vinaigrette

¼ cup Sichuan chili flakes

½ cup vegetable oil

2 garlic cloves, sliced thin

1 (1-inch) piece ginger, peeled and sliced thin

1 tablespoon Sichuan peppercorns

½ cinnamon stick

1 star anise pod

2 tablespoons soy sauce

2 tablespoons Chinese black vinegar

1 tablespoon toasted sesame oil

1 teaspoon sugar

1 tablespoon table salt

12 sprigs fresh cilantro, trimmed and cut into 2-inch pieces

6 scallions, sliced thin

recipe continues on next page

2 **For the chili oil vinaigrette:** Place chili flakes in large heatproof bowl. Place fine-mesh strainer over bowl and set aside. Combine vegetable oil, garlic, ginger, peppercorns, cinnamon stick, and star anise in small saucepan and heat over medium-high heat until sizzling. Reduce heat to low and gently simmer until garlic and ginger are slightly browned, 10 to 12 minutes. Pour through strainer into bowl with chili flakes; discard solids in strainer. Stir chili oil to combine and let cool for 5 minutes. Stir in soy sauce, vinegar, sesame oil, and sugar until combined; set aside.

3 Unwrap dough, transfer to lightly oiled counter, and, using bench scraper or knife, divide into 6 equal pieces (each 1½ inches wide). Cover with plastic and let rest for 5 minutes. Meanwhile, bring 4 quarts water and salt to boil in large pot; reduce heat to low and cover to keep hot. Working with 1 piece at a time, oil both sides of dough and flatten into 7 by 3-inch rectangle, with long side parallel to edge of counter. With both hands, gently grasp short ends of dough. Stretch dough and slap against counter until noodle is 32 to 36 inches long (noodle will be between 1⁄16 and 1⁄8 inch thick). Place noodle on counter. Pinch center of noodle with forefinger and thumb of each hand and pull apart with even pressure in both directions to rip seam in middle of noodle and create 1 continuous loop.

Cut loop to create 2 equal-length noodles. Set noodles aside on lightly oiled counter (do not let noodles touch) and cover with plastic. Repeat stretching and cutting with remaining pieces of dough.

4 Return water to boil over high heat. Add half of noodles to water and cook, stirring occasionally, until noodles float and turn chewy-tender, 45 to 60 seconds. Using wire skimmer, transfer noodles to bowl with chili vinaigrette; toss to combine. Return water to boil and repeat with remaining noodles. Divide noodles among individual bowls, top with cilantro and scallions, and serve.

Test Kitchen Tip

Bread flour, which contains more protein than all-purpose flour, is key for chewy, sturdy noodles, but they don't stretch easily until we add both a tablespoon of vegetable oil to lubricate the dough and a slow resting period, which relaxes the well-developed gluten network. The resulting dough can be pulled effortlessly, and the chewy texture is maintained.

Pulling Flat Noodles by Hand

1 Flatten 1 piece of oiled dough into 7 by 3-inch rectangle, with long side parallel to edge of counter.

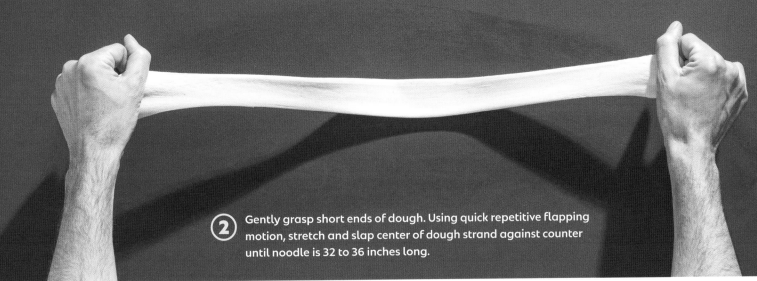

2 Gently grasp short ends of dough. Using quick repetitive flapping motion, stretch and slap center of dough strand against counter until noodle is 32 to 36 inches long.

3 Pinch center of noodle with forefinger and thumb of each hand and pull apart in both directions to create 1 continuous loop. Cut loop to create 2 equal-length noodles.

Noodle Soup with Pork and Preserved Mustard

Serves: 4 to 6 — **Total Time:** 1 hour — **Difficulty:** ●●○○

1 (12- to 16-ounce) pork tenderloin, trimmed

2 teaspoons cornstarch

2 teaspoons oyster sauce

2 teaspoons Shaoxing wine

2 teaspoons soy sauce

6 cups chicken broth

10 ounces (2 cups) shredded zhacai, divided

1 (2-inch) piece ginger, peeled and sliced thin

12 ounces fresh thin white wheat noodles

4 teaspoons vegetable oil, divided

2 garlic cloves, sliced thin

2 scallions, sliced thin

1 teaspoon sesame oil

Test Kitchen Tip

Recipe developer Joe Gitter says:

"This soup gets fast flavor in two ways: from the concentrated stir-fried topping, and from simmering a portion of the same ingredients in chicken broth, carrying the sour-spicy-savory flavor all the way through."

Though you'd rightly associate Sichuan cooking with fieriness, this elegant noodle soup showcases another hallmark of the cuisine: its embrace of the pickled and the fermented. The stir-fried pickled mustard here provides a crunchy, punchy, sauerkraut-like bite to the proceedings. Together with the tender pork slivers and gentle wheat noodles in chicken broth, this is a dish displaying a more temperate side of the Sichuanese culinary canon.   — Kevin

Zhacai can be labeled "spicy pickled mustard," "salted spicy radish," or "pickled mustard tuber." It can be sold whole or preshredded in vacuum-sealed packages. We do not recommend substituting other varieties of pickled mustard greens. If fresh wheat noodles are unavailable, substitute 8 ounces dried wheat noodles.

1 Transfer tenderloin to plate and freeze until firm, about 15 minutes. Slice pork crosswise ⅛ inch thick. Cut each slice into ⅛-inch-thick strips.

2 Whisk cornstarch, oyster sauce, Shaoxing wine, and soy sauce together in medium bowl; add two-thirds of pork and stir to break up clumps; set aside.

3 Bring broth, 1 cup water, ⅔ cup zhacai, ginger, and remaining pork to boil in large saucepan over high heat. Reduce heat to medium-low and simmer for 15 minutes. Strain broth through fine-mesh strainer into large bowl, pressing on solids to extract as much liquid as possible; discard solids. Return broth to now-empty saucepan and cover to keep warm.

4 Bring 4 quarts water to boil in large pot. Add noodles and cook, stirring often, until tender. Drain noodles and immediately divide among individual serving bowls.

5 Meanwhile, heat empty 14-inch flat-bottomed wok over high heat until just beginning to smoke. Drizzle 1 tablespoon vegetable oil around perimeter of wok and heat until just smoking. Add marinated pork and cook, tossing slowly but constantly, until cooked through, 1 to 3 minutes. Add remaining 1⅓ cups zhacai, reduce heat to medium, and cook, tossing slowly but constantly, until mustard begins to soften, about 2 minutes.

6 Push pork mixture to 1 side of wok and add garlic and remaining 1 teaspoon vegetable oil to clearing. Cook, mashing mixture into wok, until fragrant, about 30 seconds. Stir garlic into pork mixture until combined.

7 Return broth to rolling boil over high heat. Pour broth over noodles in bowls and top with pork mixture. Sprinkle with scallions and drizzle with sesame oil before serving.

Taiwanese Beef Noodle Soup

Serves: 4 to 6 — **Total Time:** 4 hours, plus 30 minutes resting — **Difficulty:** ●●●○

Broth

- ¼ cup (2 ounces) rock sugar, crushed
- ¼ cup vegetable oil
- 2 tablespoons doubanjiang (broad bean chile paste)
- 6 garlic cloves, lightly crushed and peeled
- 1 (1½-inch) piece ginger, peeled and sliced ¼ inch thick
- 1 scallion, minced
- ½ cinnamon stick
- 1 tablespoon Sichuan peppercorns
- 1 teaspoon fennel seeds
- 2 star anise pods
- 2 bay leaves
- 1 tomato, cored and chopped
- 8 cups water
- 1 small onion, coarsely chopped
- 1 carrot, peeled and coarsely chopped
- ¼ cup soy sauce
- 3 tablespoons Shaoxing wine
- 1 teaspoon table salt
- ½ teaspoon white pepper
- 3 pounds cross-cut beef shanks, trimmed

Soup

- 2 heads baby bok choy (4 ounces each), quartered lengthwise
- 12 ounces dried flat (¼-inch-wide) white wheat noodles
- 1 recipe Stir-Fried Pickled Mustard Greens (page 24)
- 2 scallions, sliced thin
- ¼ cup minced fresh cilantro leaves and tender stems

The Pangs have little to do with this recipe, other than being madly in love with it. This version of Taiwan's national dish is the creation of test cook Faye Yang, who cooked through two dozen bowls to nail down a recipe faithful enough for her Taiwanese parents to approve. For Faye, memories of this dish run deep. Growing up in New England, Faye remembers coming home on cold winter days and being greeted with the sweet, beefy, warmly spiced aromas of the broth filling her home. All children have certain taste memories lodged in their psyche; Faye's was biting into the unctuous, deeply flavorful medallions of beef shank, a delicious slick coating her lips. To this day, when Faye returns home to visit, that very same comforting bowl of the Yang family noodle soup awaits her arrival.

This recipe is Faye's loving homage. She told us how every culture has its matzo ball soup, its chicken noodles. Her goal with this dish was to evoke those fuzzy coming-home-to-a-warm-bowl memories, no matter your background. "Everyone who tastes this should feel nostalgic," Faye said. — Kevin + Jeffrey (+ Faye)

Look for beef shanks that are 2 inches thick and 2 to 4 inches in diameter. If beef shank is unavailable, you can substitute 2 pounds beef blade steaks, ¾ to 1 inch thick.

---

1 **For the broth:** Cook sugar and oil in Dutch oven over medium-low heat, stirring frequently, until sugar has melted and mixture is amber-colored, about 5 minutes. Stir in doubanjiang, garlic, ginger, and scallion and cook until doubanjiang is rust-colored, about 3 minutes. Stir in cinnamon stick, peppercorns, fennel seeds, star anise, and bay leaves and cook until fragrant, about 30 seconds. Stir in tomato and cook until softened and beginning to release its juices, about 2 minutes.

2 Stir in water, onion, carrot, soy sauce, Shaoxing wine, salt, and pepper, scraping up any browned bits. Nestle beef into broth and bring to simmer over medium-high heat. Reduce heat to medium-low, partially cover, and cook until beef is nearly tender and tip of knife inserted into beef meets some resistance, 2½ to 3 hours, flipping beef halfway through cooking.

3 Off heat, let beef rest in broth until fully tender and tip of knife inserted into beef meets little resistance, about 30 minutes. Transfer beef to cutting board and separate meat from bones in large pieces; discard bones. Tent beef with aluminum foil and set aside.

4 Set fine-mesh strainer over large bowl or container and line with triple layer of cheesecloth. Strain broth through prepared strainer, pressing on solids to extract as much liquid as possible, and let settle for 5 minutes; discard solids. Using wide, shallow spoon, skim excess fat from surface of broth. (You should have 6 cups broth; add extra water as needed to equal 6 cups. Broth and beef can be refrigerated separately for up to 4 days; let beef sit at room temperature for 30 minutes before assembling soup.)

5 **For the soup:** Bring 4 quarts water to boil in large pot. Add bok choy to boiling water and cook until crisp-tender, about 1 minute. Using tongs, transfer bok choy to plate. Return water to boil, add noodles, and cook, stirring occasionally, until nearly tender. Drain noodles and immediately divide among individual serving bowls.

6 Meanwhile, add broth to now-empty Dutch oven and bring to rolling boil over high heat. Slice beef ½ inch thick against grain on bias. Arrange beef and bok choy attractively over noodles. Ladle broth over noodles and serve, passing pickled mustard greens, scallions, and cilantro separately.

POULTRY, MEAT, FISH

Let's talk about meats. If you're a fan of Chinese food
(and we hope you are at this point), we're certain at least
one of your favorite dishes can be found in this chapter.
Here you'll learn about not only making those iconic recipes,
but also foundational Chinese cooking methods such as poaching
chicken and steaming whole fish. If you haven't veered far
from the pan-frying/oven-roasting way of cooking meats, you're
in for a succulent and delightful treat.

170

Gōngbǎo Jīdīng　宮保雞丁

Kung Pao Chicken

173

Sānbēi Jī　三杯雞

Three-Cup Chicken

175

Chǐyóu Jī　豉油雞

Soy Sauce Chicken

176

Buddhist-Style Chicken

178

Zīrán Yángròu　孜然羊肉

Stir-Fried Cumin Lamb

180

Měnggǔ Niúròu　蒙古牛肉

Mongolian Beef

184

Jièlán Niúròu　芥蘭牛肉

Stir-Fried Beef and Gai Lan

186

Huíguō Ròu　回鍋肉

Twice-Cooked Pork

188

Lǔròu Fàn　滷肉飯

Taiwanese Pork Rice Bowl

190

Mùxū Ròu　木須肉

Mu Shu Pork

Chūnbǐng　春餅

Spring Pancakes

194

Shīzitóu　獅子頭

Lion's Head Meatballs

196

Jiāngcōng Zhēng Yúliǔ
薑葱蒸魚柳

Steamed Fish Fillets with Scallions and Ginger

198

Jiāngcōng Zhēng Quányú
薑葱蒸全魚

Steamed Whole Fish with Scallions and Ginger

202

Yóubào Xiā　油爆蝦

Oil-Exploded Shrimp

205

Chǐjiāo Chǎo Xiǎn　豉椒炒蜆

Stir-Fried Clams with Black Bean Sauce

Gōngbǎo Jīdīng 宮保雞丁
Kung Pao Chicken

Serves: 4 to 6 — **Total Time:** 45 minutes — **Difficulty:** ●●○○

1 tablespoon water

¼ teaspoon baking soda

1½ pounds boneless, skinless chicken thighs, trimmed and cut into ½-inch pieces

¼ cup soy sauce, divided

1 tablespoon cornstarch

1 tablespoon Shaoxing wine

½ teaspoon white pepper

2 tablespoons plus 1 teaspoon vegetable oil, divided

3 garlic cloves, minced

2 teaspoons grated fresh ginger

1 tablespoon Chinese black vinegar

1 tablespoon packed dark brown sugar

2 teaspoons toasted sesame oil

½ cup dry-roasted peanuts

10–15 small dried Sichuan chiles, stemmed, halved lengthwise, and seeded

1 teaspoon Sichuan peppercorns, coarsely ground

2 celery ribs, cut into ½-inch pieces

5 scallions, white and light green parts only, cut into ½-inch pieces

I once had kung pao chicken at a Costco. A nice employee gave me a free sample. This kung pao chicken was sold in gigantic vacuum-sealed bags and pitched as "an easy weeknight dinner!" I tasted it and thought heck, it's not too bad! That was the moment I realized kung pao chicken—named for a 19th-century governor-general who loved the dish—had achieved cultural escape velocity, leaping from the kitchens of Chengdu to all corners of the globe. Including Costco.

And once people taste it, who could blame them for liking it? It's a spicy, tingly, crunchy mix of chicken, chiles, and toasted peanuts, gently sauced in a savory light glaze. Take it from the nice free-sample ladies: It's an easy weeknight dinner!

— Kevin

1 Combine water and baking soda in medium bowl. Add chicken and toss to coat; let sit for 5 minutes. Add 2 tablespoons soy sauce, cornstarch, Shaoxing wine, and pepper to chicken and toss until well combined; let marinate for 15 minutes.

2 Combine 1 tablespoon vegetable oil, garlic, and ginger in small bowl; set aside. Whisk vinegar, sugar, sesame oil, and remaining 2 tablespoons soy sauce in separate small bowl until sugar has dissolved; set aside.

3 Cook peanuts and 1 teaspoon vegetable oil in 14-inch flat-bottomed wok over medium-low heat, stirring constantly, until peanuts just begin to darken, 3 to 5 minutes. Transfer peanuts to plate and spread into even layer to cool. Return now-empty wok to medium-low heat. Add remaining 1 tablespoon vegetable oil, chiles, and peppercorns and cook, stirring constantly, until chiles begin to darken, 1 to 2 minutes. Add reserved garlic mixture and cook, stirring constantly, until mixture is fragrant, about 30 seconds.

4 Add chicken mixture and spread into even layer. Cover wok, increase heat to medium-high, and cook, without tossing, for 1 minute. Toss chicken and spread into even layer. Cover and cook, without tossing, for 1 minute. Add celery and cook uncovered, tossing slowly but constantly, until chicken is cooked through, about 3 minutes. Add reserved soy sauce mixture and cook, tossing constantly, until sauce has thickened, 3 to 5 minutes. Stir in scallions and peanuts. Serve.

Three-Cup Chicken

Serves: 4 to 6 — **Total Time:** 45 minutes — **Difficulty:** ●●○○

Perhaps the most celebrated dish of Taiwanese cuisine, three-cup chicken was named for the three components originally required to make it: one cup each of soy sauce, rice wine lees, and lard. As catchy as that name was, the rigidity of the three-cup ratio seemed off. In time, Taiwanese cooks tweaked the balance to be more palatable, subbed out lard for toasted sesame oil, lees for michiu, and kept the name.

The key to this dish, however, is the trio of ginger, garlic, and Thai basil in combination with the sauce. You'll find this flavor applied to dishes in Taiwanese cooking beyond chicken, such as tofu or pork ribs. It's savory and sweet, with a hint of licorice from the Thai basil.

By the way, that's not a typo in the ingredient list: 12 garlic cloves are required for this dish. But know that the garlic turns pleasingly nutty, sweet, and creamy in the sauce.   — Kevin + Jeffrey

3 tablespoons vegetable oil

1 (2-inch) piece ginger, sliced into ⅛-inch rounds

12 garlic cloves, peeled and halved

1½ pounds boneless, skinless chicken thighs, trimmed and cut into 1-inch pieces

2 tablespoons (1 ounce) crushed rock sugar

⅓ cup water

3 tablespoons michiu (Taiwanese rice wine)

3 tablespoons soy sauce

1 tablespoon dark soy sauce

2 tablespoons toasted sesame oil

1 cup fresh Thai basil leaves, plus extra for garnishing

1 Fresno chile, stemmed, seeded, and thinly sliced into rings

1 Cook vegetable oil and ginger in 14-inch flat-bottomed wok over medium-low heat until fragrant, about 3 minutes. Add garlic and cook, stirring frequently, until ginger and garlic are golden brown, about 2 minutes. Using slotted spoon, transfer ginger and garlic to bowl; transfer oil to separate bowl.

2 Heat now-empty wok over high heat until just beginning to smoke. Drizzle reserved vegetable oil around perimeter of wok and heat until just smoking. Add chicken and cook, tossing slowly but constantly, until beginning to brown, about 5 minutes. Add ginger, garlic, and rock sugar and cook, tossing slowly but constantly, until sugar has dissolved, about 1 minute.

3 Stir in water, michiu, soy sauce, and dark soy sauce. Cover, reduce heat to medium-low, and simmer, stirring occasionally, until chicken is tender, about 5 minutes. Stir in sesame oil, increase heat to high, and cook, tossing slowly but constantly, until almost all liquid has evaporated and chicken is well glazed, about 2 minutes. Off heat, stir in basil and Fresno chile. Garnish with extra basil leaves before serving.

A Chicken in Every Pot

This dish is commonly prepared in a wok, but transfer to a warm earthenware pot for a more distinctive presentation at the table.

Chǐyóu Jī 豉油雞
Soy Sauce Chicken

Serves: 4 to 6 — **Total Time:** 50 minutes, plus 1 hour resting — **Difficulty:** ●●○○

The best part about poached chicken is the texture the cooking method yields: silky, succulent, fork-tender meat. Although this quality can be achieved just by poaching in plain water with a few slices of ginger and scallions, it turns out that poaching in a deeply spiced and intense sweet-savory marinade results in that same texture— with the bonus of the plump, glistening skin suffused with soy sauce flavor.

This is one of the most crowd-pleasing ways of serving chicken to Hong Kongers. It's available at practically every corner takeout. The chicken is endlessly versatile; it's delicious on everything from plain rice to instant ramen. You might find me sneaking a piece of soy sauce chicken from the fridge before bedtime.   — Jeffrey

While any chicken will work here, we prefer to use Buddhist-style chickens (see page 176) for their flavorful meat and rich, springy skin, which best absorbs the cooking liquid. They are typically sold at Asian supermarkets with their head and feet attached; you can ask the butcher to remove those for you (save them for broth). Other chickens will taste less rich, and the skin won't be as plump. Granulated sugar can be substituted for the rock sugar. If mei kuei lu chiew is unavailable, it can be omitted. Use a Dutch oven that holds 6 quarts or more. Serve with Ginger-Scallion Sauce (page 23) if desired.

1   Bring 8 cups water, soy sauce, dark soy sauce, Shaoxing wine, rock sugar, mei kuei lu chiew, scallions, ginger, star anise, cinnamon sticks, and bay leaves to simmer in large Dutch oven over medium-high heat. Place chicken breast side up into pot. Cover, reduce heat to medium-low, and simmer gently for 15 minutes. Off heat, let chicken sit for 15 minutes.

2   Using tongs, gently flip chicken and continue to let sit, covered, until breasts register 160 degrees and thighs register at least 175 degrees, 15 to 30 minutes. Using tongs and spatula, transfer chicken to carving board and let rest for 30 minutes.

3   Strain cooking liquid through fine-mesh strainer into bowl; discard solids. Transfer ½ cup cooking liquid to small saucepan; save remaining cooking liquid for another use or discard. Whisk cornstarch into reserved cooking liquid and bring to simmer over medium heat, stirring frequently, until just thickened, about 30 seconds. Carve chicken and serve with sauce.

turn to see how to cut up a whole chicken

2½ cups soy sauce

¾ cup dark soy sauce

¾ cup Shaoxing wine

⅓ cup (3 ounces) rock sugar, crushed

¼ cup mei kuei lu chiew (rose cooking liquor)

3 scallions, cut into 2-inch lengths

1 (2-inch) piece ginger, sliced thin

4 star anise pods

2 cinnamon sticks

2 bay leaves

1 (3½- to 4½-pound) whole chicken, head, feet, and giblets removed

1 teaspoon cornstarch

Test Kitchen Tip

Recipe developer David Yu notes: "We encourage you to save the remaining cooking liquid in step 3. Often referred to as a 'master stock,' this liquid can be used again and again to poach or braise other proteins. It can be refrigerated for up to four days or frozen in smaller portions for up to three months. While chicken is most common, it's also a great cooking liquid for duck and pork."

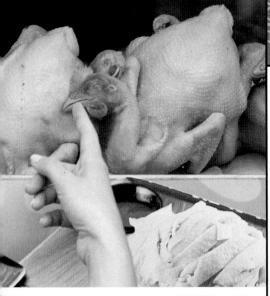

Buddhist-Style Chicken

Head to Chinatown and order a whole chicken dish, and you'll notice the difference. The chicken served there tastes richer, and the meat is firmer and the chicken-y flavors more pronounced. The cooked skin bears a shade of marigold. All chickens are not created the same, and this bird—preferred by us Chinese—is known as Buddhist-style chicken. Typically it costs double that of commodity chickens, as it takes twice as long to breed.

A common refrain among Chinese folks living in North America is that Western supermarket chickens have no flavor. Buddhist-style chickens are bred to allow the meat's flavors to shine, especially in simply prepared dishes like Soy Sauce Chicken (page 175) and Hainanese Chicken Rice (page 307).

Several years ago I was on assignment for *Saveur* magazine on the Chinese tropical island of Hainan, where chicken is beloved. I wrote that the blond chicken skin was "plump and fatty as lips. There's a luscious, gelatinous quality, and the flavor of chicken oil leaching from it is as indulgent as the fat cap of a rib-eye steak." The meat was chewier and more subtly gamy than the chicken I'd tasted in America. "What it really tastes like is an exaggerated form of chicken."

Know that if you're planning to buy one from a Chinese grocer, you likely won't see it labeled as "Buddhist-style chicken." (It might just be called chicken.) The biggest tells are if it's sold with the head and feet still attached, and whether it costs a lot more than what you're used to paying.

— Kevin

Photo Descriptions (from top to bottom): *Photo 1: A rather unlucky chicken; Photo 2: Poaching chicken on Hainan Island, China; Photo 3: Hainanese Chicken Rice from Tsui Wah restaurant in Hong Kong.*

Chopping Chicken (and Duck) Like a Chinese Chef

Rather than carving a chicken into two pieces each of wing/leg/thigh/breast, the Chinese are a bit more indelicate about the process. We love gnawing on bone-in pieces of chicken and also duck (see page 314 for that recipe), and then spitting out the bones. It's a tactile thing! If you have a cleaver, this is a good time to use it; otherwise use your heaviest (not your finest) chef's knife.

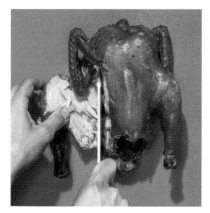

1 Using cleaver, cut off legs, 1 at a time, by severing joint between leg and body.

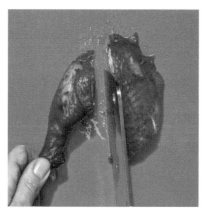

2 Cut each leg into 2 pieces—drumstick and thigh—by slicing through joint that connects them.

3 Position cleaver at middle of each drumstick and thigh, perpendicular to bone, and slice through meat to expose bone. Use nondominant hand to push down on spine of cleaver to split into 2 pieces.

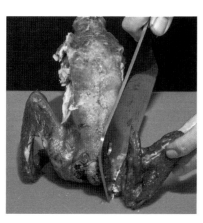

4 Flip chicken over and remove wings by slicing through each wing joint.

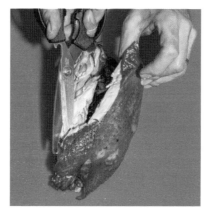

5 Turn chicken (now without legs and wings) on its side and, using scissors or cleaver, remove back from chicken breast.

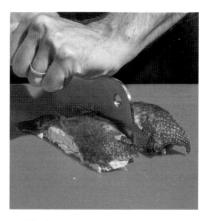

6 Flip breast skin side up and, using cleaver, cut in half through breast plate (marked by thin white line of cartilage). Cut each breast half crosswise into 4 to 6 pieces.

Zīrán Yángròu 孜然羊肉
Stir-Fried Cumin Lamb

Serves: 4 to 6 — **Total Time:** 45 minutes — **Difficulty:** ●●○○

- 2 (14- to 16-ounce) lamb shoulder chops (blade or round bone), ¾ to 1 inch thick, trimmed
- 1 tablespoon water
- ¼ teaspoon baking soda
- 1 tablespoon cumin seeds, ground
- 2 teaspoons Sichuan chili flakes
- 1¼ teaspoons Sichuan peppercorns, ground
- ½ teaspoon sugar
- 4 teaspoons dark soy sauce
- 1 tablespoon Shaoxing wine
- ½ teaspoon cornstarch
- ¼ teaspoon table salt
- 5 teaspoons vegetable oil, divided
- 4 garlic cloves, minced
- 1 tablespoon grated fresh ginger
- ½ small onion, sliced ¼ inch thick
- 2 tablespoons coarsely chopped fresh cilantro

Test Kitchen Tips

- Grinding whole cumin seeds and Sichuan peppercorns releases vibrant aromatic compounds that give the dish its wonderful fragrance.

- Stir-frying the meat in batches helps it brown and allows the juices to reduce to a sticky fond that coats each slice.

Cumin was an important spice traded along the Silk Road in what is now the Xinjiang region of northwest China. There, and across northern China, cumin endures today in the cuisine. In Beijing I experienced a bite that will forever be lodged in my taste memory: skewers of fatty lamb, grilled over charcoal, seasoned with only cumin and salt.

This stir-fry takes the gentle gaminess of lamb and pairs it with garlic, ginger, and onion slivers, and seasons it with smoky cumin. It's a jab-hook-uppercut combo of a dish, with bold spicing, biting herbaceousness, and numbing heat.   — Kevin

If lamb shoulder chops are unavailable, you can substitute 1 pound boneless leg of lamb or beef flank steak; trim the meat and cut it with the grain into 2- to 2½-inch-wide strips before freezing and slicing. You can substitute 1 tablespoon of ground cumin for the cumin seeds.

1   Cut bones from lamb and trim all visible connective tissue from meat; discard bones. (You should have about 1 pound of lamb after trimming.) Transfer lamb to plate and freeze until firm, about 15 minutes. Slice meat against grain on bias ¼ inch thick. Combine water and baking soda in medium bowl. Add lamb and toss to coat; let sit for 5 minutes.

2   Combine cumin, chili flakes, peppercorns, and sugar in small bowl. Add soy sauce, Shaoxing wine, cornstarch, and salt to lamb mixture and toss to coat.

3   Heat empty 14-inch flat-bottomed wok over high heat until just beginning to smoke. Drizzle 1 teaspoon oil around perimeter of wok and heat until just smoking. Add half of lamb mixture and cook, tossing slowly but constantly, until just cooked through, 1 to 3 minutes; transfer to clean bowl. Repeat with 1 teaspoon oil and remaining lamb mixture; transfer to bowl.

4   Heat remaining 1 tablespoon oil in now-empty wok over medium heat until shimmering. Add garlic and ginger and cook, stirring constantly, until fragrant, 15 to 30 seconds. Add onion and cook, tossing slowly but constantly, until onion begins to soften, 1 to 2 minutes. Return lamb mixture to wok and toss to combine. Sprinkle cumin mixture over lamb mixture and toss until onion takes on pale orange color. Sprinkle with cilantro and serve.

Mongolian Beef

Serves: 4 to 6   **Total Time:** 1¼ hours — **Difficulty:** ●●●○

- 1½ **pounds beef flap meat, trimmed**
- ½ **cup cornstarch**
- 2 **quarts peanut or vegetable oil for frying**
- 4 **scallions, white parts minced, green parts cut into 1-inch pieces**
- 2–4 **small dried Sichuan chiles, stemmed and halved crosswise**
- 4 **garlic cloves, minced**
- 1 **tablespoon grated fresh ginger**
- ¾ **cup water**
- ⅔ **cup packed brown sugar**
- 6 **tablespoons soy sauce**

Stone Cold Beef Frostin'

Why do we place the beef in the freezer for 15 minutes? This step makes for easier, more precise slicing, especially if you haven't sharpened your knife recently. Also: Instead of a straight-down cut, slice the beef at an angle to create more surface area for the sauce to cling to.

Breaking news: Mongolian beef is not from Mongolia. But neither is Portuguese chicken from Portugal, Lumpiang Shanghai from Shanghai, nor Baked Alaska from Alaska. Some theories on the name point to a Taiwanese chef having developed this dish, adopting "Mongolian" to make it sound vaguely exotic. But only when the dish migrated across the Pacific did Mongolian beef become a staple of American Chinese cookery. Even if you'd have trouble finding this dish in, say, the back-alley restaurants of Beijing, the flavors of Mongolian beef are familiarly Chinese: a sweet-salty sauce enrobing crispy sheets of beef tossed with wilted scallions and chile peppers.   — Kevin

Ask your butcher for a 1½-pound piece of flap meat instead of already-cut sirloin steak tips, which are more difficult to slice thin.

1   Cut beef with grain into 2½- to 3-inch-wide strips. Transfer to plate and freeze until firm, about 15 minutes. Slice strips crosswise against grain ⅛ inch thick. Toss beef with cornstarch in bowl; set aside.

2   Line rimmed baking sheet with triple layer of paper towels. Add oil to large Dutch oven until it measures about 1½ inches deep and heat over medium-high heat to 375 degrees. Carefully add one-third of beef to hot oil. Using tongs or cooking chopsticks, separate pieces so they fry individually. Fry beef, stirring occasionally, until browned and crispy, 2 to 4 minutes. Adjust burner, if necessary, to maintain oil temperature between 350 and 375 degrees. Using spider skimmer or slotted spoon, transfer beef to prepared sheet. Return oil to 375 degrees and repeat with remaining beef in 2 batches; transfer to sheet.

3   Measure out and reserve 1 tablespoon frying oil; discard remaining oil or save for another use. Heat reserved oil in empty 14-inch flat-bottomed wok over medium-high heat until shimmering. Add scallion whites, chiles, garlic, and ginger and cook, mashing mixture into wok, until fragrant, about 30 seconds. Stir in water, sugar, and soy sauce and bring to vigorous simmer. Cook until sauce is thickened and reduced to 1¼ cups, 6 to 8 minutes. Add beef and scallion greens and cook, tossing constantly, until sauce coats beef, about 1 minute. Serve.

Stir-Fried Beef
and Gai Lan
(page 184)

Stir-Fried Beef and Gai Lan

Serves: 4 — **Total Time:** 1 hour — **Difficulty:** ●●○○

1 (8-ounce) center-cut filet mignon, trimmed

1 pound gai lan, stalks trimmed

5 teaspoons Shaoxing wine, divided

1 tablespoon soy sauce, divided

2 teaspoons cornstarch, divided

¾ cup chicken broth, divided

2 tablespoons oyster sauce

1½ teaspoons toasted sesame oil, divided

2 tablespoons vegetable oil, divided

1½ teaspoons grated fresh ginger

¾ teaspoon minced garlic, divided

Pound for pound, this recipe from *Cook's Illustrated* senior editor Lan Lam packs in more fundamentals concerning good Chinese cooking than any other in this book. In one hour you'll apply three important techniques:

1. Velveting: Ever notice how meats in Chinese dishes have that tender, velvety texture? You'll learn to achieve this by marinating filet mignon with a cornstarch-thickened sauce, then cooking over high heat.

2. Wok hei: Cooking gai lan in stages (stalks first, then leaves) over very high heat creates wok hei 鑊氣, or "breath of the wok." This is the coveted smoky, charcoal flavor possible only when cooking in a very hot wok with oil.

3. Chinese sauce work: If your past attempts to cook Chinese food never quite tasted like a restaurant version, one possible explanation is the sauce. Most likely the dish didn't include oyster sauce, Shaoxing wine, or a cornstarch slurry. In this recipe you'll witness the alchemy this combination creates. — Jeffrey

If gai lan is unavailable, you can use broccolini, substituting the florets for the gai lan leaves. Do not use standard broccoli.

1 Cut beef into 4 equal wedges. Transfer to plate and freeze until very firm, 20 to 25 minutes. Meanwhile, remove leaves, small stems, and florets from gai lan stalks; slice leaves crosswise into 1½-inch strips (any florets and stems can go into pile with leaves), and cut stalks on bias into ¼-inch-thick pieces. Set aside. When beef is firm, stand 1 piece on its side and slice against grain ¼ inch thick. Repeat with remaining pieces. Transfer to bowl. Add 1 teaspoon Shaoxing wine, 1 teaspoon soy sauce, and 1 teaspoon cornstarch and toss until beef is evenly coated; set aside.

2 In second bowl, whisk together ½ cup broth, oyster sauce, ½ teaspoon sesame oil, remaining 4 teaspoons Shaoxing wine, remaining 2 teaspoons soy sauce, and remaining 1 teaspoon cornstarch; set aside. In third bowl, combine 4 teaspoons vegetable oil, ginger, and ¼ teaspoon garlic.

3 Heat empty 14-inch flat-bottomed wok over high heat until just beginning to smoke. Drizzle 1 teaspoon vegetable oil around perimeter of wok and heat until just smoking. Add gai lan stalks and cook, stirring slowly but constantly, until spotty brown and crisp-tender, 3 to 4 minutes; transfer to separate bowl.

4 Add remaining 1 teaspoon sesame oil, remaining 1 teaspoon vegetable oil, and remaining ½ teaspoon garlic to now-empty wok and cook, stirring constantly, until garlic is fragrant, about 15 seconds. Add gai lan leaves and cook, stirring frequently, until vibrant green, about 1 minute. Add remaining ¼ cup broth and cook, stirring constantly, until broth evaporates, 2 to 3 minutes. Spread mixture evenly in serving dish.

5 Add ginger-garlic mixture to now-empty wok and cook, stirring constantly, until fragrant, about 30 seconds. Add beef mixture and cook, stirring slowly but constantly, until no longer pink, about 2 minutes. Return stalks to wok and add oyster sauce mixture. Cook, stirring constantly, until sauce thickens, 30 to 60 seconds. Place mixture on top of leaves. Serve.

Gai Lan: An Early Chinese Import

When Chinese immigrants first set sail from the entrepôt of Hong Kong to San Francisco, labor contractors provided the sojourners with "all kinds of necessities and luxuries," according to Anne Mendelson, author of *Chow Chop Suey: Food and the Chinese American Journey*. Among the bountiful provisions "were seeds for everything that you could grow in both Guangdong and California . . . and I'm sure that gai lan was among them," she said.

Later, as the settlers spread to the suburbs, cooks without access to purveyors of Asian produce swapped broccoli for gai lan. (The two vegetables are different varieties of the same *Brassica oleracea* species.) Gai lan's broad, waxy leaves offer hints of minerality and bitterness (mature specimens may have started to flower) and branch from smooth, fleshy stalks that are prized for their crispness and delicate nuttiness.

How to Prep Gai Lan for Stir-Frying

1 Cut leaves off stalks.

2 Slice leaves crosswise into 1½-inch strips.

3 Cut stalks on bias into ¼-inch-thick pieces.

Huíguō Ròu 回鍋肉
Twice-Cooked Pork

Serves: 4 to 6 — **Total Time:** 1¼ hours, plus 3¼ hours cooling — **Difficulty:** ●●○○

1 pound leeks

1 pound skin-on center-cut fresh pork belly, about 2 inches thick

1 (2-inch) piece ginger, sliced into ¼-inch-thick rounds

1 tablespoon vegetable oil

1 tablespoon douchi (fermented black beans)

4 teaspoons doubanjiang (broad bean chile paste)

2 teaspoons tianmianjiang (sweet wheat paste)

2 green or red longhorn chiles, stemmed and sliced 1 inch thick on bias (optional)

1 teaspoon dark soy sauce

1 teaspoon sugar

Test Kitchen Tip

Recipe developer Kelly Song notes: "The mark of excellence for this dish is exemplified by thinly sliced pieces of pork belly, cooked to succulent perfection (twice) and coated in a savory, spicy sauce. To achieve the thinnest possible pieces, slice the pork belly skin side down after it has been boiled and chilled. Use a sharp knife, aiming to keep both fat and lean parts of each slice intact."

At America's Test Kitchen we're not the only Chinese parent-child cooking combo. Our colleague Kelly Song, a test cook for *Cook's Country,* grew up thinking her dad was the best chef in the world. What convinced her was a recipe he worked for months to perfect: twice-cooked pork. It was a dish Kelly always ordered at Sichuanese restaurants, so her father took it upon himself to replicate it at home.

Take pork belly slices and stir-fry in a fiery mix of chile paste and fermented black beans until the meat is unctuous and crisp, and then you can begin to appreciate the appeal of twice-cooked pork (the pork belly is cooked once in boiling water until tender, and "cooked" a second time in the wok, hence the name).

Kelly developed her version taking much inspiration from her dad, whom she said "held the secret to the best twice-cooked pork." She claims the ideal way to enjoy this dish is to spoon meat and sauce over white rice, allowing the pork fat–tinged chili oil to coat each grain. There's really no elegant or dainty way of eating it; you just have to shovel the contents swiftly into your mouth.

"My dad used to scold me over my mess at fancy restaurants while indulging in this dish," Kelly said, "and then smile and serve me more."
— Kevin + Jeffrey (+ Kelly)

Look for pork belly that is sold as one whole piece, about 2 inches thick, with a decent amount of fat. We prefer skin-on pork belly to achieve traditional textures and flavors; if you cannot find skin-on pork, you can use skin-off. You can substitute Fresno chiles for the optional longhorn chiles.

1 Trim root ends and dark-green parts from leeks; discard roots. Quarter white and light-green parts lengthwise, then slice crosswise into 1½-inch pieces; wash thoroughly. (You should have about 3 cups white and light-green parts.) Cut dark-green parts into 4- to 6-inch pieces and wash thoroughly.

2 Bring 2 quarts water, pork, ginger, and dark-green leek parts to boil in large saucepan. Reduce heat to medium-low, adjusting heat as needed to maintain gentle simmer. Cook until pork skin and fat can be easily pierced with paring knife, 30 to 40 minutes, adding water as needed to keep pork submerged. Transfer pork to large plate and let cool completely, about 15 minutes; discard cooking liquid and solids. Cover pork with plastic wrap and refrigerate for at least 3 hours or up to 24 hours. Place pork skin side down on cutting board and slice as thin as possible (⅛ to ¼ inch thick).

3 Heat oil in 14-inch flat-bottomed wok over medium-high heat until shimmering. Add pork and cook, tossing slowly but constantly, until meat is just beginning to brown and some fat has rendered, 2 to 4 minutes. Stir in douchi and cook until fragrant, about 30 seconds.

4 Slide pork mixture to 1 side of wok and let oil pool on opposite side (briefly tilt wok as needed to allow oil to pool).

Stir doubanjiang and tianmianjiang into oil (oil may splatter) and cook, stirring constantly, until mixture is fragrant and oil has turned red, about 30 seconds. Stir pork into oil mixture.

5 Stir in white and light-green leek parts, longhorn chiles, if using, soy sauce, and sugar. Cook, stirring constantly, until leeks are tender and just wilted, 3 to 4 minutes. Serve.

Lǔròu Fàn 滷肉飯
Taiwanese Pork Rice Bowl

Serves: 4 — **Total time:** 3¾ hours — **Difficulty:** ●●○○

- ¼ teaspoon Sichuan peppercorns
- 1 star anise pod
- 1 bay leaf
- 1 pound skin-on center-cut fresh pork belly, about 2 inches thick, cut into ½-inch pieces
- 1 tablespoon crushed rock sugar
- 4 garlic cloves, minced
- 1 (¼-inch) piece ginger
- ⅓ cup michiu (Taiwanese rice wine)
- ¼ cup fried shallots, plus extra for serving
- 2½ tablespoons soy sauce
- 1 teaspoon dark soy sauce
- ¼ teaspoon white pepper
- 4 large eggs
- 4 cups cooked short-grain white rice
- 1 recipe Stir-Fried Pickled Mustard Greens (page 24)

Pick Your Lurou

If you try this dish in southern Taiwan, you'll likely find it cooked with a leaner ground pork mince. Our version reflects the northern Taiwanese tradition of using fattier pork belly chunks.

Our colleague Faye Yang, who developed Taiwanese Beef Noodle Soup on page 166, also came up with this recipe—high in the rankings of Taiwan's most cherished home-cooked dishes. Lurou fan is a rich meat sauce (think Taiwanese bolognese) that gets spooned over rice and is served with pickled mustard greens and a hard-cooked egg.

Faye tells us her backstory: "Growing up, I always knew my mom was making lurou fan when I heard loud clangs coming from the kitchen. She'd be vigorously chopping the pork belly or pork butt with two large cleavers. The best moment was lifting the lid off the pot after it had been simmering for hours and being welcomed by a burst of porky, salty, and sweet aromas. Inside was a glossy sauce that instantly had my mouth watering. It was so delicious I'd ask for seconds, thirds, and on and on."
— Kevin + Jeffrey (+ Faye)

Look for pork belly that is sold as one whole piece, about 2 inches thick, with a decent amount of fat. We prefer skin-on pork belly to achieve traditional textures and flavors; if you cannot find skin-on pork, you can use skin-off. You can purchase fried shallots or make your own (see page 24).

1 Place peppercorns, star anise, and bay leaf in center of small piece of cheesecloth; gather edges of cheesecloth and tie with kitchen twine to form sachet. Cook pork in 14-inch flat-bottomed wok over medium heat, stirring frequently, until fat begins to render and pork begins to brown, about 7 minutes. Using slotted spoon, transfer pork to plate.

2 Pour off all but 1 tablespoon fat from wok. (Add vegetable oil as needed to equal 1 tablespoon.) Add rock sugar to fat left in wok and cook, stirring frequently, until sugar has melted and mixture is amber-colored, about 1 minute. Stir in garlic and ginger and cook until fragrant, about 30 seconds. Stir in michiu, scraping up any browned bits. Stir in pork and any accumulated juices, 2 cups water, shallots, soy sauce, dark soy sauce, pepper, and spice sachet and bring to boil. Reduce heat to low, cover, and simmer gently for 2 hours.

3 Meanwhile, bring 1 inch water to rolling boil in large saucepan over high heat. Place eggs in collapsible steamer basket. Transfer basket to saucepan. Cover, reduce heat to medium (small wisps of steam should escape from beneath lid), and cook for 8 minutes. When eggs are almost finished cooking, fill large bowl halfway with

ice and water. Using tongs or slotted spoon, transfer eggs to ice bath. Discard water in saucepan. Let eggs sit for 15 minutes. Peel eggs and transfer to medium bowl; set aside.

4   Nestle eggs into sauce and cook, covered, until pork is very tender and eggs are deep brown, 30 minutes to 1 hour, turning eggs halfway through cooking.

5   Discard spice sachet and transfer eggs to cutting board. Bring pork mixture to boil over high heat and cook, stirring frequently, until sauce thickens and begins to coat back of spoon, about 3 minutes. Divide rice among serving bowls and spoon sauce over top. Halve eggs and arrange on top of each bowl with pickled mustard greens and extra fried shallots. Serve.

Mùxū Ròu 木須肉

Mu Shu Pork

Serves: 4 — **Total Time:** 1¼ hours — **Difficulty:** ●●○○

1 (12-ounce) pork tenderloin, trimmed

¼ cup soy sauce, divided

2 tablespoons Shaoxing wine, divided

1 teaspoon sugar

1 teaspoon grated fresh ginger

¼ teaspoon white pepper

1 ounce dried shiitake mushrooms, rinsed

2 teaspoons cornstarch

3 tablespoons vegetable oil, divided

6 scallions, white and green parts separated and sliced thin, divided

2 large eggs

1 (8-ounce) can bamboo shoots, rinsed and sliced into matchsticks

3 cups thinly sliced green cabbage

1 recipe Spring Pancakes (page 192)

Hoisin sauce

While we don't think there's a connection between tacos and mu shu pork, it's a helpful visual for considering why this American Chinese classic endures.

Mu shu pork's defining feature is its delicate wrapper, called a spring pancake. Gossamer thin, stretchy, and pliable, with a lovely chew, these flour crepes hold a savory filling of stir-fried pork, shiitake mushrooms, cabbage, and bamboo shoots. While old-fashioned compared to many other dishes in this book, mu shu pork is an undeniable crowd-pleaser, as much fun to put together as it is for guests to serve themselves.   — Kevin + Jeffrey

1   Cut tenderloin in half lengthwise. Transfer to plate and freeze until firm, about 15 minutes. Slice pork crosswise ⅛ inch thick. Whisk 2 tablespoons soy sauce, 1 tablespoon Shaoxing wine, sugar, ginger, and pepper in medium bowl until sugar has dissolved. Add pork and toss to coat; let marinate for 15 minutes.

2   Microwave 1 cup water and mushrooms in covered bowl until steaming, about 1 minute. Let sit until mushrooms are softened, about 5 minutes. Drain in fine-mesh strainer, reserving ⅓ cup liquid; discard mushroom stems and slice caps thin. Whisk cornstarch, reserved mushroom liquid, remaining 2 tablespoons soy sauce, and remaining 1 tablespoon Shaoxing wine together in small bowl; set aside.

3   Heat empty 14-inch flat-bottomed wok over high heat until just beginning to smoke. Drizzle 2 teaspoons oil around perimeter of wok and heat until just smoking. Add half of scallion whites and half of pork mixture and cook, tossing slowly but constantly, until pork is no longer pink, 2 to 6 minutes; transfer to large bowl. Repeat with 2 teaspoons vegetable oil, remaining scallion whites, and remaining pork mixture; transfer to bowl with pork.

4   Heat 2 teaspoons oil in now-empty wok over medium-high heat until shimmering. Add eggs and scramble quickly using rubber spatula. Continue to cook, scraping slowly but constantly along bottom and sides of pan, until eggs just form cohesive mass, 15 to 30 seconds (eggs will not be completely dry). Transfer to bowl with pork mixture, then break up any large egg curds.

5 Heat remaining 1 tablespoon oil in now-empty wok over medium-high heat until shimmering. Whisk reserved mushroom liquid mixture to recombine. Add mushrooms and bamboo shoots to wok and cook, tossing constantly, until heated through, about 1 minute. Add cabbage, all but 2 tablespoons scallion greens, and mushroom liquid mixture and cook, tossing slowly but constantly, until liquid has evaporated and cabbage is wilted but retains some crunch, 2 to 3 minutes. Add pork mixture and eggs and stir to combine. Transfer to platter and top with remaining scallion greens. Serve with pancakes, passing hoisin separately.

turn to see how to make spring pancakes

Chūnbǐng 春餅
Spring Pancakes

Makes: 12 pancakes
Total Time: 45 minutes, plus 30 minutes resting
Difficulty: ●●○○○

You might think, "Oh, I've got flour tortillas, I could use those wrappers instead for mu shu pork." Fight the temptation. Don't use tortillas, lavash, buttermilk pancakes, or any other wrappers. These are fun to roll out and can be made well in advance and refrigerated or frozen.

1½ cups (7½ ounces) all-purpose flour
¾ cup boiling water
2 teaspoons toasted sesame oil
½ teaspoon vegetable oil

1 Using wooden spoon, mix flour and boiling water in bowl to form rough dough. When cool, transfer dough to lightly floured counter and knead until it forms ball that is tacky but no longer sticky, about 4 minutes (dough will not be perfectly smooth). Cover loosely with plastic wrap and let rest for 30 minutes.

2 Roll dough into 12-inch-long log on lightly floured counter and cut into 12 equal pieces. Turn each piece cut side up and pat into rough 3-inch disk. Brush 1 side of 6 disks with sesame oil; top each oiled side with unoiled disk to form 6 pairs, lightly pressing each pair together. Roll disks into 7-inch rounds, lightly flouring counter as needed.

3 Heat vegetable oil in 12-inch nonstick skillet over medium heat until shimmering. Using paper towels, carefully wipe out oil. Place 1 pancake in skillet and cook without moving it until air pockets begin to form between layers and underside is dry, 40 to 60 seconds. Flip pancake and cook until few light brown spots appear on second side, 40 to 60 seconds. Transfer to plate and, when cool enough to handle, peel apart into 2 pancakes. Stack pancakes moist side up and cover loosely with plastic. Repeat with remaining pancakes. Cover pancakes tightly and keep warm while preparing mu shu. (Pancakes can be wrapped tightly in plastic wrap, then aluminum foil, and refrigerated for up to 3 days or frozen for up to 2 months. Thaw wrapped pancakes at room temperature. Unwrap and place on plate. Invert second plate over pancakes and microwave until warm and soft, 60 to 90 seconds.)

Pancakes Made Two by Two

Cooking two rounds together produces pancakes twice as fast.

1 Brush 6 disks with sesame oil. Top with unoiled disks. Press pairs together, then roll into thin rounds.

2 Heat each round until air pockets form between layers and underside is dry. Flip and cook second side.

3 When pancakes are cool enough, pull apart into 2 pieces.

Shīzitóu 獅子頭

Lion's Head Meatballs

Serves: 4 to 6 — **Total Time:** 2 hours — **Difficulty:** ●●○○

¾ teaspoon baking soda

½ teaspoon table salt

2 pounds ground pork

1 large egg, lightly beaten

2 scallions, white parts minced, green parts sliced thin

2 tablespoons soy sauce

2 tablespoons Shaoxing wine

4 teaspoons sugar

2 teaspoons grated fresh ginger

½ teaspoon white pepper

4 cups chicken broth

1 small head napa cabbage (1½ pounds), quartered lengthwise, cored, and cut crosswise into 2-inch pieces

4 ounces mei fun (dried rice vermicelli)

What Baking Soda Does to Meat

Baking soda plays a key role in these meatballs: 1) Its alkalinity helps proteins dissolve to create a smoother mixture. 2) It raises the pH of the pork, which helps it retain more moisture during cooking. And both translate to pronounced tenderness in every bite.

It's become a recurring theme each time we cook an America's Test Kitchen recipe: "Oh, that's such an ATK technique," we'd say with amusement. That's code for an exacting, borderline-finicky way of making food, but one that results in a pretty spectacular finished dish (if we say so ourselves).

My colleague Annie Petito's recipe for lion's head meatballs, the tennis ball–size pork meatballs from China's eastern seaboard, has been thoroughly, lovingly put through the ATK wringer. There are baking soda solutions! Stand mixers to release myosins for juicier balls! There is even a 1½-hour oven braise!

No, these aren't traditional Chinese techniques, but the end product—delicate, rich, tender-without-peer meatballs in a soul-comforting chicken broth—would win my Shanghainese grandma's approval. — Kevin

Fully cooked ground pork may retain a slightly pink hue.

1 Adjust oven rack to lower-middle position and heat oven to 325 degrees. Whisk baking soda, salt, and 2 tablespoons water together in bowl of stand mixer. Add pork and toss to combine. Add egg, scallion whites, soy sauce, Shaoxing wine, sugar, ginger, and pepper. Fit stand mixer with paddle and beat on medium speed until mixture is well combined and has stiffened and started to pull away from sides of bowl, and pork has slightly lightened in color, 45 to 60 seconds. Using wet hands, form about ½ cup (4½ ounces) pork mixture into 3-inch round meatball; repeat with remaining mixture to form 8 meatballs in all.

2 Bring broth to boil in Dutch oven over high heat. Off heat, carefully arrange meatballs in pot (7 around perimeter and 1 in center; meatballs will not be totally submerged). Cover pot, transfer to oven, and cook for 1 hour.

3 Transfer meatballs to large plate. Add cabbage to pot in even layer and arrange meatballs over cabbage, paler side up. Cover, return pot to oven, and continue to cook until meatballs are lightly browned and cabbage is softened, about 30 minutes.

4 Meanwhile, bring 4 quarts water to boil in large pot. Remove from heat, add noodles, and let sit, stirring occasionally, until tender but not mushy. Drain noodles and distribute evenly among individual bowls. Ladle meatballs, cabbage, and broth into bowls over noodles. Sprinkle with scallion greens and serve.

Jiāngcōng Zhēng Yúliǔ 薑葱蒸魚柳

Steamed Fish Fillets with Scallions and Ginger

Serves: 4 — **Total Time:** 45 minutes — **Difficulty:** ●●○○

8 scallions, 6 chopped coarse,
  2 sliced thin

1 (3-inch) piece ginger, peeled

3 garlic cloves, sliced thin

4 (6- to 8-ounce) skinless cod fillets,
  1 inch thick

3 tablespoons soy sauce

2 tablespoons Shaoxing wine

1½ teaspoons toasted sesame oil

1½ teaspoons sugar

¼ teaspoon table salt

¼ teaspoon white pepper

2 tablespoons vegetable oil

⅓ cup fresh cilantro leaves and
  tender stems

Test Kitchen Tips

- Using a foil sling to cradle the fillets makes it easy to transfer the cooked fish to a platter without falling apart.

- Steaming the fish directly in cooking liquid allows the fish to release jus that adds flavor to the sauce.

As with the fried rice recipes in the previous chapter, we'll walk you through a beginner and an advanced version of Chinese steamed fish.

For this 101-level recipe, *Cook's Illustrated* deputy food editor Andrea Geary developed a new technique that marries Chinese and French cooking methods. She oven-steams skinless cod fillets in a flavorful Chinese cooking liquid and, just before serving, pours a sizzling ginger-infused oil over the fish. The term "meltingly tender" is a bit cliché, but no description is more accurate for the fish this recipe produces. Simple enough to whip up on a weeknight, it would also be right at home at your most elegant dinner party.

Once you're comfortable with this technique, turn the page to learn about the pleasure of steaming a whole fish on your stovetop. Don't be scared, the water is warm, quite literally.   — Jeffrey

Black sea bass, haddock, hake, and pollock are good substitutes for cod. If using a glass baking dish, add 5 minutes to the cooking time.

1   Adjust oven rack to middle position and heat oven to 450 degrees. Scatter coarsely chopped scallions over bottom of 13 by 9-inch baking pan. Coarsely chop 2 inches ginger and add to pan with scallions, then sprinkle with garlic. Slice remaining 1 inch ginger into thin matchsticks; set aside.

2   Fold 18 by 12-inch piece of aluminum foil lengthwise to create 18 by 6-inch sling and spray lightly with vegetable oil spray. Place sling lengthwise on top of aromatics in pan, with extra foil hanging over ends of pan, then place cod on sling, spaced evenly apart. (If fillets vary in thickness, place thinner fillets in middle and thicker fillets at ends.)

3   Whisk soy sauce, Shaoxing wine, sesame oil, sugar, salt, and pepper together in bowl, then pour around cod in pan. Cover pan tightly with foil and bake until cod registers 130 degrees, 12 to 14 minutes.

4 Grasping sling at both ends, carefully transfer sling and cod to deep platter. Place spatula at 1 end of fillets to hold in place and carefully slide out sling from under cod, leaving cod behind on platter. Strain remaining cooking liquid from pan through fine-mesh strainer set over bowl, pressing on solids to extract as much liquid as possible; discard solids.

Pour strained liquid over cod, then sprinkle with sliced scallions. Heat vegetable oil in 8-inch skillet over high heat until shimmering. Reduce heat to low, add reserved ginger, and cook, stirring frequently, until ginger begins to brown and crisp, 20 to 30 seconds. Quickly drizzle oil-ginger mixture over cod (oil will crackle), then sprinkle with cilantro. Serve.

Steamed Whole Fish with Scallions and Ginger

Serves: 2 to 4 — **Total Time:** 45 minutes — **Difficulty:** ●●●○

1 (1¼- to 1¾-pound) whole striped bass, 12 to 14 inches long, scaled, gutted, and fins snipped off with scissors if desired

¼ teaspoon table salt

3 scallions, white parts cut into 2-inch pieces and halved lengthwise, divided, green parts cut into 2-inch matchsticks

1 (2-inch) piece ginger, peeled and cut into thin matchsticks (¼ cup), divided

3 tablespoons vegetable oil, divided

2 tablespoons Shaoxing wine

2 tablespoons soy sauce

⅛ teaspoon white pepper

½ small Fresno chile, seeded and sliced thin crosswise

2 tablespoons coarsely chopped fresh cilantro (optional)

You Raise Me Up

If you don't have a trivet that fits in the base of your wok, you can use a large round cookie cutter; either way, it's important that the plate rests above the water level while steaming.

The 7-year-old me who was served steamed whole fish was slightly horrified. The restaurant server placed the dish directly in front of me, carp head at eye level. Judging from its facial expression, the fish wasn't having a good day.

The 17-year-old me who finally tried steamed whole fish experienced a spiritual awakening. A gentle nudge of the chopsticks against the skin revealed meat that was astoundingly delicate, the freshness of the catch evident in its sea-sweetness.

The 37-year-old me who cooked steamed whole fish realized there was no more magnificent way of cooking fresh fish. The clincher: dousing the whole steamed fish with a ladleful of sizzling hot oil, which vigorously released the perfume of scallions and ginger.

I call that personal growth.　— Kevin

Red snapper, black sea bass, and branzino are good substitutes for striped bass.

1　Rinse fish under cold running water and pat dry inside and out with paper towels. Using sharp knife, make 3 or 4 shallow slashes, about 2 inches apart, on both sides of fish. Open cavity, sprinkle with salt, and add half of scallion whites and 1 tablespoon ginger. Lightly rub fish, including head and tail, with 1 tablespoon oil.

2　Fold 18 by 12-inch piece of aluminum foil lengthwise to create 18 by 6-inch sling, and set 10-inch heatproof plate in center of sling. Spread remaining scallion whites and 1 tablespoon ginger in center of plate and arrange fish on top so that head and tail are positioned over ends of sling. Whisk Shaoxing wine, soy sauce, and pepper together in bowl, then pour over fish.

3　Bring 4 cups water to boil in 14-inch flat-bottomed wok over medium-high heat. Set wire trivet in base of wok and, using sling, center plate on top. Cover (you may need to tuck head and tail to fit) and cook until thickest part of fish registers 125 degrees, 10 to 12 minutes.

4　Using sling, carefully transfer plate to wire rack. Arrange scallion greens, remaining 2 tablespoons ginger, and Fresno attractively on top of fish. Heat remaining 2 tablespoons oil in 8-inch skillet over high heat until just smoking. Quickly drizzle oil over scallion greens and ginger (oil will crackle). Sprinkle with cilantro, if using, and serve.

Steamed Whole Fish with Scallions
and Ginger (page 198)

Yóubào Xiā 油爆蝦

Oil-Exploded Shrimp

Serves: 4 to 6 — **Total Time:** 45 minutes — **Difficulty:** ●●●○

- 1¼ pounds jumbo (16 to 20 per pound) or extra-jumbo (U15) head-on shrimp

- 2 tablespoons Shaoxing wine

- 2 tablespoons soy sauce

- ½ teaspoon cornstarch

- 1 cup peanut or vegetable oil for frying

- 1½ teaspoons crushed rock sugar

- 2 scallions, cut into 2-inch pieces

- 1 (1-inch) piece ginger, sliced thin

- 1 tablespoon Chinese black vinegar

Though oil-exploded shrimp sounds like an appetizer at a Guy Fieri restaurant, it's a literal translation of a classic dish from Shanghai, where shrimp is served in abundance. "Oil-exploded" might be better characterized as flash-fried; head-on shrimp sizzles and pops in the hot oil before being quickly stir-fried in a lightly sweet dressing. The shrimp become so crisp you can crunch through the whole thing—shell, head, and all—like a kettle chip of the sea. — Kevin + Jeffrey

Head-on shrimp are available at many Asian supermarkets. If you can't find them, you can substitute 1 pound jumbo or extra-jumbo unpeeled, head-off shrimp. Patting the shrimp dry will minimize splattering, though some is inevitable.

1 Using kitchen shears, snip through back of each shrimp shell, starting at head and working toward tail. Snip off legs if desired for a cleaner look. Remove vein, leaving shell intact. Pat shrimp dry with paper towels. Set wire rack in rimmed baking sheet and line half of rack with triple layer of paper towels. Whisk Shaoxing wine, soy sauce, and cornstarch together in small bowl; set aside.

2 Heat oil in 14-inch flat-bottomed wok over medium-high heat to 400 degrees. Using spider skimmer or slotted spoon, carefully add half of shrimp (oil will splatter) and cook, stirring slowly but constantly, until shells turn light pink, 20 to 30 seconds. Adjust burner, if necessary, to maintain oil temperature between 375 and 400 degrees. Using spider skimmer, transfer shrimp to unlined side of prepared rack. Return oil to 400 degrees and repeat with remaining shrimp; transfer to unlined side of rack.

3 Return oil to 400 degrees. Carefully add half of fried shrimp to oil and cook, stirring with spider skimmer slowly but constantly, until shells turn dark orange and start to crisp at cut edges, 30 to 45 seconds. Transfer shrimp to lined side of prepared rack. Return oil to 400 degrees and repeat with remaining shrimp.

4 Whisk Shaoxing wine mixture to recombine. Pour off all but 1 tablespoon oil from wok and wipe edges of wok clean with paper towels. Add rock sugar and cook over medium-low heat, stirring frequently, until sugar has melted and mixture is amber-colored, about 3 minutes. Add scallions and ginger and cook, stirring frequently, until fragrant, about 30 seconds. Increase heat to high, add shrimp and Shaoxing wine mixture, and cook, tossing slowly but constantly, until sauce has thickened and coats shrimp, about 1 minute. Off heat, stir in vinegar. Serve.

Test Kitchen Tip

Recipe developer Joe Gitter notes: "Oil-blanching shrimp—briefly submerging them in very hot oil—causes the shells to rapidly pull away from the flesh, crisping up and becoming edible. High heat is essential for this but risks overcooking the delicate shrimp. Cooking in batches and twice frying keeps interiors juicy by minimizing time spent in the oil."

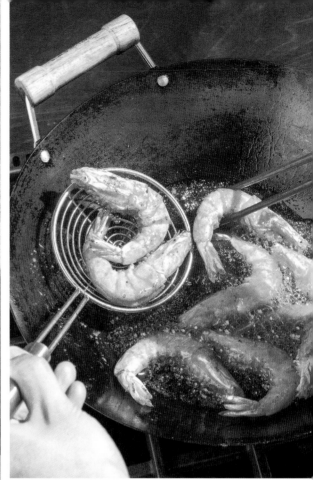

Stir-Fried Clams with Black Bean Sauce

Serves: 4 to 6 — **Total Time:** 30 minutes — **Difficulty:** ●○○○

There's a part of Hong Kong, called Castle Peak, where muddy beaches line the base of the adjacent hills. When I was a teenager, my friends and I would come here on hot summer days to go swimming.

One day we saw a group of fishermen digging for clams at low tide. My friends and I thought: "What's stopping us from doing the same?" It's a public beach! So this became a frequent activity for us, both for fun and for practicality. We'd return home carrying two heavy buckets filled to the brim with fresh clams. Of course we had to soak them overnight to draw out the sandy impurities, but by the next afternoon we'd have free lunch!

This dish is what we'd always make with our freshly dug clams—always, always, always. It's quintessentially Hong Kong, stir-fried with the delightful pungent flavors of fermented black beans. Seeing this photo of the dish makes me feel young again. — Jeffrey

Discard any raw clams with an unpleasant odor or a cracked or broken shell, as well as any with an open shell that won't close when tapped. Don't risk it!

1 Bring 4 cups water to boil in 14-inch flat-bottomed wok over medium-high heat. Add clams, cover, and cook, shaking wok occasionally to redistribute, until clams open, 3 to 8 minutes. Using slotted spoon, transfer clams to bowl (discard any unopened clams) and cover to keep warm. Discard cooking liquid and wipe wok clean with paper towels.

2 Whisk broth, oyster sauce, cornstarch, Shaoxing wine, and sesame oil together in small bowl. Heat now-empty wok over high heat until just smoking, about 3 minutes. Reduce heat to medium, drizzle vegetable oil around perimeter of wok, and heat until just smoking. Add ginger, douchi, and garlic and cook, stirring frequently, until fragrant, about 30 seconds. Stir in broth mixture, bring to simmer, and cook until sauce has thickened, about 1 minute. Add clams and Fresno and gently toss to coat. Sprinkle with scallion before serving.

2 pounds manila or littleneck clams, 1½ to 2 inches in diameter, scrubbed

¾ cup chicken broth

2 tablespoons oyster sauce

1 tablespoon cornstarch

1 tablespoon Shaoxing wine

1 teaspoon toasted sesame oil

2 tablespoons vegetable oil

1 (1-inch) piece ginger, peeled and cut into thin matchsticks (1 to 2 tablespoons)

1 tablespoon douchi (fermented black beans), rinsed and lightly smashed

1 garlic clove, minced

1 Fresno chile, stemmed, seeded, and thinly sliced into rings

1 scallion, sliced thin

Test Kitchen Tip

Recipe developer David Yu notes: "The fermented black beans, along with other aromatics, brings a fragrant savoriness to the sauce that complements the sweetness and slight salinity of the clams. Be sure to scoop up a bit of sauce with each clam to enjoy the flavor combination."

VEGETABLES AND TOFU

It may be true that many Chinese-cooking neophytes view the cuisine as meat-centric, heavily Kung Pao'd or General Tso'd. They therefore may be surprised by the sophistication and elegance of the Chinese approach to cooking vegetables. In this chapter we'll showcase recipes that are minimally adorned and that allow the produce to shine. And we'll present dishes that take a humble vegetable (or tofu) and dress it in the grandest way possible.

Suànróng Chǎo Qīngcài 蒜茸炒青菜

Stir-Fried Tender Greens with Garlic

Serves: 4 — **Total Time:** 20 minutes — **Difficulty:** ●○○○

Chinese stir-fries can be complex, with a wide variety of ingredients each added at a prescribed time. Or they can be supersimple, like these tender greens with garlic.

This dish is an example of ching chau 清炒, which in Cantonese means "clear stir-fry." It is considered the purest form of stir-fry, in which usually only a single ingredient is cooked with light seasoning to allow the flavors, freshness, and colors of that ingredient to shine. There is no sauce in the dish, but the stir-fry oil may be infused with a little ginger or garlic.

Once our greens start to wilt we sprinkle in some salt to allow the seasoning to better adhere to the tender leaves. The greens then need just a little extra time before they are fully cooked. Cooking them in very high heat gives them a vivid, bright color that otherwise can be achieved only through blanching. — Jeffrey

For more information on Chinese greens, see page 28.

4 teaspoons vegetable oil, divided

2 garlic cloves, chopped, divided

1 pound red or green amaranth, watercress, or stemmed flat-leaf spinach, divided

¼ teaspoon table salt, divided

1 Heat empty 14-inch flat-bottomed wok over high heat until just beginning to smoke. Drizzle 2 teaspoons oil around perimeter of wok and heat until just smoking. Add half of garlic, then immediately add half of greens. Cook, tossing greens slowly but constantly, until just beginning to wilt, about 30 seconds. Sprinkle with ⅛ teaspoon salt and continue to cook until greens are vibrant and just tender, 30 seconds to 2 minutes; transfer to bowl.

2 Repeat with remaining 2 teaspoons oil, remaining garlic, remaining greens, and remaining ⅛ teaspoon salt. Off heat, return first batch of greens to wok and toss to combine. Serve.

A Green of Many Colors

Any tender green can be cooked by this simple method, but none will look more dazzling than amaranth, or xiancai, sometimes called yin choy or Chinese spinach. Streaked with purple, red, or gold, its leaves retain their vibrancy cooked this way.

Fŭrŭ Jiāosī Tōngcài 腐乳椒絲通菜

Ong Choy with Fermented Bean Curd

Serves: 4 — **Total Time:** 30 minutes — **Difficulty:** ●○○○

Fermented bean curd is a secret weapon in the arsenal of some of our favorite Chinese chefs. It's highly funk-tastic, faintly boozy, and sinus-clearing intense in a Roquefort blue cheese kind of way. Just a cube or two from a jar (they're soft and the size of casino dice) brings a savory can't-put-a-finger-on-it undertow to dishes. A very successful chef friend who has sold thousands of bowls of cold sesame noodles has fermented bean curd to thank for helping to pay down his mortgage.

Dip your toes into the exciting world of fermented bean curd by incorporating it with ong choy. This simple stir-fry is bright and appealingly bitter, with just a bit of cheesy funk to make your day interesting.   — Kevin

We prefer green ong choy (distinguished by its larger leaves and more vibrant stems) to white ong choy, as it releases less liquid during cooking. Yu choy and chrysanthemum greens work well in place of the ong choy.

1   Cut ong choy tops (leaves with tender stems) from stalks. Cut tops into 4-inch lengths. Cut stalks into 2-inch lengths. Halve stalks lengthwise if more than ¼ inch in diameter. Rinse both separately under cold water, spin dry, and place on paper towel–lined rimmed baking sheet to dry thoroughly, keeping stalks separate from leaves and tender stems.

2   Using back of fork, mash fermented bean curd, bean curd liquid, Shaoxing wine, and sugar together in bowl (mixture does not need to be fully smooth); set aside.

3   Heat empty 14-inch flat-bottomed wok over high heat until just smoking. Drizzle oil around perimeter of wok and heat until just smoking. Add garlic and cook, stirring constantly, until fragrant and beginning to brown, about 15 seconds. Stir in chiles, then immediately add ong choy stalks and cook, tossing slowly but constantly, until stalks start to soften and turn vibrant green, about 1½ minutes.

4   Add ong choy leaves and tender stems and cook, tossing slowly but constantly, until leaves and stems are just starting to wilt and stalks are crisp-tender, about 1½ minutes. Push greens to 1 side of wok and add bean curd mixture to clearing. Mash mixture into wok, then stir into greens until fully combined, about 30 seconds. Season with salt to taste. Serve.

1 **pound ong choy (water spinach),** trimmed

1½ **tablespoons white or red fermented bean curd, plus 2 teaspoons fermented bean curd liquid**

1 **tablespoon Shaoxing wine**

½ **teaspoon sugar**

4 **teaspoons vegetable oil**

3 **garlic cloves, sliced thin**

3 **small dried Sichuan chiles, stemmed, seeded, and torn into small pieces**

We Love Ong Choy

Ong choy, or water spinach, is known as the "hollow" vegetable because of its tubular stalks, which offer texture while the leaves trap flavorful sauce. Cutting both into bite-size pieces makes them far easier to eat than full-length ong choy, which can be over 16 inches long. Giving the stalks a head start in the wok turns them crisp-tender, while the leaves become silky but not soggy.

Suānlà Báicài 酸辣白菜
Hot and Sour Napa Cabbage

Serves: 4 to 6 — **Total Time:** 45 minutes — **Difficulty:** ●○○○

1 head napa cabbage (2 pounds)

2 tablespoons soy sauce

2 tablespoons Chinese black vinegar

1 tablespoon oyster sauce

1 tablespoon cornstarch

2½ teaspoons sugar

2 tablespoons peanut or vegetable oil

3–5 small dried Sichuan chiles, stemmed, halved lengthwise, and seeded

1 scallion, white and green parts separated and sliced thin

1 tablespoon grated fresh ginger

1 tablespoon minced garlic

It's All about the Angle

While napa cabbage's crinkly leaves ably hold on to sauce, it takes a bit of deliberate knife work to encourage the sauce to coat the smooth cabbage ribs. When prepping the ribs, cut them at an acute (roughly 45-degree) angle. Doing so creates more surface on which the sauce can settle and exposes much more of their capillary structure (think: cutting fresh flower stems on a bias to increase water intake), which will soak up the sauce. Cutting at an angle also thins the ribs so that they cook quickly and evenly.

Cook's Illustrated senior editor Steve Dunn tells a story of how every month he and his kitchen colleagues would frequent a Sichuan restaurant in the Boston suburbs. As Steve puts it, this napa cabbage stir-fry cooked in the sour-hot style "was the most unassuming part of the spread but would disappear as soon as it hit the table. Its combination of malty black vinegar backlit with aromatics, savory sweetness, wok hei, and dried chile heat was beguiling."

Steve worked out the recipe, timed when to incorporate each component in the wok, and beautifully struck the balance of sweet, sour, and spicy. Make this once and chances are it'll disappear as soon as it hits your table.

— Kevin + Jeffrey (+ Steve)

1 Discard any outer leaves from cabbage that are bruised or torn. Peel away enough leaves to yield 1½ pounds (16 to 20 leaves). Reserve smaller leaves near core for other use. Stack 3 leaves of similar size and, using sharp knife, remove white portion from center. Keeping pieces stacked, cut cabbage whites crosswise at 45-degree angle into 1-inch slices and place in medium bowl. Cut cabbage greens into 2-inch pieces and place in second medium bowl. Repeat with remaining leaves.

2 Whisk soy sauce, vinegar, oyster sauce, cornstarch, and sugar together in small bowl.

3 Heat empty 14-inch flat-bottomed wok over high heat until just beginning to smoke. Drizzle oil around perimeter of wok and heat until just smoking. Add chiles and cook, stirring constantly, until beginning to brown, about 30 seconds. Add scallion whites, ginger, and garlic and cook, stirring constantly, until fragrant, about 1 minute.

4 Add sliced cabbage whites. Cook, tossing slowly but constantly, until cabbage begins to turn translucent at edges, 2 to 3 minutes. Add cabbage greens and cook, tossing slowly but constantly, until greens begin to collapse and wilt, about 1½ minutes.

5 Whisk soy sauce mixture to recombine and pour over cabbage mixture. Cook, stirring constantly, until cabbage is evenly coated and sauce has thickened, about 30 seconds. Sprinkle with scallion greens and serve.

Angle-Cutting Napa Cabbage

1 Stack 3 cabbage leaves of similar size and, using sharp knife, remove portion from center.

2 Holding thick white ribs in a stack, cut crosswise at 45-degree angle into 1-inch slabs.

3 Cut greens into 2-inch pieces and place in second bowl.

Suànróng Xiǎobáicài 蒜蓉小白菜
Baby Bok Choy with Ginger and Garlic

Serves: 4 — **Total Time:** 45 minutes — **Difficulty:** ●○○○

- 4 **teaspoons vegetable oil, divided**
- 1 **tablespoon grated fresh ginger**
- 1 **garlic clove, minced**
- 2 **tablespoons oyster sauce**
- 2 **teaspoons toasted sesame oil**
- ½ **teaspoon cornstarch**
- 8 **small heads baby bok choy (1½ to 2 ounces each), halved lengthwise, washed thoroughly, and spun dry**
- 2 **tablespoons water**

Gastronomically speaking, China is more continent than country. One vegetable you'll find across many regions of Chinese cooking is bok choy. These hearty members of the cabbage family grow quickly and in most climates, contributing to their ubiquity.

The key to cooking bok choy has always been striking a textural balance: How do you time it so the firm stalks soften to a tender crispness before the green leaves get too limp? Cooking with baby bok choy—as opposed to its larger counterpart—solves some of the dilemma. We also cut the baby bok choy in half lengthwise, which has the added benefit of providing more direct access to where most of the dirt and grit hide, making the vegetable easier to clean.   — Jeffrey

If using heads larger than 2 ounces each, quarter them instead of halving. We spin the bok choy dry after washing to avoid adding too much water to the wok.

1   Combine 1 teaspoon vegetable oil, ginger, and garlic in small bowl; set aside. Whisk oyster sauce, sesame oil, and cornstarch together in second small bowl; set aside.

2   Heat empty 14-inch flat-bottomed wok over high heat until just beginning to smoke. Reduce heat to medium, drizzle remaining 1 tablespoon vegetable oil around perimeter of wok, and heat until just smoking. Add bok choy and water (water will sputter), cover, and cook, shaking wok occasionally, for 2 minutes.

3   Uncover, toss bok choy, then push to 1 side of wok. Add ginger-garlic mixture to clearing and cook, mashing mixture into wok, until fragrant, about 20 seconds. Stir ginger-garlic mixture into bok choy and continue to cook, tossing slowly but constantly, until all water has evaporated, stems are crisp-tender, and leaves are wilted, 1 to 2 minutes. Add oyster sauce mixture and cook, stirring constantly, until sauce is thickened and coats bok choy, about 15 seconds. Serve.

Test Kitchen Tip

Recipe developer José Maldonado notes: "As bok choy grows, grit collects between the base of the leaves. Gently peel back the leaves as you rinse them. Let the water do all the work. The leaves are fragile, and too much pressure can snap a leaf clean from its base, affecting your presentation."

Háoyóu Jièlán 蠔油芥蘭
Gai Lan with Oyster Sauce

Serves: 4 — **Total Time:** 30 minutes — **Difficulty:** ●○○○

5 teaspoons vegetable oil, divided

1 garlic clove, minced

¼ teaspoon Sichuan chili flakes

3 tablespoons chicken broth

3 tablespoons oyster sauce

1 tablespoon Shaoxing wine

1 teaspoon dark soy sauce

1 teaspoon toasted sesame oil

1 teaspoon cornstarch

1½ pounds gai lan, trimmed

¼ cup water

Gai lan, also called Chinese broccoli or Chinese kale, is the sturdy giant of the Asian produce world—it can grow to the size of a baseball bat. We love the crunchiness of the stalks and the vibrant taste of the leaves, and it's one of the more nutrition-dense vegetables you can cook. This dish is a simple and classic Cantonese treatment for gai lan, using oyster sauce, chicken broth, and a touch of cornstarch to help the sauce lightly cling to the greens.   — Jeffrey

1   Combine 1 teaspoon vegetable oil, garlic, and chili flakes in small bowl; set aside. Whisk broth, oyster sauce, Shaoxing wine, soy sauce, sesame oil, and cornstarch in second small bowl; set aside.

2   Trim leaves from bottom 3 inches of gai lan stalks and reserve. Cut tops (leaves and florets) from stalks. Quarter stalks lengthwise if more than 1 inch in diameter, and halve stalks if less than 1 inch in diameter. Keep leaves and tops separate from stalks.

3   Heat empty 14-inch flat-bottomed wok over high heat until just beginning to smoke. Reduce heat to medium, drizzle 2 teaspoons vegetable oil around perimeter of wok, and heat until just smoking. Add stalks and water (water will sputter). Cover and cook until gai lan is bright green, about 5 minutes. Uncover, increase heat to high, and continue to cook, tossing slowly but constantly, until all water has evaporated and stalks are crisp-tender, 1 to 3 minutes; transfer to separate bowl.

4   Heat now-empty wok over high heat until just beginning to smoke. Drizzle remaining 2 teaspoons vegetable oil around perimeter of wok and heat until just smoking. Add half of gai lan tops and reserved leaves and cook, tossing slowly but constantly, until beginning to wilt, 1 to 3 minutes. Add remaining gai lan tops and reserved leaves and continue to cook, tossing slowly but constantly, until completely wilted, about 3 minutes.

5   Push gai lan to 1 side of wok. Add garlic mixture to clearing and cook, mashing mixture into wok, until fragrant, about 30 seconds. Stir garlic mixture into gai lan. Whisk broth mixture to recombine, then add to wok with stalks and any accumulated juices and cook, tossing constantly, until sauce has thickened and coats gai lan, about 30 seconds. Serve.

Test Kitchen Tip

If you can't find gai lan, broccolini is a good substitute. Trim the broccolini stems and cut the tops (leaves and florets) from the stems, keeping them separate, and halve any stems thicker than ½ inch.

Kevin's Chinese Dining Etiquette

(or How Not to Bring Eternal Shame to Your Ancestors)

1. Rarely will you dine at a Chinese restaurant and order an entrée solely for yourself. Assume communal rules and everybody shares.

2. Never point the ends of a chopstick toward anyone you like.

3. Don't jab chopsticks into your food, or leave them sticking straight up in food.

4. Never play air drums with your chopsticks, especially not "In the Air Tonight" by Phil Collins.

5. If there are two sets of chopsticks in front of you, only one pair should touch your mouth. The other is for picking up food from communal dishes.

6. The Chinese like bony foods. It's fine to leave bones on your plate.

7. Don't act surprised if someone places a piece of food on your plate. They're showing respect.

8. Pour tea for the eldest person at the table first. Pour for yourself last.

9. If someone pours you tea, extend your index and middle fingers and tap twice on the table. It's shorthand for a bow and expresses gratitude.

10. If you need a refill for your teapot, balance the lid on the edge of the pot. A waiter will notice and pour more hot water.

11. Chinese folks are known to use toothpicks at the table openly (sorry). The polite ones will use a napkin or their other hand to shield the view.

12. If you're dining at a restaurant with a lazy Susan, never rotate the turntable while someone is in the middle of taking a serving from it.

13. "Cheers!" in Mandarin Chinese is gānbēi 乾杯 (pronounced "gan bay").

14. Not exactly dining etiquette, but if you're out with clients and they hand you a business card, accept it with both hands, thumbs on top.

15. The best strategy for dining at a Chinese restaurant? Bring a Chinese friend. (Yes, I'll be your friend.)

16. Arguing to pay the bill is a long-standing (and exasperating) Chinese tradition. The bigger the fuss you make and the more wildly you gesticulate with your arms, the more respect you're showing to dining mates—even if you have zero intention of paying.

— Kevin

Gānbiān Sìjìdòu 乾煸四季豆
Sichuan Green Beans

Serves: 4 — **Total Time:** 40 minutes — **Difficulty:** ●●○○

Certain foods taste better charred and burnt: roasted corn, the cheese atop a French onion soup, a s'more. Green beans also firmly belong on this list. They improve with scorched heat, the dark, blistered spots softening to a caramelized sweetness.

Chinese restaurants with gas-powered burners have no problem getting woks hot enough to achieve this result. Many professional kitchens use deep fryers. However, achieving that beautifully blistered exterior at home has been a tough challenge.

Cook's Illustrated deputy editor Andrea Geary solved this riddle by taking advantage of a home appliance that can hit very high temperatures: your oven broiler. First we get the green beans ripping hot and spotty dark under the broiler, and then we cook them a second time in the wok, alongside pickled mustard greens and ground pork that turns into savory, garlicky, crispy bits.   — Kevin

Yacai is sometimes labeled suimiyacai. We do not recommend substituting other varieties of pickled mustard.

1   Adjust oven rack 8 inches from broiler element and heat broiler. Combine beans with 1 tablespoon vegetable oil in bowl and toss to coat. Spread on rimmed baking sheet (do not wash bowl). Broil beans until softened and charred in places, 10 to 15 minutes, flipping beans halfway through broiling. Return beans to bowl, add salt, and toss to distribute evenly. Cover with plate. Stir Shaoxing wine, soy sauce, and sugar together in small bowl until sugar is dissolved, and set aside.

2   Combine remaining 1½ tablespoons vegetable oil, chiles, and peppercorns in 14-inch flat-bottomed wok and cook over medium-low heat until fragrant, about 1 minute. Add garlic and ginger and cook, stirring constantly, until fragrant, about 1 minute. Add pork, and mash and smear into wok until pork and garlic mixture are evenly combined. Increase heat to medium-high and continue to cook, chopping meat into ¼-inch chunks with edge of spatula, until pork is cooked through, about 2 minutes.

3   Add beans and yacai and toss to combine. Add Shaoxing wine mixture and cook, stirring constantly, until no liquid remains in wok, 1 to 2 minutes. Drizzle with sesame oil and serve.

1½ **pounds green beans, trimmed**

2½ **tablespoons vegetable oil, divided**

½ **teaspoon table salt**

1 **tablespoon Shaoxing wine**

1½ **teaspoons soy sauce**

1 **teaspoon sugar**

2–4 **dried small Sichuan chiles, stemmed, halved lengthwise, and seeded**

½ **teaspoon Sichuan peppercorns**

1 **tablespoon minced garlic**

1 **tablespoon grated fresh ginger**

3 **ounces ground pork**

2 **tablespoons yacai**

1 **teaspoon toasted sesame oil**

The Secret to Charred Beans

The key to charred, dense, concentrated green beans? Dehydration. In place of deep frying, we use a hybrid broiling-steaming method. The broiling condenses the beans and creates spotty charring. Letting the beans gently steam in their residual heat in a covered bowl ensures that they become fully tender.

Eggplant with Black Bean Sauce

Serves: 4 — **Total Time:** 45 minutes — **Difficulty:** ●●○○

- 1½ pounds Chinese or Japanese eggplant, cut into 1½-inch pieces
- 1 teaspoon kosher salt
- ⅓ cup plus 3 tablespoons vegetable oil, divided
- 2 garlic cloves, sliced thin
- 1½ tablespoons Sichuan chili flakes
- 1 (½-inch) piece ginger, peeled and sliced thin
- 1 star anise pod
- ¼ cup hoisin sauce
- ¼ cup douchi (fermented black beans), rinsed
- ¼ cup plus 2 tablespoons Shaoxing wine, divided
- 1 tablespoon sugar
- 1 green bell pepper, stemmed, seeded, and cut into 1-inch pieces
- ¼ cup water
- 6 scallions, white parts sliced thin, green parts cut into 1-inch pieces
- 12 sprigs fresh cilantro, cut into 2-inch pieces

Here's another example of a very Chinese recipe using a not-very-Chinese method. This one involves a surprising but effective way of cooking eggplant: with your microwave.

Raw eggplants are spongy little devils, with a lot of water tucked away in their flesh. Getting eggplants to that browned, silky, nonmushy state requires removing that moisture, which typically involves salting to draw it out, then blotting the excess liquid.

A microwave accomplishes this in one-third the time. How? You're drawing out moisture in the form of steam, while salting the eggplant beforehand expedites the process. The result: ready-to-cook eggplant pieces primed to soak up any delicious sauces tossed their way—in this case, a bold Sichuan chili oil with pungent fermented black beans and herbaceous cilantro. — Kevin

Chinese or Japanese eggplant, which both have thinner skin and fewer seeds than globe eggplant, are good options for this dish. If unavailable, globe or Italian eggplant can be substituted.

1 Toss eggplant with salt in medium bowl. Line large plate with double layer of coffee filters and lightly spray with vegetable oil spray. Spread eggplant in even layer over prepared plate. Microwave until eggplant feels dry and pieces shrink to about 1 inch, about 10 minutes, flipping eggplant halfway through microwaving. Transfer immediately to paper towel–lined plate.

2 Cook ⅓ cup oil, garlic, chile flakes, ginger, and star anise in 14-inch flat-bottomed wok over medium-high heat until sizzling. Reduce heat to low and gently simmer until garlic and ginger are softened but not browned, about 5 minutes. Transfer oil mixture to medium bowl and let cool for 5 minutes. Stir in hoisin, douchi, 2 tablespoons Shaoxing wine, and sugar. Wipe wok clean with paper towels.

3 Heat now-empty wok over high heat until just beginning to smoke. Drizzle 2 tablespoons oil around perimeter of wok and heat until just smoking. Add eggplant and cook, tossing eggplant slowly but constantly, until pieces are charred on most sides, 5 to 7 minutes. Add remaining 1 tablespoon oil and bell pepper and cook, tossing slowly but constantly, until bell pepper is lightly charred, about 3 minutes.

4 Reduce heat to medium and add remaining ¼ cup Shaoxing wine and water, scraping up any browned bits. Cook, tossing constantly, until liquid is reduced by half, about 15 seconds. Stir in scallion greens and cook, tossing constantly, until slightly wilted, about 15 seconds. Off heat, stir in garlic–black bean sauce until combined. Top with scallion whites and cilantro and serve.

Suànróng Hóngshāo Qiézi 蒜蓉紅燒茄子

Braised Eggplant with Soy, Garlic, and Ginger

Serves: 4 to 6 — **Total Time:** 1 hour — **Difficulty:** ●●○○

1½ cups water

¼ cup Shaoxing wine

2 tablespoons soy sauce

4 teaspoons sugar

2 teaspoons doubanjiang
(broad bean chile paste)

1 teaspoon cornstarch

1 pound Chinese or Japanese
eggplant

1 tablespoon vegetable oil

1 garlic clove, minced

1 teaspoon grated fresh ginger

½ teaspoon toasted sesame oil

2 scallions, sliced thin

A Five-Year-Old Eggplant Expert

My earliest memory of shopping at
the produce market with my mother
involved eggplants. She taught me to
look for shiny and heavy ones with a
deep lavender gloss. Yes, I became an
expert eggplant shopper at age five.

I'm not afraid to admit I'm wrong. The way I'd always cooked eggplant involved using
a lot of oil—and I mean *a lot*. Old delicious habits die hard. Then on *Hunger Pangs*
I made this ATK version, which uses all of 1 tablespoon oil (plus ½ teaspoon sesame
oil to finish). This dish checked off all the boxes I grew up with: a meltingly tender
and creamy texture, with flavors that deeply penetrate the eggplant. It took only
70-something years, but this is the way I'll be braising eggplant going forward.
— Jeffrey

*Two medium (8- to 10-ounce) globe or Italian eggplants may be substituted for
the Chinese eggplant. (Larger eggplants will disintegrate when braised.) For intact
pieces, it's important to cut the eggplant so each piece has some skin attached.*

1   Whisk water, Shaoxing wine, soy sauce, sugar, doubanjiang, and cornstarch in
medium bowl until sugar has dissolved. Cut each eggplant crosswise into 3- to 4-inch
lengths. Halve each piece lengthwise, then cut each half into ¾-inch-thick wedges.

2   Heat empty 14-inch flat-bottomed wok over high heat until just smoking.
Reduce heat to medium-high, drizzle vegetable oil around perimeter of wok, and
heat until shimmering. Add garlic and ginger and cook, mashing mixture into wok,
until fragrant, about 30 seconds. Spread eggplant evenly in wok (pieces will not
form single layer). Pour Shaoxing wine mixture over eggplant and bring to boil.
Reduce heat to medium-low, cover, and simmer gently until eggplant is soft and
has decreased in volume enough to form single layer on bottom of wok, about
15 minutes, gently shaking wok to settle eggplant halfway through cooking (some
pieces will remain opaque).

3   Uncover and continue to cook, swirling wok occasionally, until liquid is thickened
and reduced to just a few tablespoons, 12 to 14 minutes. Drizzle with sesame oil and
sprinkle with scallions. Serve.

Chuānwèi Suānlà Tǔdòusī 川味酸辣土豆絲
Sichuan Hot and Sour Potatoes

Serves: 4 — **Total Time:** 30 minutes — **Difficulty:** ●●●○

We joke that potatoes are perfect for both the very young and the very old—you know, people who are "teeth-challenged." That approach to cooking spuds is a very Western one, where the flesh is often mashed, baked, or boiled to within an inch of disintegration.

The Sichuanese tend to enjoy potatoes for their semiraw bite and crunchiness, like fresh jicama in a salad. In this recipe, potatoes are sliced into matchsticks and barely stir-fried—just enough to start crisping and pick up the tingly aromatics.
— Jeffrey

Look for potatoes that are about 4 inches in length. Slicing the potatoes into thin matchsticks is crucial for the success of this dish. You can do this with a sharp knife; however, a mandoline ensures even slices; we use it to slice ⅛-inch planks and then cut those into matchsticks by hand. We prefer yellow waxy potatoes such as Yukon Golds for this recipe, but any potato will work.

1   Slice potatoes into ⅛-inch planks, then cut planks into ⅛-inch matchsticks. Transfer potatoes to bowl and submerge in cold water. Soak for 10 minutes, then drain in colander. Transfer to paper towel–lined plate and set aside.

2   Heat oil and peppercorns in 14-inch flat-bottomed wok over medium heat, stirring constantly, until peppercorns are sizzling and fragrant but not darkened, about 2 minutes. Using slotted spoon, remove peppercorns and discard, reserving oil. Add Thai chile to oil in wok and cook, stirring constantly, until fragrant, about 15 seconds. Increase heat to high, add potatoes, and cook, tossing slowly but constantly, until potatoes are crisp-tender, about 2 minutes. Add scallions, salt, and sugar and toss to combine. Off heat, add vinegar and toss to combine. Serve warm or at room temperature.

- 1 pound large yellow waxy potatoes, peeled
- 1½ tablespoons vegetable oil
- ¾ teaspoon Sichuan peppercorns
- 1 Thai chile, stemmed and sliced thin
- 2 scallions, sliced into 3-inch-long thin matchsticks
- 1 teaspoon table salt
- ½ teaspoon sugar
- 4 teaspoons Chinese white rice vinegar

Test Kitchen Tip

Recipe developer Hannah Fenton notes: "Briefly soaking the matchstick-cut potatoes (which have plenty of surface area) draws out excess starch, preventing them from becoming gummy, clumping, or sticking to the wok. The cold water also stiffens the potatoes, ensuring their signature 'crisp-tender' texture."

Xīhóngshì Chǎo Jīdàn 西紅柿炒雞蛋
Stir-Fried Tomatoes and Eggs

Serves: 4 — **Total Time:** 25 minutes — **Difficulty:** ●○○○

- 4 scallions, white parts sliced thin, green parts cut into 1-inch pieces
- 3 tablespoons vegetable oil, divided
- 3 garlic cloves, sliced thin
- 2 teaspoons grated fresh ginger
- 8 large eggs
- 2 tablespoons Shaoxing wine
- 1 teaspoon toasted sesame oil
- 1 teaspoon table salt, divided
- 1 (28-ounce) can whole peeled tomatoes, drained with juice reserved, cut into 1-inch pieces
- 2 teaspoons sugar

Test Kitchen Tip

Recipe developer Joe Gitter notes: "Whisking Shaoxing wine and sesame oil into the eggs dilutes their proteins, making it more difficult for them to form tight curds. The extra moisture also produces more steam to puff the eggs. Finally, cooking the eggs over medium-high heat ensures that the curds are light rather than creamy."

In keeping with Chinese parental law, punishable by a lifetime of disappointment if not obeyed, I was forced to take piano lessons at age four. Like a lot of kids, the first song I learned to play was "Twinkle, Twinkle, Little Star."

You might be surprised to learn that stir-fried tomatoes and eggs is the "Twinkle, Twinkle, Little Star" of Chinese cookery, often the first dish a child is taught to stir-fry. You have to try really hard to mess this one up.

If the combination of tomatoes and eggs sounds peculiar ("How I wonder what you are," I'm sure you're thinking), know that the sweet-savoriness of the tomatoes plus tender, billowy curds of just-set scrambled eggs make a magnificent pairing.

No dish comes together quicker on a Tuesday night than this.   — Kevin

1   Combine scallion whites, 1 tablespoon vegetable oil, garlic, and ginger in small bowl; set aside. Whisk eggs, Shaoxing wine, sesame oil, and ½ teaspoon salt together in separate bowl.

2   Heat empty 14-inch flat-bottomed wok over high heat until just beginning to smoke. Reduce heat to medium-high, drizzle remaining 2 tablespoons vegetable oil around perimeter of wok, and heat until just smoking. Add egg mixture and, using rubber spatula, scrape slowly but constantly along bottom and sides of wok until eggs just form cohesive mass, 1½ to 2½ minutes (eggs will not be completely dry); transfer to clean bowl.

3   Add scallion white mixture to now-empty wok and cook over medium heat, mashing mixture into wok, until fragrant, about 30 seconds. Add tomatoes and their juice, sugar, and remaining ½ teaspoon salt and simmer until almost completely dry, 5 to 7 minutes. Stir in eggs and scallion greens and cook, breaking up any large curds, until heated through, about 1 minute. Serve.

Homemade Tofu
(page 234)

Zìzhì Dòufǔ 自製豆腐

Homemade Tofu

Makes: 14 ounces — **Total Time:** 1¼ hours, plus 13 hours soaking and resting — **Difficulty:** ●●○○

8 ounces (1¼ cups) dried soybeans, picked over and rinsed

2 teaspoons liquid nigari

Tofu is an important food in the diets of one-third of the world's population. Made from cooking ground soybeans in liquid and pressing the curds into custardy blocks, tofu is supremely versatile (as you'll see in the coming pages). By itself it doesn't taste like much, but it's a true chameleon ingredient in that it takes on the flavor of its surroundings. It can be served hot, cold, or at room temperature, and it's so adaptable it can be made into a silky-smooth dessert, a crispy fried appetizer, or the centerpiece entrée at a dinner party.

So why make tofu at home? This is like asking why someone would want to make homemade chicken stock or bake sourdough bread. The answer is that it's immensely satisfying to do so—a pleasure to watch the good work you put in pay off handsomely.   — Kevin

While truly fresh tofu is hard to come by, tofu is no more difficult to make than yogurt. We do it in a few relatively easy steps: making soy milk from soy beans, curdling the hot soy milk with the mineral salt nigari, and then pressing the resulting curds. Liquid nigari can be found online and at Asian supermarkets. It's important to bring the strained soy milk in step 4 to at least 165 degrees before adding the nigari, because otherwise the tofu might not coagulate properly. We developed this recipe using a 5½ by 4-inch tofu mold and press kit; other mold sizes and styles may affect the pressing time in step 7.

Keep Me Searching for a Tofu Mold

You can find tofu molds online, but if you don't want to invest in one, poke three even holes in the bottom of a quart-size plastic berry container and then cut off the lid and trim it to fit just inside the container. Line the container with muslin or cheesecloth and scoop the curds into the container just as you would with a mold. Cover the curds with the excess muslin/cheesecloth and place the trimmed plastic lid on top.

1   Place soybeans in large bowl or container and add enough water to cover by 2 inches. Soak soybeans at room temperature for at least 12 hours or up to 18 hours. Drain and rinse well.

2   Working in batches, process one-third of soaked soybeans and 3 cups water in blender until mostly smooth, about 3 minutes; transfer mixture to large Dutch oven. Repeat processing twice more with remaining soybeans and 3 cups water for each batch.

3 Set colander over large bowl and line with triple layer of cheesecloth. Bring soybean mixture to simmer over medium-high heat, stirring frequently with rubber spatula to prevent scorching and boiling over, and cook until slightly thickened, about 10 minutes.

4 Slowly pour soybean mixture into prepared colander and let drain. Being careful of hot liquid, pull edges of cheesecloth together and twist to form pouch. Using tongs, firmly squeeze soybean pulp to extract as much liquid as possible. (You should have about 8 cups of soy milk; discard soybean pulp or reserve for another use.) Return soy milk to clean Dutch oven and heat to gentle simmer (165 to 175 degrees) over medium-high heat, stirring frequently to prevent scorching. Remove pot from heat.

5 Combine ½ cup water and nigari in 1-cup liquid measuring cup. While slowly stirring milk in figure-eight motion, add ¼ cup nigari mixture. Immediately stop stirring, cover, and let milk mixture sit undisturbed for 2 minutes. Drizzle remaining ¼ cup nigari mixture on surface of milk mixture and gently stir using figure-eight motion until combined, about 6 stirs. Cover and let sit undisturbed until curds form and whey is pooling on top and around sides of pot, about 20 minutes.

6 Line tofu mold with triple layer of cheesecloth and place in colander set over large bowl. Using slotted spoon, gently transfer milk curds to prepared mold, retaining as much of curds' natural structure as possible. Cover top of curds with excess cheesecloth and arrange mold press plate on top.

7 Weight plate with heavy brick or large can and press tofu until desired firmness is reached, about 30 minutes for medium-firm and 40 minutes for firm. Gently transfer tofu to storage container and cover with water. Let sit until tofu is fully set, at least 10 minutes. (Tofu can be refrigerated for up to 1 week; change water daily.)

Pressing Homemade Tofu

1 Gently transfer milk curds to mold. Use slotted spoon with small holes or fine-mesh strainer to avoid disturbing structure of curds.

2 Arrange mold press plate on top of curds and weight with heavy brick or large can until desired firmness is reached.

Jiācháng Dòufǔ 家常豆腐
Homestyle Tofu

Serves: 4 — **Total Time:** 45 minutes — **Difficulty:** ●●○○

The "homestyle" in homestyle tofu isn't some vague folksy descriptor. It refers to a specific flavor combination popular in Sichuan cooking—a little spicy, a little savory, a little sweet. But it just as well describes the way I prepare the dish at home, which is with a little bit of this and that from my pantry.

Though tofu is the star of the show, we're just as fond of the crunchy vegetal supporting cast: bell peppers, bamboo shoots, and carrots, lightly dressed by the piquant sauce.

If you want to master the wok, this dish provides excellent training.   — Jeffrey

This recipe can also be made using a 12-inch nonstick skillet; increase the oil to 2 cups in step 2.

1   Halve tofu lengthwise, then cut crosswise into ¾-inch-thick slabs. Spread tofu on paper towel–lined rimmed baking sheet and gently pat dry with additional paper towels. In small bowl combine soy sauce, cornstarch, sugar, and oyster sauce; set aside.

2   Line large plate with triple layer of paper towels. Heat oil in 14-inch flat-bottomed wok over medium-high heat to 375 degrees. Using spider skimmer or slotted spoon, carefully add tofu in even layer and cook until crisp and well browned on both sides, about 10 minutes, flipping tofu halfway through cooking. Transfer tofu to prepared plate to drain.

3   Pour off all but 3 tablespoons oil from wok. Heat oil left in wok over medium-high heat until just smoking. Add bell pepper, carrot, and bamboo shoots and cook, tossing slowly but constantly, until crisp-tender, about 3 minutes. Push vegetables to 1 side of wok and add garlic, scallion whites, ginger, and doubanjiang to clearing. Cook, mashing garlic mixture into wok, until fragrant, about 30 seconds. Stir garlic mixture into vegetables. Add water and tofu and cook, tossing slowly but constantly, until tofu has warmed through and absorbed some liquid, 3 to 5 minutes.

4   Whisk soy sauce mixture to recombine, then add to wok and cook, tossing gently, until sauce has thickened, about 30 seconds. Sprinkle with scallion greens and serve.

14 ounces firm tofu

2 teaspoons soy sauce

2 teaspoons cornstarch

1 teaspoon sugar

1 teaspoon oyster sauce

1 cup vegetable oil

1 green bell pepper, stemmed, seeded, and cut into 1-inch pieces

1 carrot, peeled and sliced ¼ inch thick on bias

½ cup canned sliced bamboo shoots, drained, rinsed, and patted dry

3 garlic cloves, sliced

2 scallions, white and green parts separated and sliced thin

1 (1-inch) piece ginger, peeled and sliced into thin matchsticks

1 tablespoon doubanjiang (broad bean chile paste)

¾ cup water

Test Kitchen Tip

Recipe developer Carmen Dongo notes: "The vegetables here provide color and textural contrast. Other vegetables would certainly work; check your fridge and pantry for your favorite vegetable staples."

Liángbàn Dòufǔ 凉拌豆腐
Spicy Cold Tofu

Serves: 4 — **Total Time:** 20 minutes — **Difficulty:** ●○○○

2 tablespoons soy sauce

1 tablespoon toasted sesame oil

1½ teaspoons Chinese white rice vinegar

1 teaspoon sugar

1 teaspoon minced fresh ginger

1 garlic clove, minced

1 Thai chile, stemmed and sliced thin

1 scallion, white and green parts separated and sliced thin

14 ounces silken tofu, chilled

¼ cup fresh cilantro leaves and tender stems

½ teaspoon sesame seeds, toasted

There's something luxurious and refined about chilled silken tofu in the way it slips and slides across your palate. And yet making this dish could not be more effortless.

Focus your energies instead on the presentation. Find a rustic-looking plate, shingle the silken tofu as uniformly as you can, and pick out only the choicest cilantro leaves, strewing them about in an artfully haphazard way.

This elegant recipe, developed by our colleague José Maldonado, is the September *Vogue* of tofu dishes.   — Kevin

For a milder dish, remove the chile seeds before slicing.

1 Whisk soy sauce, oil, vinegar, sugar, ginger, and garlic in medium bowl until sugar has dissolved. Stir in Thai chile and scallion whites.

2 Slice tofu crosswise into ¾-inch-thick slabs or cut into 1-inch pieces. Arrange tofu attractively on serving platter. Spoon dressing over tofu and sprinkle with scallion greens, cilantro, and sesame seeds. Serve.

One Hundred Years of Solid Food

This dish is often served with century eggs to add a more savory element. If desired, peel and cut 1 or 2 century eggs into thin wedges and arrange around the platter before serving.

Mápó Dòufǔ 麻婆豆腐

Mapo Tofu

Serves: 4 to 6   **Total Time:** 1 hour — **Difficulty:** ●●○○

28 ounces soft tofu, cut into ½-inch cubes

1 cup chicken broth

6 scallions, sliced thin

8 ounces ground pork

1 teaspoon vegetable oil, plus extra as needed

9 garlic cloves, minced

⅓ cup doubanjiang (broad bean chile paste)

1 tablespoon grated fresh ginger

1 tablespoon douchi (fermented black beans)

1 tablespoon Sichuan chili flakes

1 tablespoon Sichuan peppercorns, toasted and coarsely ground

2 tablespoons hoisin sauce

2 teaspoons toasted sesame oil

2 tablespoons water

1 tablespoon cornstarch

Give It a Rest, Why Don't Ya

Like many good stews and braises, this dish will continue to taste great if stored in the refrigerator for up to 24 hours. Reheat gently in a saucepan.

The most famous culinary export of Sichuan is named for an old widow whose face was scarred by smallpox. Lovely thought, right? The legend goes that an elderly woman with a pockmarked face ran a restaurant near Chengdu and was famous for this dish. People traveled far and wide to sample it, and in time it garnered the name mapo tofu, or "pockmarked old woman tofu."

While this poor lady surely wouldn't be thrilled with the branding, her contribution to the culinary canon is indelible. For those unfamiliar, mapo tofu is a thrilling introduction to Sichuan cuisine—an audacious, unapologetically fiery showcase for tofu and the spices that made the region famous. Cooks from Japan to Peru have since adapted mapo tofu to local tastes, but this original Sichuan version is hard to beat, continuing to break sweat, race heartbeats, and produce sniffs of spicy satisfaction.   — Kevin

1   Place tofu, broth, and scallions in large bowl and microwave, covered, until steaming, 5 to 7 minutes. Let stand while preparing remaining ingredients.

2   Cook pork and vegetable oil in 14-inch flat-bottomed wok over medium heat, breaking up meat with wooden spoon, until meat just begins to brown, 5 to 7 minutes. Using slotted spoon, transfer pork to separate bowl. Pour off all but ¼ cup fat from wok. (If necessary, add vegetable oil to equal ¼ cup.)

3   Add garlic, doubanjiang, ginger, douchi, chili flakes, and peppercorns to fat left in wok and cook over medium heat until spices darken and oil begins to separate from paste, 2 to 3 minutes.

4   Gently pour tofu with broth into wok, followed by hoisin, sesame oil, and cooked pork. Cook, stirring gently and frequently, until simmering, 2 to 3 minutes. Whisk water and cornstarch together in small bowl. Add cornstarch mixture to wok and continue to cook, stirring frequently, until sauce has thickened, about 3 minutes. Serve.

JEFFREY'S GREATEST HITS

Jeffrey here. This is a special chapter for me. The recipes here
are all cherished dishes straight out of my personal notebook—
from my childhood, my travels, my many attempts with my wife,
Catherine, to re-create a specific taste memory. These 11 dishes,
culled from hundreds I've developed, mean the most to me.

Why I Cook

For the first few years of my life the only mangoes I saw were green and hard, hanging from tree branches. Before they had a chance to ripen they were picked, sliced into strips, and dried or pickled.

That changed when I was five years old, traveling on a train with my parents as we moved from my birthplace in Guangzhou to Hong Kong, 100 miles south. Each time the train pulled into a station, hawkers swarmed the platform, offering snacks to hungry passengers. They sold bananas, lychees, and apples, as well as marinated chicken thighs and hard-boiled eggs. Also offered were live chickens and ducks in bamboo cages. The entrepreneurial sellers were persistent; even as the train departed they ran along the tracks, hoping to close one more sale.

When we walked out of the train station in Hong Kong we saw a hundred times more hawkers selling their wares—every kind of fruit and vegetable, flower and plant, tropical fish and small pet. At one point a yellow color caught my eye.

My dear mother said they were mangoes from the Philippines. She picked a few choice ones from the seller and handed me my first fresh, ripe mango. I peeled the thick skin and took a bite. I had never tasted anything so sweet, juicy, and magnificent before. I still can't taste a mango without thinking about that day when I was five.

Every childhood memory I have revolves around food. Outside our home in the working-class neighborhood of Diamond Hill, there were assorted fruit trees that grew longans and lychees. Around the corner was a fence where honeysuckle climbed, with its sweet nectar and edible blossoms. Not far from that was a tall kapok tree. When its fruit fell in the autumn, my mother would dry its cotton-like fibers for porridge.

Though Diamond Hill had a stone quarry for many years, there weren't actual diamonds to be found there, and Hong Kong wasn't yet the gleaming metropolis on the South China Sea that it is today. Farmers plowed from sunrise to sunset in the large field in front of our house. All around me were hard-working people trying to make an honest living.

The fruit and vegetable sellers, butchers, and fishmongers worked hard at the loud and colorful wet market. What I remember most at that age was my mother bringing me there several times a week, rain or shine. We had no television or radio in our home, and few toys, so shopping with Mom became my entertainment. She patiently explained how to choose the best ingredients. You couldn't rely just on sight. You had to pick something up, squeeze it, smell it, weigh it in your hands. You had to knock against it and listen to the reverberations.

When choosing lotus root, she said it's best to pick one with a little mud residue. She claimed the mud forms a barrier that keeps the root from drying out. Likewise with winter melons—seek out ones with a layer of white fuzz.

My mom taught me that when shopping for fish to look under the gills. The color should be bright red, without any sliminess. The eyes on the fish should be shiny and not sunken, the flesh firm, not soft. And it should never smell fishy. I can't think of many young children who became experts at shopping for fish at the wet market.

When we returned home I would stand beside her on an upside-down Coca-Cola crate and watch her cook. This wasn't so much about learning as it was about her sneaking bites of food for me to taste. Even when I wasn't paying close attention, I still absorbed her techniques by osmosis. She was my personal Food Network, in living color.

Cooking in the 1960s was far simpler. We didn't own refrigerators, microwaves, ovens, or rice cookers. The only equipment we had were an iron wok, two clay pots, some bowls, and just enough chopsticks. Our pantry staples consisted of soy sauce, cooking wine, vinegar, salt, and sugar in crocks on the counter. Measuring cups or spoons? We had only our fingers to use for measuring. Oil temperature was gauged by sticking a bamboo chopstick in the oil and waiting for tiny bubbles to form at the tip. I'm thankful for learning how to cook with such limited means, because it made me rely on the true tools for success in the kitchen: our five senses.

* * *

In my teenage years I started cooking for my family, which also included two younger sisters—Szwina and Rita—who obsessed over food as much as I did. Unlike today, when you can find any recipe on your phone in seconds, satiating a cooking curiosity was not easy. There weren't many cookbooks published in Hong Kong back then, much less televised cooking shows.

When it came to food, we followed our instincts. Whenever we were lucky enough to dine out as a family, we'd dissect every dish that crossed our table. How was the sauce made? What equipment was used to cook it? What's that unidentifiable flavor that tastes so incredible?

Photo Descriptions (from top to bottom): *Photo 1: Jeffrey at age 2 with his mother, 1953; Photo 2: Jeffrey prepping for a cooking demonstration, 2001; Photo 3: The Pang family featuring Kevin's embarrassing hair on The Great Wall of China, 1995.*

Investigating restaurant dishes became Puzzle Night for the Pangs. Our discussions were lively, sometimes heated, but they were mysteries we always tried solving as a family. In time my mother tried replicating dishes we tasted. The process involved a few tries, sometimes more, but many dishes joined the regular rotation in our household.

While my father held his own as a cook—he loved beef tripe with pickled mustard greens— my mother's dishes are the ones I still daydream about. She loved braising pork belly for me; I loved eating it all. She made a lamb stew that took everybody's breath away. When my parents fought, it wasn't over grievances or bad behavior, but about who should cook that night!

Food permeated every part of family and social life. When my relationship with Catherine became serious, she realized the best way to ingratiate herself with my family was to learn to cook (by her admission, she couldn't boil water). So she took cooking lessons from a local culinary school. She was soon accepted into our family with open arms.

Years after culinary classes and having two kids of our own, we would face our greatest cooking challenge yet.

In the 1980s many Hong Kong families made the decision to emigrate overseas. For our children's future, Catherine and I decided to move to Canada. A little more than a year passed between the time our immigration application was accepted and the day we boarded the plane. Beyond all the complicated logistics of moving to a new country, there was an important loose end to tie up: deciding on which recipes to document, master, and bring with us to our new life halfway across the world.

It was a race against time. Catherine consulted with both her parents and mine, as well as with relatives and friends, furiously jotting down recipes in her blue spiral notepad. There were dishes we couldn't leave without knowing how to make: radish cake, Hakka-style tofu, scallion pancakes, shrimp-paste fried chicken, stir-fried sticky rice, to name a few. What made our task especially difficult was the absence of any precise measurements. Many of her notes read like this: "A bit of soy sauce, a pinch of five-spice powder, cook until done." Every jigsaw puzzle was missing a few pieces.

Thankfully, we weren't alone in our new life. Many other families from Hong Kong settled in our Toronto neighborhood, and we formed a tight support system. Most of our friends weren't as cooking-obsessed as Catherine and me, and this turned out to be a good deal for them, because

our house hosted countless dinner gatherings.
We always had a fun time, but there was an
ulterior motive: Catherine and I used these
opportunities to refine those imprecise,
incomplete recipes we brought with us. Not only
did every attempt at Portuguese chicken and
pork chop rice improve upon the last, subsequent
versions of all our recipes achieved a taste
closer to our memories from yesteryear. And
these meals created new memories for our friends
and our young family. You're holding many of
those recipes in your hands right now.

* * *

The last conversation I had with my mother was
on September 2, 2005, the day before she died.
She was in the cruel throes of late-stage
Alzheimer's, her faculties mostly gone and her
memory faded. But as always we talked about
food. In her weakened voice she pleaded with
me to hurry back to Hong Kong and visit. "I'll
cook something great for you," she promised.
Then I asked what she would make. Immediately
she snapped to her feisty old self. "You think
I don't remember? Of course I remember! I'll
make you poached chicken and lotus root soup,
your favorite!"

Of course she remembered.

* * *

We live on opposite sides of the world now,
me in Seattle and my sisters in Hong Kong.
The three of us and Catherine are the only
Pangs from our generation left, and we're lucky
to still have each other. We talk to each other
as much as possible, and while we always begin
by exchanging the obligatory pleasantries, very
quickly the conversation will veer toward what
really needs to be discussed: cooking.

Szwina and Rita will tell me about the latest
dishes they've tried. And just like old times
we'll fall down the rabbit hole, trying to
figure out how to re-create them. How was this
sauce made? What cooking equipment was used?
What's this unidentifiable flavor that tastes
so incredible? Just last week we spent one
hour talking—on the verge of arguing—about
stir-frying lobster. I cherish these
conversations; there's always another puzzle
waiting to be solved.

— Jeffrey

Photo Descriptions (from left to right): *Photo 1: Jeffrey with parents and Catherine, mid-1980s; Photo 2: Jeffrey traveling in Japan, 1970s; Photo 3: Jeffrey with baby Kevin on shoulders, 1981; Photo 4: Jeffrey's birthday party, early 1980s; Photo 5: Catherine with mother, 2012; Photo 6: Szwina, Jeffrey, and Rita Pang, 2018.*

Dòuchǐ Jī 豆豉雞
Stir-Fried Chicken in Black Bean Sauce

Serves: 4 — **Total Time:** 1 hour, plus 30 minutes refrigeration — **Difficulty:** ●●○○

4 (5- to 7-ounce) bone-in chicken thighs, trimmed

2 tablespoons soy sauce, divided

1 large egg white

1 teaspoon cornstarch

¼ teaspoon table salt

Pinch black pepper

2 tablespoons water

2 teaspoons sugar

2 teaspoons Shaoxing wine

½ teaspoon toasted sesame oil

1 cup peanut or vegetable oil

½ green bell pepper, cut into 1-inch pieces

½ red bell pepper, cut into 1-inch pieces

1 small shallot, sliced thin

4 garlic cloves, minced

1 scallion, cut into 1-inch pieces

1 tablespoon douchi (fermented black beans), rinsed and patted dry

1 teaspoon grated fresh ginger

Storing Fermented Black Beans

After opening a package, tightly cover the black beans and store in the fridge, where they'll keep indefinitely.

Fermented black beans, sold inexpensively in jars and cardboard cylinders, are a top-five staple in Cantonese kitchens. The salty, earthy funk pairs wonderfully with meats and seafood. I view their versatility the way Italians view tomato paste. I love making this colorful dish on a Tuesday night: juicy stir-fried dark meat chicken with that classic, delicious combination of black beans, ginger, and garlic. — Jeffrey

This recipe can also be made using a 12-inch nonstick or cast-iron skillet; increase the peanut oil to 2 cups in step 3.

1   Place 1 chicken thigh skin side down on cutting board. Using sharp paring knife, cut slit along length of thigh bone to expose bone. Using tip of knife, cut meat from bone, being careful not to cut through skin. Slip knife under bone to separate bone from meat. Discard bone and trim any remaining cartilage from thigh, leaving skin intact on meat. Repeat with remaining thighs. Cut chicken into 1-inch pieces.

2   Combine 2 teaspoons soy sauce, egg white, cornstarch, salt, and pepper in large bowl; add chicken and toss to coat. Cover and refrigerate for at least 30 minutes or up to 2 hours. Combine water, sugar, Shaoxing wine, sesame oil, and remaining 4 teaspoons soy sauce in small bowl; set aside.

3   Line large plate with triple layer of paper towels. Heat peanut oil in 14-inch flat-bottomed wok over medium-high heat to 375 degrees. Using spider skimmer or slotted spoon, carefully add chicken in even layer and cook until well browned and cooked through, 8 to 10 minutes, flipping as needed. Transfer chicken to prepared plate to drain.

4   Pour off all but 2 tablespoons oil from wok. Heat oil left in wok over medium-high heat until just smoking. Add bell peppers and shallot and cook, tossing slowly but constantly, until crisp-tender, about 2 minutes. Push vegetables to 1 side of wok and add garlic, scallion, douchi, and ginger to clearing. Cook, mashing garlic mixture into wok until fragrant, about 30 seconds. Stir garlic mixture into vegetables. Add chicken and sauce mixture and cook, tossing constantly, until sauce has thickened, about 30 seconds. Serve.

Hong Kong–Style
Portuguese
Chicken
(page 252)

Hong Kong-Style Portuguese Chicken

Serves: 4 — **Total Time:** 1 hour, plus 30 minutes refrigeration — **Difficulty:** ●●○○

- 3 tablespoons vegetable oil, divided
- 1 tablespoon cornstarch
- 2 teaspoons fresh ginger juice
- 2 teaspoons soy sauce
- 2 teaspoons Shaoxing wine
- 1 teaspoon white pepper
- 1 teaspoon sugar
- 1 teaspoon table salt, divided, plus table salt for boiling potatoes
- ½ teaspoon chicken bouillon powder (optional)
- 2 pounds boneless, skinless chicken thighs, trimmed and cut into 2-inch pieces
- 1 pound small red potatoes, unpeeled, halved
- 1 small onion, halved and sliced thin
- 1 tablespoon Madras curry powder
- 1 (14-ounce) can coconut milk
- ⅔ cup canned condensed cream of chicken soup
- 3 tablespoons evaporated milk
- 1 ounce Parmesan cheese, grated (½ cup)

For Cantonese kids, this is their mac and cheese, foundational to their Hong Kong childhood. It is the dish they beg their parents to cook on a weeknight, and it is the dish they order at a diner as teenagers, so comforting and with so much bang for the buck.

And once they become parents themselves, it is the first dish they learn to cook for *their* kids, so easy to whip up and certain to please.

What we call Portuguese chicken (with apologies to the nation of Portugal) is actually a dish of Macau, through and through. The Portuguese role in this dish was having once colonized Macau, a valuable sliver of land a 45-minute boat ride to the west of Hong Kong. The Portuguese introduced ingredients such as potatoes, coconut milk, and curry powder to the region, culinary trophies of their expanding empire.

The Hong Kong version of Macau's Portuguese chicken is a true fusion dish. Marinated dark meat chicken is cooked in a creamy coconut-curry gravy, topped with Parmesan, and broiled until the top gets charred and crusty. Neither child nor adult can resist sauce and chicken spooned over rice.

After our family immigrated to Canada, so passionate was I about this dish that my mother scheduled Portuguese chicken on our meal planner every Wednesday. Now that I'm a father to a growing boy, I plan on doing the same.   — Kevin

---

Fresh ginger juice is important to the flavor of this dish; do not use store-bought ginger juice. Look for small red potatoes measuring 1 to 2 inches in diameter.

---

1   Combine 1 tablespoon oil, cornstarch, ginger juice, soy sauce, Shaoxing wine, pepper, sugar, ½ teaspoon salt, and bouillon powder, if using, in large bowl; add chicken and toss to coat. Cover and refrigerate for at least 30 minutes or up to 2 hours.

2   Cover potatoes with 1 inch water in large saucepan. Add ½ teaspoon salt and bring to boil over high heat. Reduce heat to simmer and cook until paring knife slips in and out of center of potato with no resistance, 5 to 10 minutes. Drain potatoes; set aside.

3   Heat empty 14-inch flat-bottomed wok over high heat until just beginning to smoke. Reduce heat to medium, drizzle remaining 2 tablespoons oil around perimeter of wok, and heat until just smoking. Add onion and remaining ½ teaspoon salt and cook, tossing slowly but constantly, until onion begins to soften, about 2 minutes. Add curry powder and cook, stirring constantly, until fragrant, about 1 minute.

4   Add chicken with marinade and cook, tossing slowly but constantly, until beginning to brown, about 5 minutes. Add potatoes, coconut milk, and condensed soup and bring to simmer. Cook, stirring occasionally, until chicken is cooked through and sauce is thickened and begins to coat chicken, 5 to 10 minutes. Off heat, stir in evaporated milk.

5   Adjust oven rack 6 inches from broiler element and heat broiler. Transfer chicken and sauce to 13 by 9-inch broiler-safe baking dish and sprinkle with Parmesan. Broil until Parmesan is spotty brown, 3 to 5 minutes. Serve.

A Few Bullet Points from Kevin

- Sure, you could lovingly simmer a cream sauce with chicken broth, white wine, bay leaves, and cream, toast the spices—all that jazz. Except not one Cantonese parent has time to do this on a Wednesday night. Instead, we've collectively agreed to take a shortcut: condensed cream of chicken soup. It's not cheating if everyone does it.

- Why a splash of evaporated milk to finish? This is a relic of a time decades ago when refrigerators weren't common in Hong Kong. Evaporated milk in cans wasn't perishable, and so the Cantonese used it and grew accustomed to that dairy taste. If you want to finish with half-and-half instead, by all means do so.

- A number of recipes in this cookbook call for fresh ginger juice, including this one. There are a couple reasons we add it to meat marinades. Chinese cooks claim the sharpness of ginger juice neutralizes "bloody" tastes from the raw meat. In addition, ginger juice contains enzymes that act as a meat tenderizer.

Preparing Ginger Juice

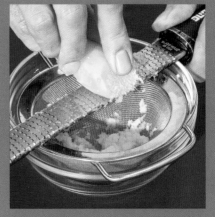

1   Grate peeled fresh ginger directly into fine-mesh strainer set over bowl.

2   Press grated ginger firmly into fine-mesh strainer using back of spoon to extract as much ginger juice as possible. Reserve ginger juice; discard expressed grated ginger.

Xiājiàng Zhájī 蝦醬炸雞
Shrimp-Paste Fried Chicken

Serves: 4 to 6 — **Total Time:** 1 hour, plus 2 hours refrigeration — **Difficulty:** ●●●○

3 tablespoons Chinese shrimp paste

1 large egg white

2 tablespoons Shaoxing wine

1½ tablespoons fresh ginger juice

4 teaspoons oyster sauce

1 tablespoon packed brown sugar

1 teaspoon white pepper

½ teaspoon toasted sesame oil

3 pounds chicken wings, trimmed, cut at joints, wingtips discarded

2 quarts peanut or vegetable oil for frying

½ cup all-purpose flour

½ cup cornstarch

¼ teaspoon baking soda

⅔ cup water

Wing Tip

We prefer to buy whole wings and butcher them ourselves because they tend to be larger than wings that come split. If you can find only split wings, look for larger ones. Twelve whole wings should equal 3 pounds and yield 24 pieces (12 drumettes and 12 flats).

Around the 1970s the first Kentucky Fried Chicken opened in Hong Kong. The lines for the colonel's chicken went out the door, and our family was among those wowed by this American style of fried chicken.

This was one of those dishes our mother tried to reverse engineer. She bought drumsticks and wings and fried them every which way. In the end, little about her recipe resembled KFC's, save the craggy batter. Front and center is Chinese shrimp paste and oyster sauce, which give the wings an unexpected but appealing funkiness. Pro tip: Fry this with an open window or proper ventilation.   — Jeffrey

Be sure to purchase Chinese shrimp paste, such as Koon Chun brand, distinguished by its purplish-gray color, smooth texture, and assertive briny smell. (Don't be put off by the smell; the taste is far milder.) Fresh ginger juice is important to the flavor of this dish; to make it, see page 253. Do not use store-bought ginger juice.

1   Combine shrimp paste, egg white, Shaoxing wine, ginger juice, oyster sauce, sugar, pepper, and sesame oil in large bowl; add chicken and toss to coat. Cover and refrigerate for at least 3 hours or up to 24 hours.

2   Set wire rack in rimmed baking sheet. Set second wire rack in second sheet and line with triple layer of paper towels. Add peanut oil to 14-inch flat-bottomed wok or large Dutch oven until it measures about 1½ inches deep and heat over medium-high heat to 350 degrees.

3   Whisk flour, cornstarch, and baking soda together in second large bowl. Whisk in water until smooth. Add half of wings and gently toss to coat. Using hands, remove wings from batter and place in single layer on unlined rack. Let rest for 1 minute to allow excess batter to drip off. Working quickly, use tongs or cooking chopsticks to carefully lower 1 wing at a time into hot oil, moving pieces around as needed so they fry individually. Fry until wings are light golden brown, 5 to 7 minutes. Adjust burner as needed to maintain oil temperature between 325 and 350 degrees. Using spider skimmer or slotted spoon, transfer wings to towel-lined rack. Return oil to 350 degrees and repeat with remaining chicken.

4   Return oil to 350 degrees over medium-high heat. Working in 1 batch, fry all chicken a second time until deep golden brown and crisp, 5 to 7 minutes; return chicken to rack lined with fresh paper towels and let sit for 5 minutes. Serve.

Chuānwèi Niújiàn 川味牛腱

"Taste of Sichuan" Beef Shank

Serves: 4 to 6 — **Total Time:** 2¾ hours — **Difficulty:** ●●●○

My aunt—my mother's sister—taught me how to make this dish in the 1980s. She lived in Taiwan most of her adult life, so I'm putting quotation marks around "Taste of Sichuan" because of her limited connections to Sichuan. This succulent and homey stew, perfect with steamed rice, is her interpretation of Sichuanese flavors.

Because beef was a luxury in olden days, shank—a relatively inexpensive, tough-as-boots cut—became popular with home cooks. The compromise? It requires a long cook time just to achieve a tender-with-a-chew texture. But in the process the collagen in the beef shank gets released and melts into gelatin, which gives this dish a rich and decadent quality.   — Jeffrey

If beef shank is unavailable, you can substitute beef blade steaks, ¾ to 1 inch thick.

1   Bring beef and 2 quarts cold water to boil in 14-inch flat-bottomed wok or large Dutch oven over high heat. Reduce to simmer and cook for 5 minutes. Drain and rinse beef. Wipe wok clean with paper towels.

2   Heat empty wok over high heat until just beginning to smoke. Reduce heat to medium-high, drizzle 1 tablespoon vegetable oil around perimeter of wok, and heat until just smoking. Add sliced ginger and cook, stirring constantly, until fragrant, about 30 seconds. Add beef, 8 cups water, and star anise and bring to boil. Reduce to simmer and cook until beef is just tender, about 1½ hours. Transfer beef and cooking liquid to bowl. Wipe wok clean with paper towels.

3   Heat remaining 2 tablespoons vegetable oil in now-empty wok over medium heat until shimmering. Add garlic and grated ginger and cook, stirring constantly, until fragrant, about 30 seconds. Add rock sugar and doubanjiang and cook, stirring constantly, until sugar is melted and mixture is amber-colored, about 2 minutes. Add beef with cooking liquid, Shaoxing wine, vinegar, soy sauce, and salt and toss to combine. Bring to simmer, then reduce heat to low, cover, and cook until beef is fully tender, about 30 minutes.

4   Uncover and continue to simmer until sauce is thickened and begins to coat beef, about 5 minutes. Discard star anise. Stir in sesame oil and serve.

3 pounds boneless beef shank, trimmed and cut into 2-inch pieces

3 tablespoons vegetable oil, divided

1 (3-inch) piece ginger, sliced thin, plus 1 tablespoon grated fresh ginger

3 star anise pods

10 garlic cloves, minced

2 tablespoons (1 ounce) crushed rock sugar

1½ tablespoons doubanjiang (broad bean chile paste)

2 tablespoons Shaoxing wine

2 tablespoons Chinese black vinegar

1 tablespoon soy sauce

¼ teaspoon table salt

¼ teaspoon toasted sesame oil

Best Supporting Actor

As with Red-Braised Pork Belly (page 316), we don't recommend eating this all by itself. This filling dish is best with a bowl of steamed rice. Think of the meat, along with a few spoonfuls of sauce, as a garnish for the rice: A little goes a long way.

Hétáo Xiā 合桃蝦

Honey-Walnut Shrimp

Serves: 4 — **Total Time:** 1 hour, plus 45 minutes cooling and refrigerating — **Difficulty:** ●●○○

½ cup walnuts

2 tablespoons water

2 tablespoons sugar

¼ teaspoon plus ⅛ teaspoon table salt, divided

1 pound jumbo shrimp (16 to 20 per pound), peeled and deveined

1 large egg white

1 teaspoon Shaoxing wine

¼ teaspoon white pepper

¼ cup Kewpie mayonnaise

1 tablespoon lemon juice

1 tablespoon sweetened condensed milk

1 teaspoon honey

2 quarts peanut oil for frying

½ cup cornstarch

Kindly Use Kewpie or We'll Alert the Authorities

Kewpie mayonnaise is made from egg yolks and rice vinegar (among other proprietary ingredients) and has a hollandaise quality to it. (It's the same type of mayo used in a spicy tuna maki roll.) Seriously, do not substitute!

At a previous job Catherine's colleagues had heard the two of us were cooking buffs, so once for a company potluck they requested we make honey-walnut shrimp. The only problem was, we never had the dish growing up in Hong Kong. It exists, but it's nowhere as popular as it is in the United States. (Especially at Panda Express!)

At first we were skeptical. Crispy fried shrimp shellacked in mayonnaise? Then we tried it and asked ourselves: "Where has this dish been all our lives?!"

Catherine and I put on our culinary detective hats. After many tries we arrived at this, our interpretation of the American Chinese favorite. Our secret ingredients are Kewpie, the much-loved Japanese mayonnaise, as well as condensed milk, which adds a distinct sweetness to the sauce. You now have in your hands the very recipe that's made Catherine office-potluck-famous.   — Jeffrey

Store-bought candied walnuts can be substituted for homemade. Because we're heating oil to 425 degrees, it is important to use peanut oil for frying.

1   Line rimmed baking sheet with parchment paper. Toast nuts in 8- or 10-inch nonstick skillet over medium heat until fragrant and spotty brown, about 3 minutes. Quickly add water, sugar, and ⅛ teaspoon salt and stir with rubber spatula to coat nuts evenly. Cook, stirring often, until sugar mixture caramelizes and nuts begin to clump together, 2 to 3 minutes. Transfer nuts to prepared sheet and spread in even layer. Let cool completely, about 30 minutes, then break nuts apart with hands; set aside. (Candied walnuts can be stored in airtight container for up to 1 week.)

2   Pat shrimp dry with paper towels. Whisk egg white, Shaoxing wine, pepper, and remaining ¼ teaspoon salt together in large bowl; add shrimp and toss to coat. Refrigerate for 15 minutes. Combine mayonnaise, lemon juice, condensed milk, and honey in separate large bowl; set aside.

3   Set wire rack in rimmed baking sheet and line with triple layer of paper towels. Add oil to 14-inch flat-bottomed wok or large Dutch oven until it measures about 1½ inches deep and heat over medium-high heat to 425 degrees.

4   Add cornstarch to medium bowl. Working with 1 shrimp at a time, dredge in cornstarch, pressing firmly to adhere, then shake off excess and transfer to large plate. Working quickly, use tongs or cooking chopsticks to pick up half of shrimp by tails and carefully transfer to hot oil, moving pieces around as needed so they fry individually. Fry shrimp until light golden brown and crisp, about 4 minutes.

Adjust burner, if necessary, to maintain oil temperature between 400 and 425 degrees. Using spider skimmer or slotted spoon, transfer shrimp to prepared rack. Return oil to 425 degrees and repeat with remaining shrimp.

5   Add shrimp and candied walnuts to bowl with mayonnaise mixture and gently toss to coat. Serve.

Ròusuì Zhēngshuǐdàn 肉碎蒸水蛋
Steamed Egg Custard with Ground Pork

Serves: 2 — **Total Time:** 45 minutes — **Difficulty:** ●●○○

- 3 ounces ground pork
- 2 teaspoons soy sauce, divided
- 2 teaspoons vegetable oil, divided
- ½ teaspoon cornstarch
- ⅛ teaspoon white pepper
- 1 teaspoon sugar
- 1 teaspoon toasted sesame oil
- 7 ounces lightly beaten egg (about 4 eggs)
- ½ teaspoon table salt
- ½ scallion, sliced thin

The Key to Silky Eggs

Ten minutes might seem like a long time for the custard to set on the wire rack. But letting it sit covered allows the carryover heat to work its gentle magic. The result? A silky-smooth interior and a top surface that doesn't collapse.

Several chapters back, I mentioned how my father in his youth would make monthly 14-hour trips on foot to attend school, sustained during those long walks by his favorite snack: hard-boiled eggs with a pinch of salt.

He passed on his fondness for eggs to my generation. We always kept three types of eggs around: fresh eggs, salted eggs, and century eggs. Not a day would go by without an egg making its way into a family meal.

This dish, one of my mother's signatures, is an example of extracting a lot out of very little. It's amazing that four eggs and some scant pork can create something so elegant and refined. The savory egg custard is so silky, chawanmushi-like in its velvetiness, it could be served at a Michelin-starred restaurant. But it's not. Maybe my mom was a more sophisticated cook than she let on.   — Jeffrey

---

For an accurate measurement of eggs, lightly beat four eggs, then measure out the desired amount. Use an 8-inch shallow serving bowl or 9-inch pie plate for steaming to ensure even cooking. Depending on the thickness of your bowl, you may need to increase the steaming time in step 3.

---

1 Combine ground pork, 1 teaspoon soy sauce, 1 teaspoon vegetable oil, cornstarch, and pepper in bowl; set aside. Whisk 1 tablespoon water, remaining 1 teaspoon soy sauce, sugar, and sesame oil together in small bowl; set aside.

2 Bring 4 cups water to boil in 14-inch flat-bottomed wok. Place 8-inch shallow serving bowl in 10-inch bamboo steamer basket. Reduce heat to maintain simmer, set steamer basket in wok, and cover with steamer lid. Heat until bowl is warmed through, 1 minute. Meanwhile, whisk egg and salt together in large bowl. While whisking constantly, slowly drizzle 1 cup hot (140-degree) water into eggs until thoroughly combined.

3 Carefully remove bowl from steamer basket. Pour egg mixture through fine-mesh strainer into bowl. Cover bowl tightly with plastic wrap, return to steamer basket, and cover. Steam custard until it registers 165 degrees (custard will be just set in center), 12 to 16 minutes, adjusting heat as needed to maintain simmer. Carefully transfer steamer basket with bowl to wire rack. Let sit, covered, until custard is fully set, about 10 minutes. Discard water and wipe wok dry.

4 Heat now-empty wok over high heat until just beginning to smoke. Reduce heat to medium, drizzle remaining 1 teaspoon vegetable oil around perimeter of wok, and heat until just smoking. Add pork mixture and cook, breaking up meat with wooden spoon, until just beginning to brown, about 3 minutes. Top custard with pork mixture and sprinkle with scallion. Drizzle with sauce and serve.

Hakka Stuffed Tofu
with Egg Dumplings
(page 264)

Hakka Stuffed Tofu with Egg Dumplings

Serves: 4 to 6 — **Total Time:** 2 hours, plus 1 hour refrigeration — **Difficulty:** ●●●○

1 (3-inch) piece ginger, halved lengthwise

4 scallions (2 cut into 2-inch pieces, 2 sliced thin)

1⅓ cups water, divided

4 teaspoons plus ¼ teaspoon cornstarch, divided

1 tablespoon Shaoxing wine

1½ teaspoons soy sauce

1 teaspoon oyster sauce

1 teaspoon toasted sesame oil

¼ teaspoon white pepper

½ teaspoon sugar

8 ounces ground pork

1 (14-ounce) block firm tofu

3 large eggs

¾ teaspoon table salt, divided

3 tablespoons vegetable oil, divided

½ head napa cabbage (1 pound), cored and cut into 2-inch pieces

4 cups chicken broth

I am of Hakka ancestry. Our people migrated from northern China centuries ago, eventually settling along the South China Sea by present-day Hong Kong. Not long ago calling someone Hakka was pejorative, like calling that person a gypsy. The words for Hakka 客家 mean "guest family," implying nomads.

Wheat flour was abundant in the north, and dumplings and breads were Hakka daily staples. In the south they found the main crops to be rice and soybeans. But many continued to retain a fondness for the dumplings enjoyed by generations of their ancestors. So the Hakka people improvised: They took cubes of tofu, stuffed them with meat filling, and simmered them in broth with napa cabbage. These "dumplings" instantly reminded them of where they came from.

The egg dumplings in this recipe aren't Hakka but a reflection of Catherine's Shanghai heritage, so this dish is a true Pang family mash-up. The eggs are stuffed with the same meat filling and are pan-fried and shaped like bars of gold bullion. The Chinese like food with symbolism, so maybe eating this will bring good fortune—no promises, though you do have our gratitude for trying our cherished family special dish. — Jeffrey

1 Crush ginger and scallion pieces with meat pounder or back of knife. Transfer ginger and scallion pieces to bowl with ⅓ cup water and let sit until flavors meld and water turns green, about 20 minutes. Strain mixture through fine-mesh strainer into medium bowl, pressing on solids to extract as much liquid as possible; discard solids.

2 Whisk 1 tablespoon cornstarch, Shaoxing wine, soy sauce, oyster sauce, sesame oil, pepper, and sugar into ginger-scallion water. Add pork and stir to combine. Cover and refrigerate for at least 1 hour or up to 3 hours.

3 Halve tofu lengthwise, then cut crosswise into 1-inch-thick slabs. Spread tofu on paper towel–lined rimmed baking sheet and let drain for 20 minutes. Gently pat tofu dry with paper towels. Using small spoon or melon baller, scoop out divot 1 inch wide by ¾ inch deep in center of each tofu piece, making sure to leave edges and bottom of tofu intact. Sprinkle divots with 1 teaspoon cornstarch, then lightly pack each divot with 1 tablespoon pork filling. (You will have extra filling.) Transfer to plate and refrigerate until ready to use.

4   Lightly beat eggs, ¼ teaspoon salt, and remaining ¼ teaspoon cornstarch together. Stir in remaining pork filling.

5   Heat 1 tablespoon vegetable oil in 12-inch nonstick skillet over medium heat until shimmering. Spoon 8 heaping 1-tablespoon portions of egg mixture into skillet, spaced evenly apart. Use rubber spatula to gently shape each portion of egg mixture into even, round layer. Let omelets cook, undisturbed, until bottoms are just set but tops are still slightly wet, about 30 seconds. Fold omelets in half and continue to cook until bottoms are spotty brown, about 1 minute; transfer to plate. Repeat with 1 tablespoon vegetable oil and remaining egg mixture; transfer to plate.

6   Heat remaining 1 tablespoon vegetable oil in Dutch oven over medium-high heat until shimmering. Add cabbage and cook, stirring occasionally, until beginning to soften, 5 to 7 minutes. Add broth, remaining 1 cup water, and remaining ½ teaspoon salt. Spread cabbage into even layer. Nestle tofu pieces pork filling side up in cabbage, then arrange omelets around tofu. Bring mixture to boil, then reduce heat to medium-low, cover, and simmer until pork filling in tofu is cooked through, about 15 minutes. Sprinkle with sliced scallions. Serve.

A Couple Tips from Jeffrey

- It's been mentioned before, but it bears repeating: Avoid using European-style chicken broths that are flavored with carrot, celery, and onion. Chinese-style broths have a more pronounced chicken flavor and taste less sweet. If you're not using homemade broth (page 25), we like Swanson Chicken Stock.

- While this dish is flavorful enough as is, we love serving hoisin sauce and Sriracha as accompaniments. Just a few dabs each on the stuffed tofu will do.

Preparing Hakka Stuffed Tofu

1   Cut out divot 1 inch wide by ¾ inch deep in center of tofu piece.

2   Sprinkle divots with cornstarch.

3   Lightly pack each piece of tofu with pork filling.

Gǎngshì Jú Zhūpá Fàn 港式焗豬扒飯
Hong Kong-Style Baked Pork Chop Rice

Serves: 4 — **Total Time:** 1½ hours, plus 1 hour refrigeration — **Difficulty:** ●●●○

Catherine — When I was a teenager, I had cousins whose parents belonged to a country club in Hong Kong. Sometimes I was lucky enough to tag along, and dining at the members-only restaurant made me feel so fancy. On the menu was baked pork chop rice. To me it was the epitome of high-class. The dish was a Cantonese take on Western food—fried pork chop, tomato sauce, sizzling cheese—and eating it always transported me to a different world.

Jeffrey — Like my wife, every time I ate this dish it made me feel so refined. I didn't encounter much cheese growing up, so watching the platter topped with bubbling Parmesan arrive at the table was a thrill. Add to that a sweet, sour, crispy bone-in pork chop with fluffy fried rice underneath? It's irresistible.

Fresh ginger juice is important to the flavor of this dish; to make it see page 253. Do not use store-bought ginger juice. While we prefer jasmine rice, any medium- or long-grain rice will work. Day-old rice works best; in a pinch you can use our Faux Leftover Rice (page 131).

1   Whisk Maggi seasoning, cornstarch, Worcestershire, Shaoxing wine, ginger juice, garlic, ½ teaspoon salt, sugar, and ¼ teaspoon pepper together in large bowl.

2   Place 1 chop on cutting board, cover with sheet of plastic wrap, and pound to ¼-inch thickness, being careful to avoid bone. Repeat with remaining chops. Add chops to bowl with marinade and toss to coat. Cover and refrigerate for at least 1 hour or up to 4 hours.

3   Beat 1 egg in shallow dish. Spread flour in second shallow dish. Working with 1 chop at a time, remove from marinade (do not pat dry) and dip into egg, turning to coat well and allowing excess egg to drip back into dish. Coat evenly on all sides with flour, pressing on chop to adhere; transfer to rimmed baking sheet.

- 2 tablespoons Maggi liquid seasoning
- 4 teaspoons cornstarch
- 1 tablespoon Worcestershire sauce
- 2 teaspoons Shaoxing wine
- 2 teaspoons fresh ginger juice
- 3 garlic cloves, minced
- 1 teaspoon table salt, divided
- ½ teaspoon sugar
- ¼ teaspoon plus ⅛ teaspoon black pepper, divided
- 4 (8- to 10-ounce) bone-in pork rib chops, ½ to ¾ inch thick
- 3 large eggs, divided
- 1 cup all-purpose flour
- 3 cups peanut or vegetable oil for frying
- 2 scallions, sliced thin
- 4 cups cooked jasmine rice, room temperature, large clumps broken up with fingers
- 1 small onion, halved and sliced thin
- 3 ounces cherry tomatoes, halved
- ½ cup frozen peas, carrots, and sweet corn medley, thawed
- 1 (10.75-ounce) can condensed tomato soup
- 1½ ounces Parmesan cheese, grated (¾ cup)

recipe continues on next page

4 Set wire rack in second rimmed baking sheet and line with triple layer of paper towels. Add oil to large Dutch oven until it measures about ½ inch deep and heat over medium-high heat to 350 degrees. Carefully lower 1 chop into oil and fry until golden brown and registers 135 to 140 degrees, 2 to 3 minutes per side. Adjust burner as needed to maintain oil temperature between 325 and 350 degrees. Transfer chop to prepared rack. Return oil to 350 degrees and repeat with remaining chops. Reserve 2 tablespoons frying oil; discard remaining oil or save for another use.

5 Beat remaining 2 eggs in bowl until well combined. Heat empty 14-inch flat-bottomed wok over high heat until just beginning to smoke. Reduce heat to medium, drizzle 2 teaspoons reserved oil around perimeter of wok, and heat until just smoking. Add eggs and cook, stirring frequently, until very little liquid egg remains, 30 to 60 seconds; transfer to plate.

6 Add 1 teaspoon reserved oil and scallions to now-empty wok and cook over medium heat, stirring constantly, until fragrant, about 30 seconds. Sprinkle rice over scallions and stir until combined. Spread into even layer. Sprinkle remaining ½ teaspoon salt evenly over rice mixture. Continue to cook, stirring frequently and pressing on rice with spatula to break up clumps, until grains are separate and heated through, 2 to 5 minutes. Add cooked eggs and cook, stirring frequently and using edge of spatula to break eggs into small pieces, until warmed through, about 2 minutes. Transfer fried-rice mixture to 13 by 9-inch broiler-safe baking dish and nestle fried pork chops into fried-rice mixture.

7 Add remaining 1 tablespoon reserved oil and onion to now-empty wok and cook over medium-high heat, tossing slowly but constantly, until onion begins to soften, about 2 minutes. Stir in tomatoes and vegetable medley and toss to combine. Add condensed soup and remaining ⅛ teaspoon pepper and bring to simmer, stirring occasionally, until sauce is slightly thickened, about 2 minutes.

8 Adjust oven rack 6 inches from broiler element and heat broiler. Pour sauce over pork chops and rice mixture. Sprinkle Parmesan evenly over sauce. Transfer dish to oven and broil until cheese is spotty brown, 3 to 5 minutes. Serve.

The Incorruptible Beauty of Maggi Seasoning

Maggi seasoning, globally recognizable by its yellow-and-red-labeled bottles, might as well be secretary-general of the United Nations: It's the great unifier of cuisines, from Polish and Filipino to Mexican and Chinese. Technically a fermented wheat protein with glutamic acids, the condiment might be more appealingly described as a second cousin to soy sauce. A few dashes give soups and stews a meaty backbone. We Cantonese are less subtle about our Maggi love—we'll slosh it aggressively over noodles, fried rice, grilled meats—anything and everything.

Zhēnjiāng Tángcù Páigǔ 鎮江糖醋排骨
Sticky Spareribs with Chinkiang Vinegar

Serves: 4 — **Total Time:** 1 hour — **Difficulty:** ●●○○

The food of Shanghai generally tends to be sweeter than in other parts of China. Shanghai is where Catherine's family comes from, and her great-grandmother used to make these delectably sweet and sour pork ribs for her. The great-grandmother moved to New York City when Catherine was 11, however, and that was seemingly that.

Decades later, in the 1990s, Catherine visited her in New York. The conversation naturally veered toward cooking, and Catherine asked about making those ribs she so fondly remembered. Sadly, her great-grandmother had forgotten how. Catherine and I eventually worked out the recipe, and it's become a favorite. But that's not what's important. The lesson is that if there's someone you care about, don't leave anything—whether a recipe or how you truly feel—unsaid.　— Jeffrey

These ribs aren't tender to the bone; they have a purposeful chew. Eating them involves a bit of mouth maneuvering to remove the bones and cartilage. But that's the joy of the dish. Pork riblets are spareribs cut flanken-style, across the bone, into 1- to 2-inch-wide strips. They are sold in Asian markets and elsewhere; check with your butcher. Chinkiang (Chinese black) vinegar and rock sugar give the ribs a complex, subtly earthy sweet and sour flavor.

1½ pounds pork riblets, trimmed, cut between bones into individual ribs

1 tablespoon vegetable oil

2 tablespoons (1 ounce) crushed rock sugar

1 (2-inch) piece ginger, sliced into thin rounds

½ cup Chinese black vinegar

⅓ cup Shaoxing wine

2 teaspoons dark soy sauce

1½ teaspoons chicken bouillon powder (optional)

1½ teaspoons toasted sesame oil

½ teaspoon white pepper

1 teaspoon sesame seeds, toasted

1 Bring ribs and 2 quarts cold water to boil in 14-inch flat-bottomed wok or large Dutch oven over high heat. Reduce heat to low and simmer gently for 5 minutes. Drain ribs and rinse well, then pat meat dry with paper towels.

2 Heat empty wok over high heat until just smoking. Reduce heat to medium-high, drizzle vegetable oil around perimeter of wok, and heat until just smoking. Add rock sugar and cook, stirring constantly, until sugar has melted and is amber-colored, about 1 minute. Add ginger and cook, stirring constantly, until fragrant, 15 to 30 seconds. Stir in ribs, ½ cup water, vinegar, Shaoxing wine, dark soy sauce, and bouillon powder, if using, and bring to boil. Reduce heat to medium-low, cover, and simmer until ribs are just tender but still have slight chew, 15 to 20 minutes.

3 Uncover, increase heat to high, and vigorously simmer, stirring frequently, until sauce is thickened and coats pork, 5 to 7 minutes. Stir in sesame oil and pepper. Sprinkle with sesame seeds. Serve.

A Few Drops for Brightness

In this recipe, black vinegar gets simmered until it develops a malty, syrupy sweetness. But I love the acidity of black vinegar before it gets reduced, so I'll often add a few drops over the ribs to give the finished dish brightness.

Shēngchǎo Nuòmǐfàn 生炒糯米飯
Stir-Fried Sticky Rice

Serves: 4 to 6 — **Total Time:** 30 minutes, plus 45 minutes soaking — **Difficulty:** ●●○○

3 cups glutinous short-grain rice, rinsed

1½ ounces dried shiitake mushrooms, rinsed

2 tablespoons dried shrimp

1 tablespoon Shaoxing wine

1 tablespoon soy sauce

1½ teaspoons dark soy sauce

1 teaspoon sugar

1 teaspoon toasted sesame oil

½ teaspoon table salt

Pinch white pepper

2 large eggs

¼ cup vegetable oil, divided

6 ounces lap cheong (Chinese sausage), cut into ½-inch pieces

3 ounces lap yuk (Chinese cured pork belly), cut into ½-inch pieces

2 scallions, white and green parts separated and sliced thin

1 tablespoon grated fresh ginger

The Weakest Link

For easier cutting of the lap cheong and lap yuk, microwave on a plate covered with a single layer of wet paper towels until warmed through and just softened, about 30 seconds. Let cool slightly before cutting.

If ever there was a Cantonese winter dish, stir-fried sticky rice is it. After all, Hong Kong temperatures in December drop down to 60 degrees Fahrenheit. Brrrrrr!

Joking aside, this dish is the product of a time when few households owned refrigerators. We stored cured sausage and pork belly by hanging them from a kitchen ceiling hook. It's amazing these pantry staples could create something so warming.

How does stir-fried sticky rice differ from your standard fried rice? The heavier grains of glutinous rice make the dish heartier and more filling, like making spaghetti carbonara with lasagna sheets—different, but no less satisfying.   — Jeffrey

When shopping, look for short-grain rice labeled "glutinous" or "sweet"; do not substitute other varieties. If lap yuk is unavailable, increase the lap cheong to 9 ounces.

1   Soak rice in 6 cups warm water (110 degrees) for 45 minutes. Rinse and drain well; set aside.

2   Microwave 1 cup water and mushrooms in covered bowl until steaming, about 1 minute. Let sit until softened, about 5 minutes. Lift mushrooms from bowl with fork and discard liquid. Squeeze mushrooms dry, stem, and chop. Microwave 1 cup water and dried shrimp in separate covered bowl until steaming, about 1 minute. Let sit until softened, about 5 minutes. Lift shrimp from bowl with fork and discard liquid. Set mushrooms and shrimp aside.

3   Whisk Shaoxing wine, soy sauce, dark soy sauce, sugar, sesame oil, salt, and pepper together in bowl; set aside.

4   Beat eggs in separate bowl until well combined. Heat empty 14-inch flat-bottomed wok over high heat until just beginning to smoke. Drizzle 1 tablespoon vegetable oil around perimeter of wok and heat until just smoking. Working quickly, add eggs and gently tilt wok and use rubber spatula to shape eggs into even, thin layer. Let cook, undisturbed, until bottom is just set but top is still slightly wet, about 30 seconds. Fold omelet in half to create half-moon shape. Holding plate in 1 hand, tilt wok to slide omelet onto plate. Let sit until cool enough to handle, then slice into ¼-inch-thick ribbons; set aside.

5 Heat now-empty wok over high heat until just beginning to smoke. Drizzle 1 tablespoon vegetable oil around perimeter of wok and heat until just smoking. Add lap cheong and lap yuk and cook, tossing constantly, until fat begins to render, about 1 minute. Add mushrooms, shrimp, scallion whites, ginger, and sauce and cook, tossing constantly, until combined, about 1 minute; transfer to bowl.

6 Heat now-empty wok over high heat until just beginning to smoke. Drizzle remaining 2 tablespoons vegetable oil around perimeter of wok and heat until just smoking. Add rice and cook, tossing slowly but constantly until coated. Stir in ½ cup water and reduce heat to medium. Cover and cook until water is absorbed, about 2 minutes. Stir in additional ½ cup water and continue to cook, covered, until water is absorbed, about 2 minutes. Repeat adding ½ cup water and cooking twice more until rice is fully cooked (2 cups water in total).

7 Stir in sausage and mushroom mixture and cook until heated through, about 1 minute. Season with salt to taste. Sprinkle with scallion greens and top with egg before serving.

Radish Cake
(page 276)

Radish Cake

Serves: 8 to 10 — **Total Time:** 2½ hours, plus 4 hours cooling — **Difficulty:** ●●●●

- ¼ ounce dried shiitake mushrooms, rinsed
- 2 ounces (½ cup) dried shrimp
- ¼ ounce dried scallops (optional)
- 2½ pounds Chinese radishes or daikon, peeled
- 1¾ cups (8 ounces) rice flour
- 1½ cups chicken broth
- ¾ cup (3 ounces) cornstarch
- 6 tablespoons vegetable oil, divided
- 3 ounces lap cheong (Chinese sausage), cut into ¼-inch pieces
- 3 ounces lap yuk (Chinese cured pork belly), cut into ¼-inch pieces
- 1 shallot, chopped
- 1 scallion, sliced thin
- 4 teaspoons sugar, divided
- 1½ teaspoons soy sauce
- 1 teaspoon Shaoxing wine
- 1 (1-inch) piece ginger, sliced thin
- ½ teaspoon table salt

Binging with Radish

Radish cake isn't just served for Chinese New Year. Any dim sum restaurant worth its salt will offer it (some places call it turnip cake). Add a dab of soy sauce and Sriracha? Perfect.

In the days leading up to Chinese New Year, my mother always took me to the wet market to buy ingredients for radish cake. She'd call every worker there "Tall Man," as the vendors appeared extra tall because they wore wooden sandals to avoid standing on wet ground. Making radish cake became an event for our family. We'd steam the cake, and then, on New Year's Day, we'd slice and pan-fry pieces until golden. The result was extraordinary: squishy, crispy squares, studded with savory bits of preserved meats. Making radish cake is an undertaking, but we consider it a celebration meal. It's the all-time favorite of my daughter, Karen. — Jeffrey

A food processor works well for shredding the radishes. If lap yuk is unavailable, use 6 ounces of lap cheong. Serve with soy sauce and chili sauce.

1 Microwave 1 cup water and mushrooms in covered bowl until steaming, about 1 minute. Let sit until softened, about 5 minutes. Lift mushrooms from bowl with fork and discard liquid. Squeeze mushrooms dry, stem, and cut into ¼-inch pieces. Microwave 1½ cups water, dried shrimp, and dried scallops, if using, in separate covered bowl until steaming, about 1 minute. Let sit until softened, about 5 minutes. Lift shrimp and scallops from bowl with fork and discard liquid. Chop shrimp and shred scallops into ¼-inch pieces. Set mushrooms, shrimp, and scallops aside.

2 Fit food processor with shredding disk. Halve or quarter radishes as needed to fit through processor feed tube, then process radishes. Drain radishes in fine-mesh strainer set over large bowl, gently pressing on radishes to extract juice. Measure out and reserve 1 cup juice; discard any remaining juice. (If necessary, add water to equal 1 cup.) Whisk rice flour, chicken broth, and cornstarch in large bowl until smooth; set aside.

3 Line 8-inch round baking pan with parchment paper and lightly spray with vegetable oil spray. Heat empty 14-inch flat-bottomed wok over high heat until just beginning to smoke. Reduce heat to medium-high, drizzle 1 tablespoon oil around perimeter of wok, and heat until just smoking. Add lap cheong and lap yuk and cook, stirring constantly, until lightly browned and fat is slightly rendered, about 2 minutes. Push meat to 1 side of wok, add shallot to clearing, and cook, stirring frequently, until softened, about 1 minute. Stir shallot into meat. Add scallion, 1 teaspoon sugar, soy sauce, Shaoxing wine, and reserved mushrooms, shrimp, and scallops and cook, stirring constantly, until fragrant and heated through, about 1 minute. Transfer to separate bowl.

4   Heat 1 tablespoon oil in now-empty wok over medium heat until shimmering. Add ginger and cook, stirring constantly, until fragrant, about 30 seconds. Add salt, radishes, reserved radish juice, and remaining 1 tablespoon sugar and bring to simmer. Gently simmer, adjusting heat as needed, until radishes are softened and turning translucent, about 15 minutes, stirring occasionally. Remove ginger.

5   Reduce heat to low. Whisk rice flour mixture to recombine and add to wok. Stir until mixture is well combined and thickens to texture of mashed potatoes. Add lap cheong mixture and stir until combined. Transfer radish mixture to prepared pan. Wipe wok clean with paper towels.

6   Bring 4 cups water to boil in now-empty wok. Transfer filled pan to 10-inch bamboo steamer basket and cover. Reduce heat to maintain vigorous simmer and set steamer in wok. Steam until cake is firm to touch and toothpick inserted into center of cake comes out clean, 50 to 60 minutes. Add more water to bottom of wok, 1 cup at a time, as needed to maintain simmering water.

7   Carefully transfer pan to wire rack and let cool for 10 minutes. Loosen cake from sides of pan with small knife, then invert onto wire rack and peel off parchment. Let cool completely, about 4 hours. (Radish cake can be refrigerated for up to 24 hours.)

8   Trim edges from cooled cake to form 6-inch square. Slice trimmed edges about ½ inch thick and set aside. Halve square, then slice each half crosswise to make 24 slices total, each slice about ½ inch thick. Heat 1 tablespoon oil in 12-inch nonstick skillet over medium-high heat until shimmering. Place 8 slices in skillet and cook until golden brown on both sides, 3 to 5 minutes per side, using 2 spatulas to gently flip slices; transfer to paper towel–lined baking sheet. Repeat with 2 tablespoons oil and remaining 16 slices in 2 batches. Repeat with remaining 1 tablespoon oil and reserved trimmed edges. Serve.

Frying Radish Cake

1   Trim edges of cake to form 6-inch square, halve square, then cut crosswise into 24 slices, each about ½ inch thick.

2   Cook slices until golden brown, 3 to 5 minutes per side, using 2 spatulas to gently flip slices.

DEEP FRIED AND DELICIOUS

Sponsored content: This chapter of *A Very Chinese Cookbook* is brought to you by Hot Oil™! It turns meats extra-crispy! Adds golden browning for exceptional flavor! Is beloved by diners age 4 to 94! Makes a loud and satisfying crackle between your teeth and turns frowns upside down! Hey, now, is that your cardiologist wagging a finger? Tell Dr. Killjoy to take that finger, add two more, and pick up a crunchy and succulent deep-fried pork chop instead! Hot Oil™: If it ain't cooked in it, it ain't deep-fried and delicious.

Deep Frying 101

Should You Fry in a Wok or Dutch Oven?
Both woks and Dutch ovens are excellent vessels for deep frying. A large cast-iron Dutch oven (6 to 7 quarts) heats slowly but retains heat well during frying. The straight sides contain splattering and accommodate a clip-on temperature probe. A carbon-steel wok heats more quickly (don't walk away while frying!). Its sloped shape means it requires less oil, and its broad sides contain splatters and afford great visibility and access to the pan.

Best of Both Pans
When a recipe ends with frying, as with American-Style Egg Rolls or Sesame Balls, both woks and Dutch ovens have their appeal. When you're frying a food first and then later stir-frying it to coat with a sauce or seasoning (true for several recipes in this chapter), frying in your Dutch oven and then transferring the food over to the wok to stir-fry can be more efficient. That way you don't have to wait for the pot of oil to cool before proceeding, or contend with pouring out a lot of hot oil. (This matters especially when frying in more than 2 cups of oil.)

Choose the Right Oil
Several recipes in this book require frying at temperatures higher than you may be accustomed to. It's important to use an oil with a high smoke point (the point at which the oil begins to break down). Peanut oil, with a high smoke point (around 450 degrees), is our preferred choice when frying at temperatures above 400 degrees. Vegetable oil is another good frying oil when shallow frying and deep frying at temperatures up to 400 degrees.

Pick the Right Tool
Gently use a spider skimmer or slotted spoon when adding smaller foods to, or removing them from, the frying oil—any excess oil will drain through their holes.

Avoid Greasiness
Food fried at the right temperature will naturally absorb less oil, so maintaining proper temperature is key. In addition, we often transfer fried food to a paper towel–lined wire rack to drain away excess oil.

Season Quickly
Season food with salt immediately after frying. Salt sticks better to hot foods.

Protect Yourself and Avoid Distractions
Keep in mind that frying usually produces a small amount of splatter; always wear an apron to protect against any oil that escapes from the pot. Minimize distractions, and keep small children and pets away from the frying. Avoid true crime podcasts while deep frying. Always follow the temperature cues in the recipe. Oil that starts to lightly smoke is a sign it's overheated—turn off the heat until the oil cools to the correct temperature.

Reusing and Disposing of Oil
Never pour frying oil down the drain! After frying, cover the pan and let the oil cool completely. Once the oil is cool, you can use a liquid measuring cup and funnel to pour it into its original container and throw it away. But unless the oil overheated and started to smoke, or was used to fry fish, it's fine to reuse it up to three times once you strain it. To strain oil, line a fine-mesh strainer with a coffee filter and place it over a large container. Pour the oil through the filter and allow it to drain (this may require several additions of oil). Discard any solids.

Get Rid of Post-Fry Funky Smell
Let a saucepan of equal parts vinegar and water boil for 10 minutes. This is a quick way to get rid of any lingering frying smell (also works for fishy smells).

Four Steps to Deep-Fry Like a Winner

1 Get an Even Fried Coating: Giving small pieces of batter-dipped food a quick rest on a wire rack set in a rimmed baking sheet allows excess batter to fall away, helping to keep the pieces from sticking together during frying.

2 Avoid Splashing: Carefully add smaller pieces of food using a spider skimmer or slotted spoon. To keep larger items from sticking together, use tongs or cooking chopsticks to hold each piece in the oil for a few seconds to let the coating set before releasing. When frying uncoated foods, pat them dry before adding to the oil to minimize splatter.

3 Fry in Small Batches: Frying food in small batches keeps the oil temperature from dropping excessively, ensuring the coating doesn't absorb too much oil and allowing the exterior to remain light and crispy. Small batches also mean that pieces are less likely to stick to each other. Even so, a gentle stir can help to separate foods as they cook in the oil. Cooking chopsticks or tongs are great tools for this.

4 Monitor the Heat: Proper oil temperature is critical for producing fried food that's light, crisp, and not greasy. Maintain the oil temperature specified in the recipe by adjusting your burner as needed. Use an instant-read thermometer with either a wok or Dutch oven, or attach a clip-on thermometer to the side of a Dutch oven (see page 38 for more information).

Dry Chili Chicken

Serves: 4 to 6 — **Total Time:** 1½ hours, plus 30 minutes resting — **Difficulty:** ●●○○

⅔ cup cornstarch

⅓ cup all-purpose flour

½ teaspoon baking powder

¾ cup water

1½ pounds boneless, skinless chicken thighs, trimmed and cut into 1-inch pieces

1 tablespoon soy sauce

1 tablespoon Shaoxing wine

2 quarts peanut or vegetable oil for frying

¼ cup Sichuan chili flakes

1½ teaspoons sugar

½ teaspoon table salt

¼ teaspoon monosodium glutamate (optional)

6 garlic cloves, minced

4 scallions, sliced thin

1 (1-inch) piece ginger, peeled and cut into thin matchsticks (1 tablespoon)

4 ounces (3 cups) small dried Sichuan chiles

2 tablespoons Sichuan peppercorns

½ cup chopped fresh cilantro

1 teaspoon sesame seeds, toasted

Three Cups of Chiles? Really?

Their purpose in this recipe is mainly for dramatic presentation. If you cut down on the quantity, we won't make a fuss.

Ever play the children's game Let's Go Fishin', the one where fish spin around the motorized lake and you have to catch them with a magnetic rod? Dry chili chicken (or Chongqing chicken, named for the Sichuan city) requires a similar level of hand-eye coordination. The game is this: There's a sea of peppers, more for decorative effect than for consumption. Nestled throughout are nuggets of batter-fried chicken thighs, deeply marinated and dusted with tingly spices. To win, you must fish out the crisp chicken with chopsticks before everyone else at your table does.

This recipe, developed by test cook David Yu, is honest-to-goodness one of the tastiest things you can make out of this book. Do it, friends.   — Kevin

1   Whisk cornstarch, flour, and baking powder together in bowl. Whisk in water until smooth, then refrigerate for 30 minutes. Meanwhile, toss chicken, soy sauce, and Shaoxing wine in second bowl; cover and refrigerate for 30 minutes.

2   Set wire rack in rimmed baking sheet. Set second wire rack in second sheet and line with triple layer of paper towels. Add oil to large Dutch oven until it measures about 1½ inches deep and heat over medium-high heat to 400 degrees.

3   Whisk batter to recombine. Add chicken and toss to coat. Using hands, remove half of chicken from batter and place in single layer on unlined rack. Let rest for 1 minute to allow excess batter to drip off. Working quickly, use spider skimmer or slotted spoon to lower chicken pieces into hot oil. Using tongs or cooking chopsticks, separate pieces so they fry individually. Fry chicken until light golden brown, about 2 minutes. Adjust burner, if necessary, to maintain oil temperature between 375 and 400 degrees. Using spider skimmer, transfer chicken to towel-lined rack. Return oil to 400 degrees and repeat with remaining chicken; transfer to rack.

4   Return oil to 400 degrees over medium-high heat. Working in 2 batches, fry chicken a second time until deep golden brown and crisp, 2 to 4 minutes; return chicken to rack lined with fresh paper towels.

5   Whisk chili flakes, sugar, salt, and monosodium glutamate, if using, together in small bowl. Measure out and reserve ¼ cup frying oil; discard remaining oil or save for another use.

6 Heat empty 14-inch flat-bottomed wok over medium-high heat until just beginning to smoke. Reduce heat to medium-low, drizzle reserved oil around perimeter of wok and heat until just smoking. Add garlic, scallions, and ginger and cook, tossing constantly, until fragrant, about 2 minutes. Add chiles and peppercorns and cook, tossing constantly, until just toasted, about 1 minute. Add chicken and sprinkle spice mix evenly over top. Cook, tossing constantly, until chicken is well coated, about 1 minute. Off heat, add cilantro and gently toss to incorporate. Sprinkle with sesame seeds and serve.

Zuǒ Zōngtáng Jī 左宗棠雞
General Tso's Chicken

Serves: 4 to 6 — **Total Time:** 1 hour, plus 30 minutes marinating — **Difficulty:** ●●●○

1½ cups water

½ cup hoisin sauce

¼ cup distilled white vinegar

3 tablespoons soy sauce

3 tablespoons sugar

1½ cups plus 2 tablespoons cornstarch, divided

1½ pounds boneless, skinless chicken thighs, trimmed and cut into 1-inch pieces

3 large egg whites

½ cup all-purpose flour

½ teaspoon baking soda

2 quarts peanut or vegetable oil for frying

2–4 small dried Sichuan chiles, stemmed and halved lengthwise

2 tablespoons grated fresh ginger

4 garlic cloves, minced

Crust for Life

Fortifying cornstarch with all-purpose flour helps the crust remain crispy even when doused in sauce. But to get next-level crunch, we toss a couple spoonfuls of the marinade into the coating, creating craggy bits that cling to the chicken and grab onto sauce.

The 19th-century general Zuo Zongtang gallantly led forces against rebels during his Qing military days. But outside China, Zuo—also called General Tso—is best known for a sweet, savory, battered and deep-fried chicken dish.

As far as we know, General Tso had little to do with his namesake dish. Journalist Jennifer 8. Lee, in her book *The Fortune Cookie Chronicles*, tracked the dish's origin to a chef who once worked in Changsha, near General Tso's birthplace. His name was Peng Chang-kuei, and he created the dish of chicken and chile peppers in Hunan Province, then brought it to Taiwan when he opened a restaurant there. As to the general, Zuo Zongtang was a figure valiant enough to associate with the dish.

It wasn't until General Tso's chicken appeared on Chinese restaurant menus in 1970s New York City that the dish rocketed to popularity. Along the way it evolved to suit American tastes: It became sweeter, the chicken chunks larger and more overtly fried, and it was sometimes served on a bed of broccoli. These days, if you ask American Chinese restaurant owners, they'll likely tell you General Tso's chicken is ordered more often than any other dish.   — Kevin + Jeffrey

We prefer this recipe made with chicken thighs, but you can also make it with boneless, skinless chicken breasts; reduce the frying time to 3 minutes.

1   Whisk water, hoisin, vinegar, soy sauce, sugar, and 2 tablespoons cornstarch together in bowl. Toss chicken with 6 tablespoons hoisin mixture in separate bowl. Cover and refrigerate for 30 minutes.

2   Whisk egg whites in shallow dish until foamy. Mix remaining 1½ cups cornstarch, flour, baking soda, and 2 tablespoons hoisin mixture in second shallow dish until mixture resembles coarse meal. Remove chicken from marinade and pat dry with paper towels. Toss half of chicken with egg whites until well coated, then dredge chicken in cornstarch mixture, pressing gently to adhere. Transfer chicken to plate and repeat with remaining chicken.

3   Line rimmed baking sheet with triple layer of paper towels. Add oil to large Dutch oven until it measures about 1½ inches deep and heat over medium-high heat to 350 degrees. Working quickly, use spider skimmer or slotted spoon to lower half of chicken pieces into hot oil. Using tongs or cooking chopsticks, separate pieces so they fry individually. Fry chicken until golden brown and crispy, about 4 minutes. Adjust burner, if necessary, to maintain oil temperature between 325 and 350 degrees.

Using spider skimmer, transfer chicken to prepared sheet. Return oil to 350 degrees and repeat with remaining chicken; transfer to prepared sheet.

4   Measure out and reserve ¼ cup frying oil; discard remaining oil or save for another use. Heat empty 14-inch flat-bottomed wok over medium-high heat until just beginning to smoke.

Reduce heat to medium-low, drizzle reserved oil around perimeter of wok, and heat until just smoking. Add chiles, ginger, and garlic and cook until fragrant, about 1 minute. Add remaining hoisin mixture, bring to simmer, and cook, stirring constantly, until dark brown and thickened, about 2 minutes. Add chicken and cook, tossing constantly, until well coated with sauce, about 1 minute. Serve.

Xìngrén Jī 杏仁雞
Almond Chicken

Serves: 4 to 6 — **Total Time:** 1¼ hours — **Difficulty:** ●●●○

Sauce

- 1 cup chicken broth
- 1 tablespoon cornstarch
- 2 teaspoons Shaoxing wine
- 2 teaspoons hoisin sauce
- 2 teaspoons soy sauce

Chicken

- 3 (6- to 8-ounce) boneless, skinless chicken breasts, trimmed
- 2½ teaspoons table salt, divided
- 1¼ teaspoons black pepper, divided
- ½ cup sliced almonds, toasted, divided
- 2 cups all-purpose flour, divided
- 1 cup cornstarch
- 1 teaspoon garlic powder
- 1 teaspoon baking powder
- ½ teaspoon baking soda
- 1¼ cups mild lager
- 1 large egg, lightly beaten
- 2 quarts peanut or vegetable oil for frying
- 5 cups shredded iceberg lettuce
- 3 scallions, sliced thin

Our next stop in *A Very Chinese Cookbook*'s world tour is Detroit, Michigan, home of a curious dish that's a staple of American Chinese restaurants in the Motor City. Almond chicken starts with chicken cutlets that are beer-battered and deep-fried, the pieces arranged on a bed of iceberg lettuce. A velvety brown sauce is spooned over the crispy chicken, which is finished with scallions and chopped toasted almonds sprinkled all over.

An innovation of recipe developer Christie Morrison: Chopped almonds are incorporated into the batter, giving the already crisp chicken more texture and a subtly sweet and nutty taste. On a personal note, I'm grateful to Christie, who's also the culinary producer of *Hunger Pangs*. She's the calming voice who makes me much less nervous while filming! Thanks, Christie.   — Jeffrey

---

1 For the sauce: Whisk all ingredients together in small saucepan. Bring to boil over medium-high heat and cook, stirring frequently, until thickened, about 30 seconds. Remove from heat and cover to keep warm, stirring occasionally.

2 For the chicken: Line rimmed baking sheet with parchment paper. Set wire rack in second rimmed baking sheet and line rack with triple layer of paper towels. Halve chicken breasts horizontally to form 6 cutlets. Pat cutlets dry with paper towels and sprinkle with ½ teaspoon salt and ½ teaspoon pepper.

3 Finely chop ¼ cup almonds. Whisk chopped almonds, 1 cup flour, cornstarch, garlic powder, baking powder, baking soda, 1 teaspoon salt, and remaining ¾ teaspoon pepper together in large bowl. Whisk in beer and egg until smooth. Combine remaining 1 teaspoon salt and remaining 1 cup flour in shallow dish.

4 Working with 1 cutlet at a time, dip in batter to coat thoroughly, letting excess drip back into bowl. Dredge cutlets in flour mixture, shaking off excess, and place on parchment-lined sheet.

5 Add oil to 14-inch flat-bottomed wok or large Dutch oven until it measures about 1½ inches deep and heat over medium-high heat to 350 degrees. Using tongs, carefully add 3 cutlets to oil and fry, stirring gently to prevent pieces from sticking together, until cutlets are golden and register 160 degrees, about 4 minutes, flipping halfway through frying. Adjust burner, if necessary, to maintain oil temperature

between 325 and 350 degrees. Using spider skimmer or slotted spoon, transfer cutlets to towel-lined rack. Return oil to 350 degrees and repeat with remaining cutlets; transfer to rack.

6 Arrange lettuce evenly on platter. Slice each cutlet crosswise ½ inch thick. Arrange chicken on lettuce, drizzle with ½ cup sauce, and sprinkle with scallions and remaining ¼ cup almonds. Serve, passing remaining sauce separately.

Xiāngchéng Niúròu 香橙牛肉
Crispy Orange Beef

Serves: 4 to 6 — **Total Time:** 1 hour, plus 1 hour freezing — **Difficulty:** ●●●○

1½ pounds beef flap meat, trimmed

3 tablespoons soy sauce, divided

6 tablespoons cornstarch

10 (3-inch) strips orange zest, sliced thin lengthwise (¼ cup), plus ¼ cup juice (2 oranges)

2 tablespoons water

2 tablespoons Shaoxing wine

4 teaspoons sugar

1 tablespoon Chinese white rice vinegar

1 tablespoon dark soy sauce

1½ teaspoons toasted sesame oil

2 quarts peanut or vegetable oil for frying

1 serrano chile, stemmed, seeded, and sliced thin lengthwise

2 tablespoons grated fresh ginger

3 garlic cloves, minced

½ teaspoon Sichuan chili flakes

2 scallions, sliced thin

Crispy orange beef is a certifiable American Chinese classic. But its lineage can be traced to Hunan Province and a dish with an interesting name: aged skin beef.

The "aged skin" refers to tangerine peel that's been dried in the sun, ideally for many years. We don't expect you to dry your own tangerines for this recipe, so we mimicked the flavor by caramelizing strips of fresh orange zest in a hot wok. To ensure the citrus flavor comes through fragrant and bright, we also juice the just-zested oranges for the glaze—don't even think about using juice from a bottle for this recipe!   — Jeffrey

Ask your butcher for a 1½-pound piece of flap meat instead of already-cut sirloin steak tips, which are more difficult to slice thin. Use a vegetable peeler on the oranges and make sure that the strips contain some pith.

1   Cut beef with grain into 2½- to 3-inch-wide strips. Transfer to plate and freeze until firm, about 15 minutes. Slice strips crosswise against grain ⅛ inch thick. Toss beef with 1 tablespoon soy sauce in bowl. Add cornstarch and toss until evenly coated. Spread beef in single layer on wire rack set in rimmed baking sheet and freeze until beef is very firm but not completely frozen, about 45 minutes.

2   Whisk orange juice, water, Shaoxing wine, sugar, vinegar, dark soy sauce, sesame oil, and remaining 2 tablespoons soy sauce together in bowl; set aside.

3   Line second rimmed baking sheet with triple layer of paper towels. Add peanut oil to large Dutch oven until it measures about 1½ inches deep and heat over medium-high heat to 375 degrees. Using spider skimmer or slotted spoon, carefully add one-third of beef to oil. Using tongs or cooking chopsticks, separate pieces so they fry individually. Fry beef, stirring occasionally, until golden brown, about 1½ minutes. Adjust burner, if necessary, to maintain oil temperature between 350 and 375 degrees. Using spider skimmer, transfer beef to towel-lined sheet. Return oil to 375 degrees and repeat with remaining beef in 2 batches; transfer to sheet.

4   Measure out and reserve 2 tablespoons frying oil; discard remaining oil or save for another use. Heat empty 14-inch flat-bottomed wok over high heat until just beginning to smoke. Reduce heat to medium-high, drizzle reserved frying oil around perimeter of wok, and heat until just smoking. Add orange zest and serrano and cook, stirring frequently, until about half of orange zest is golden brown, about 2 minutes. Add ginger, garlic, and chili flakes and cook, stirring frequently, until garlic is beginning to brown, about 45 seconds. Add orange juice mixture and cook, stirring frequently, until slightly thickened, about 45 seconds. Add scallions and beef and toss to coat. Serve.

Jīngshì Tángcù Lǐjǐ 京式糖醋里脊

Beijing-Style Sweet and Sour Pork

Serves: 4 to 6 — **Total Time:** 1¼ hours — **Difficulty:** ●●●○

Pork

2 (12-ounce) pork tenderloins, trimmed

2 tablespoons Shaoxing wine

2 tablespoons soy sauce

1 tablespoon vegetable oil

2 teaspoons table salt, divided

½ teaspoon white pepper

1½ cups (7½ ounces) potato starch

½ cup (2½ ounces) all-purpose flour

1 teaspoon baking powder

1 cup plus 2 tablespoons water

2 quarts peanut or vegetable oil for frying

Sauce

½ cup water

½ cup Chinese white rice vinegar

½ cup sugar

2 tablespoons dark soy sauce

2 tablespoons soy sauce

4 garlic cloves, minced

1 tablespoon grated fresh ginger

2 teaspoons potato starch

¼ teaspoon white pepper

2 tablespoons sesame seeds, toasted

3 Thai chiles, stemmed and sliced thin (optional)

If the photo here doesn't match the image of sweet and sour pork in your head—glowing fluorescent red with pineapple chunks and green bell peppers—it's because the dish isn't a monolith. Think of American barbecue: In Texas it's dominated by beef brisket, in North Carolina it's pork shoulder, in Kansas City it's a rack of baby back ribs. The same can be said about sweet and sour pork in China, a dish with at least three regional variations.

This rendition comes from Beijing and was developed by our colleague Kelly Song. There's a story behind it: When Kelly was 10, one day after her violin lesson her family visited a Chinese restaurant, where they ordered their usual twice-cooked pork (see page 186). On this particular day Kelly's dad said: "Let's get the Beijing-style sweet and sour pork, too." When the dish arrived it looked nothing like the versions Kelly had eaten before. The pork wasn't chunked but instead was shaped like batons and was speckled with sesame seeds in a dark ruby sauce. This wasn't turned-up-to-11 sweet and sour pork—it was more balanced and refined, less fluorescent red, much more shatteringly crisp, and just as satisfying in its savory-vinegar punch.

It stayed with Kelly all these years. If you make her recipe, it may stay with you, too. — Kevin + Jeffrey (+ Kelly)

---

1 **For the pork:** Cut tenderloins in half lengthwise. Transfer to plate and freeze until firm, about 15 minutes. Slice each half crosswise on bias into ½-inch strips, each about 3 inches long. Combine Shaoxing wine, soy sauce, vegetable oil, 1 teaspoon salt, and pepper in large bowl. Add pork strips and toss until evenly coated; set aside. Whisk potato starch, flour, baking powder, and remaining 1 teaspoon salt together in second large bowl. Whisk in water until smooth; set aside.

2 Set wire rack in rimmed baking sheet and line with triple layer of paper towels. Add peanut oil to large Dutch oven until it measures about 1½ inches deep and heat over medium-high heat to 350 degrees.

3 Whisk batter to recombine. Add half of pork and gently toss to coat. Using tongs or cooking chopsticks, lift pieces of pork from batter, dragging them gently against side of bowl to remove excess batter, and lower into oil; separate pieces as needed so they fry individually. Fry until pork is light golden brown, 4 to 6 minutes.

Adjust burner, if necessary, to maintain oil temperature between 325 and 350 degrees. Using spider skimmer or slotted spoon, transfer pork to prepared rack. Return oil to 350 degrees and repeat with remaining pork; transfer to rack.

4   Heat oil to 375 degrees. Fry pork a second time all at once until deep golden brown and crisp, 4 to 6 minutes; return to rack lined with fresh paper towels.

5   **For the sauce:** Measure out and reserve 2 tablespoons frying oil; discard remaining oil or save for another use. Whisk water, vinegar, sugar, dark soy sauce, soy sauce, garlic, ginger, potato starch, pepper, and reserved frying oil together in 14-inch flat-bottomed wok and bring to boil over medium heat, stirring occasionally with rubber spatula, until mixture is thickened and syrupy and has reduced to about 1¼ cups, about 2 minutes. Off heat, add pork and toss until each piece is evenly coated, about 1 minute. Sprinkle with sesame seeds and Thai chiles, if using, and serve.

Taiwanese Fried Pork Chops

Serves: 4 — **Total Time:** 1¼ hours, plus 1 hour marinating — **Difficulty:** ●●○○

- 1 tablespoon soy sauce
- 1 tablespoon michiu (Taiwanese rice wine)
- 2 garlic cloves, minced to paste
- 1½ teaspoons sugar
- 1½ teaspoons water
- ¾ teaspoon five-spice powder
- ½ teaspoon table salt
- ¼ teaspoon white pepper
- 2 (8- to 10-ounce) bone-in pork rib chops, ¾ to 1 inch thick, trimmed
- 2 large eggs
- 1 cup coarse sweet potato starch
- 3 cups peanut or vegetable oil for frying

Make It a Combo

In Taiwan these pork chops are found mainly in cities, where they're enjoyed by train commuters and other working folks as paigu fan, a plate of chops, rice, and vegetables. Serve the meat as paigu fan with lots of rice and accoutrements: stir-fried napa cabbage, Stir-Fried Pickled Mustard Greens (page 24), and Tea Eggs (page 44).

For those who insist the American South is home to the world's crispiest, crunchiest, deepest-fried foods, Taiwan would like a quick word.

The Taiwanese deep-fry chicken, pork, and oysters in a way that's recognizable by the distinct craggy exterior—it's got the bumpy texture of a popcorn ceiling. This is accomplished by coating foods with an ingredient somewhat unknown in the Western hemisphere: coarse sweet potato starch, which is crumbly in its raw state and fries up extraordinarily crunchy. (Doubly so in these pork chops from recipe developer Annie Petito, as they're fried twice for good luck and measure.)

On top of that, the Taiwanese love marinating with a combination of white pepper, sweetly aromatic five-spice powder, and other flavorful components such as soy sauce, garlic, and michiu. The result is profoundly flavorful, sweet and spiced and everything nice. — Kevin

If rib chops are unavailable, blade chops can be used. The bones of the chops are great for nibbling, which is why we include them for serving. Coarse (or "thick") sweet potato starch gives the chops their distinct crunch. You can substitute coarse tapioca starch.

1 Whisk soy sauce, michiu, garlic, sugar, water, five-spice powder, salt, and pepper together in large bowl.

2 Place 1 chop on cutting board. Cover with sheet of plastic wrap and pound to ¼-inch thickness, being careful to avoid bone. Repeat with remaining chop. Add chops to bowl with marinade and toss to evenly coat. Cover and refrigerate for 1 hour or up to 4 hours.

3 Beat eggs in shallow dish. Spread sweet potato starch in second shallow dish. Working with 1 chop at a time, remove from marinade (do not pat dry) and dip into egg, turning to coat well and allowing excess egg to drip back into dish. Coat evenly on all sides with sweet potato starch, pressing on chop to adhere. Transfer to rimmed baking sheet.

4 Line second rimmed baking sheet with triple layer of paper towels. Add oil to 14-inch flat-bottomed wok or large Dutch oven until it measures about ½ inch deep and heat over medium-high heat to 350 degrees. Using tongs, carefully lower 1 chop into oil. Fry until just starting to brown on both sides, about 1 minute per side. Transfer chop to towel-lined sheet. Return oil to 350 degrees and repeat with remaining chop; transfer to sheet.

5 Heat oil to 375 degrees. Return 1 chop to oil and cook until golden brown on both sides, about 1 minute per side; transfer to sheet lined with fresh paper towels. Return oil to 375 degrees and repeat with remaining chop. Let chops rest for 5 minutes. Carve meat from bone and slice ½ inch thick. Serve meat with bones.

Sìchuān Zhá Yúliǔ 四川炸魚柳
Sichuan Deep-Fried Fish Fillets

Serves: 4 to 6 — **Total Time:** 1 hour, plus 30 minutes resting — **Difficulty:** ●●●○

⅔ cup cornstarch

⅓ cup all-purpose flour

½ teaspoon baking powder

¾ cup plus 1 tablespoon water, divided

¼ teaspoon baking soda

1 pound skinless flounder fillets, ¼ to ½ inch thick, cut into 2 by 1-inch pieces

2 tablespoons Shaoxing wine

¼ teaspoon table salt

2 quarts peanut or vegetable oil for frying

4 garlic cloves, minced

1 tablespoon doubanjiang (broad bean chile paste)

1 tablespoon grated fresh ginger

2 teaspoons Sichuan peppercorns, toasted and coarsely ground

½ teaspoon sugar

¼ teaspoon monosodium glutamate (optional)

1 celery rib, sliced very thin on bias

2 teaspoons Sichuan chili flakes

There Are Other Fish in the Sea

Cod, black sea bass, striped bass, and sole are good substitutes for flounder.

Call it kismet. Recipe developer Joe Gitter was a late arrival at one of our research dinners at the Sichuanese restaurant 5 Spices House in Boston's Chinatown, appearing just as folks were paying up. He was content with bringing home everyone's leftovers, but for his benefit we felt compelled to reorder one of the evening's dishes: hot and spicy fish fillets, which had been the consensus favorite that night. (Imagine if crispy fish and chips took a semester abroad in Chengdu.) "It's just not the same if you don't taste this hot and fresh," we told Joe, who agreed to wait 10 minutes for the cooks to prepare it.

Not to infer too much poetic meaning from that one moment, but if not for our insistence Joe's eyes wouldn't have bulged and glowed upon first bite. He wouldn't have fallen hard for the dish, and the many weeks ultimately spent developing this extraordinary recipe wouldn't have happened. Then, recipe tragically omitted, this book wouldn't have become an international bestseller and made us gazillionaires (or so we think). Wouldn't the world be a poorer place? Like I said, kismet. — Kevin

1 Whisk cornstarch, flour, and baking powder together in bowl. Whisk in ¾ cup water until smooth; refrigerate for 30 minutes. Meanwhile, combine baking soda and remaining 1 tablespoon water in second bowl. Add flounder, gently toss to coat, and let sit for 5 minutes. Add Shaoxing wine and salt and gently toss to combine; refrigerate for 30 minutes.

2 Set wire rack in rimmed baking sheet. Set second wire rack in second sheet and line half of rack with triple layer of paper towels. Add oil to large Dutch oven until it measures about 1½ inches deep and heat over medium-high heat to 400 degrees.

3 Whisk batter to recombine. Add flounder and gently toss to coat. Using hands, remove half of flounder from batter and place in single layer on unlined rack. Let rest for 1 minute to allow excess batter to drip off. Working quickly, use tongs or cooking chopsticks to carefully lower 1 piece of flounder at a time into hot oil; separate pieces as needed so they fry individually. Fry flounder until light golden brown, about 3 minutes. Adjust burner as needed to maintain oil temperature between 375 and 400 degrees. Using spider skimmer or slotted spoon, transfer fish to unlined side of rack. Return oil to 400 degrees and repeat with remaining fish.

4   Return oil to 400 degrees. Return all flounder to oil and cook until deep golden brown, about 4 minutes. Adjust burner as needed to maintain oil temperature between 375 and 400 degrees. Transfer flounder to lined side of rack.

5   Measure out and reserve 3 tablespoons frying oil; discard remaining oil. Heat empty 14-inch flat-bottomed wok over high heat until just beginning to smoke. Reduce heat to medium-low, drizzle reserved oil around perimeter of wok, and heat until just smoking. Add garlic, doubanjiang, and ginger and cook, stirring frequently, until fragrant, about 30 seconds. Add peppercorns, sugar, and monosodium glutamate, if using, and toss to combine. Add flounder and cook, tossing gently but constantly, until well coated, about 1 minute. Add celery and chili flakes and cook, tossing constantly, until celery begins to soften, about 30 seconds. Serve.

MSG Is Your Friend

Can we talk? Look me in the eye. Cradle your hands in mine. Up to this point in the book, your ol' pal Kevin hasn't steered you wrong, right? I hope you've made some tasty food and I've earned your trust. Because there's something I've been meaning to tell you.

You might have heard that MSG (monosodium glutamate) is bad for you, that this powdery additive induces headaches, causes faces to swell and hearts to race, and possibly makes people grow curly tails.

Well, it's just not true. It's as bogus as claims that Thanksgiving turkey makes you sleepy or that you can cure hangovers by drinking more alcohol. If someone claims they're allergic to MSG, chances are they're not. (Some people actually are, but this is extremely rare.)

The truth is, if you eat tomatoes, hard cheeses, or mushrooms, you're already consuming glutamates in amounts greater than what a Chinese restaurant would serve. Glutamates are responsible for those foods tasting savory and rich on the palate. You've probably heard the Japanese word for that flavor: umami. That's why we add it to recipes like dry chili chicken and chili crisp; it makes them taste better.

How exactly did MSG get a bad rap? The phrase "Chinese Restaurant Syndrome" has circulated since the 1960s, referring to a host of ailments you supposedly could experience if you consume food laced with this mysterious white powder of the Orient. Although the science behind the claim was flawed, the sentiment took hold in popular culture. MSG became a convenient three-letter bogeyman, to the point Chinese restaurants became compelled to shout "No added MSG!" on their menu.

For restaurant owners, this is wholly a decision born of business survival. Sadly, many customers continue to perceive whether a restaurant publicly disavows MSG as a purity test: Either you say it, or online reviewers make a stink. Ironically, restaurants that declare they don't use MSG are certainly cooking with soy sauce, which is practically MSG in liquid form.

So what is the explanation if you *do* feel headachy after eating Chinese food? What if MSG powder was, in fact, added, as we do with certain recipes in this book? Keep in mind that correlation doesn't equal causation. Most likely you just ate too much salty rich food in one sitting and didn't drink enough water. If you'd inhaled several Quarter Pounders with Cheese in one sitting, you'd probably be feeling Chinese Restaurant Syndrome, too.

The bottom line: Like bacon, beer, fudge, and other things delicious, MSG is perfectly fine in moderation. A billion Chinese folks will tell you the same.

— Kevin

Salted Egg Fried Shrimp
(page 300)

Salted Egg Fried Shrimp

Serves: 4 to 6 — **Total Time:** 1 hour, plus 30 minutes resting — **Difficulty:** ●●●●

- ⅔ cup cornstarch
- ⅓ cup all-purpose flour
- ½ teaspoon baking powder
- 1 pound jumbo shrimp (16 to 20 per pound), peeled and deveined
- 1 teaspoon michiu (Taiwanese rice wine)
- ¾ teaspoon table salt, divided
- ⅛ teaspoon white pepper
- 6 salted duck egg yolks (3 ounces)
- 2 quarts peanut oil for frying
- 2 tablespoons unsalted butter
- 2 garlic cloves, minced
- 2 scallions, sliced thin
- 1 teaspoon sugar
- ¼ teaspoon monosodium glutamate (optional)

This recipe is unbelievable, but not in the trite, overused way we casually toss this word around. It's just hard to believe—if you've never tried it—how salted egg yolks could be the catalyst for such exceptionally tasty fried foods.

In Chinese we call something fried with salted egg yolk 金沙, meaning "golden sand." As the hardened yolks get crumbled and sautéed in a hot wok with butter, they emulsify into fine ultrarich pebbles that adhere to anything crispy in sight. And when the buttery yolk sauce coats crackly fried shrimp, it's like two people locking eyes from across the dance floor: They were meant for each other.

If we're resorting to hyperbole to convince you to cook a dish, we better truly mean the words we use. And we do: Salted egg fried shrimp is amazing, incredible, sensational, and so unexpectedly delicious you won't believe it until you try it.
— Kevin + Jeffrey

Extra-large shrimp (21 to 25 per pound) will also work here; avoid shrimp smaller than this as they will overcook. Salted duck egg yolks are often kept in the freezer section of the market. Salted whole duck eggs will also work; however, you will need to peel and remove the white before proceeding with steaming. Because we're heating oil to 425 degrees, it is important to use peanut oil for frying.

1   Whisk cornstarch, flour, and baking powder together in bowl. Whisk in ¾ cup water until smooth; refrigerate for 30 minutes.

2   Using paring knife and holding shrimp with outer curve facing you, cut along back of shrimp ½ inch deep to butterfly, taking care not to cut in half completely. Toss shrimp with michiu, ½ teaspoon salt, and pepper in bowl; set aside.

3   Bring 1 cup water to boil in 14-inch flat-bottomed wok. Reduce heat to simmer. Arrange egg yolks in collapsible steamer basket, then set basket in wok. Cover and steam yolks until softened, about 6 minutes. Transfer yolks to medium bowl and mash with fork to coarse powder. Wipe wok clean with paper towels.

4   Set wire rack in rimmed baking sheet. Set second wire rack in second sheet and line with triple layer of paper towels. Add oil to large Dutch oven until it measures about 1½ inches deep and heat over medium-high heat to 425 degrees.

5   Whisk batter to recombine. Add shrimp and toss to coat. Using hands, remove shrimp from batter and place in single layer on unlined rack. Let rest for 1 minute to allow excess batter to drip off.

6   Working quickly with half of shrimp, pick up shrimp by tail with tongs or cooking chopsticks and carefully lower into hot oil; separate pieces as needed so they fry individually. Fry shrimp until golden brown and crisp, about 4 minutes. Adjust burner, if necessary, to maintain oil temperature between 400 and 425 degrees. Using spider skimmer or slotted spoon, transfer shrimp to towel-lined rack. Return oil to 425 degrees and repeat with remaining shrimp; transfer to rack.

7   Discard oil or save for another use. Add butter to now-empty wok and heat over medium heat until butter is melted. Add garlic and scallions and cook, stirring constantly, until fragrant, about 1 minute. Add yolks and cook, stirring constantly, until mixture is well combined, turns fluid, and begins to foam, about 3 minutes. Stir in remaining ¼ teaspoon salt, sugar, and monosodium glutamate, if using. Off heat, add shrimp and gently toss to coat. Serve.

Test Kitchen Tip

Recipe developer David Yu notes: "Melting and emulsifying the salted yolks with the butter is crucial in allowing the sauce to evenly coat and adhere to each shrimp. Take your time with this step, as cooking over heat that's too high can scorch the sauce. After tossing the shrimp and sauce together off heat, the salted egg coating will resolidify just enough to develop its namesake golden sand texture while remaining slightly soft. Emulsification with butter protects the yolks from solidifying all the way."

Preparing Salted Egg Yolks

1   Quickly steam salted duck egg yolks to soften them enough to mash.

2   Mash softened yolks into fine crumble with fork to ensure that yolks emulsify and melt into sauce.

Jiāoyán Xiānyóu 椒鹽鮮魷
Salt and Pepper Squid

Serves: 4 to 6 — **Total Time:** 1 hour, plus 35 minutes resting — **Difficulty:** ●●●○

- ⅔ cup cornstarch
- ⅓ cup all-purpose flour
- ½ teaspoon baking powder
- 1⅛ teaspoons table salt, divided
- ½ teaspoon plus pinch white pepper, divided
- ⅔ cup water
- 2 quarts peanut oil for frying
- 1 pound squid, bodies sliced crosswise ¾ inch thick, extra-long tentacles trimmed to match length of shorter ones
- ¼ teaspoon monosodium glutamate (optional)
- Pinch five-spice powder
- 5 garlic cloves, minced
- 1 tablespoon grated fresh ginger
- 1 green or red longhorn chile, stemmed and sliced thin into rounds
- 1 Fresno chile, stemmed and sliced thin into rounds
- 2 scallions, sliced thin

Kevin Dreams of Calamari

One day I'm going to open a calamari restaurant called "Just Tentacles." It'll serve salt and pepper squid, Rhode Island–style calamari, ika geso—but made with fried tentacles only, the best part. I'm currently seeking investors.

To the trailblazer brave enough to think these terrifying mollusks could be fried and eaten, our eternal gratitude. Because fried calamari rules. And the Chinese approach to fried calamari features a unique flavor classified as "salt and pepper."

Know that "salt and pepper" isn't simply salt plus pepper. It involves floral white pepper, the barest hint of five-spice powder, plus MSG to round out the savoriness. This spice mix is sprinkled on the just-fried squid, and everything gets tossed in the wok with garlic, ginger, and chile. Glorious.   — Kevin

---

As we're heating oil to 425 degrees, it is important to use peanut oil for frying. For ideal texture, buy whole squid, not precut. Can't find longhorn chiles? Use 2 Fresnos.

---

1   Whisk cornstarch, flour, baking powder, 1 teaspoon salt, and ½ teaspoon pepper together in bowl. Whisk in water until smooth; refrigerate for 30 minutes.

2   Set wire rack in rimmed baking sheet. Set second wire rack in second sheet and line with triple layer of paper towels. Add oil to large Dutch oven until it measures about 1½ inches deep and heat over medium-high heat to 425 degrees.

3   Whisk batter to recombine. Add squid and toss to coat. Using hands, remove squid from batter (allowing excess to drip back into bowl) and place in single layer on unlined rack. Let rest for 1 minute to allow excess batter to drip off.

4   Working quickly, use spider skimmer or slotted spoon to lower one-third of squid into hot oil. Using tongs or cooking chopsticks, separate pieces so they fry individually. Fry squid until light golden brown, about 2 minutes. Adjust burner, if necessary, to maintain oil temperature between 400 and 425 degrees. Using spider skimmer or slotted spoon, transfer squid to towel-lined rack. Return oil to 425 degrees and repeat with remaining squid in 2 batches; transfer to rack.

5   Measure out and reserve 1 tablespoon frying oil; discard remaining oil or save for another use. Combine remaining ⅛ teaspoon salt, remaining pinch pepper, monosodium glutamate, if using, and five-spice powder in small bowl. Heat 14-inch flat-bottomed wok over medium-high heat until just beginning to smoke. Drizzle reserved oil around perimeter of wok and heat until just smoking. Add garlic and ginger and cook, stirring constantly, until garlic is beginning to brown and ginger is fragrant, about 1 minute. Add chiles and cook, stirring constantly, until softened, about 2 minutes. Add squid, scallions, and salt mixture and gently toss to coat. Serve.

ON SPECIAL OCCASION

We Chinese love us a loud and festive celebration, with endless platters of food and bottomless pours of baijiu. For such times we break out the A-list recipes, the dishes meant to elicit gasps of wonderment. If these very special recipes don't flip your switch, call the electrician.

Hǎinán Jī Fàn 海南雞飯
Hainanese Chicken Rice

Serves: 4 to 6 — **Total Time:** 2¾ hours — **Difficulty:** ●●●○

Father and son might not see eye to eye on everything (what such duo does?), but one thing on which we can both agree: Hainanese chicken rice might be the most delicious and satisfying dish extant. If we could eat only one thing for the rest of our lives, we'd shout Hainanese chicken rice in stereo.

The Singaporean cult favorite—this version meticulously developed by our colleague Hannah Fenton—is greater than the sum of its parts. Yes, the poached chicken is luscious and silky, the cool cucumbers a crunchy counterbalance. The rice, which cooks in the chicken poaching liquid, gets perfumed with garlic and pandan leaves, every grain slick with chicken fat. The trio of sauces hit all the salty-spicy-sour-sweet notes. The essence of chicken is expressed in the warm bowl of broth.

It's only when the components come together on one plate that the ensemble plays harmoniously, like a rich musical chord. It's glorious.   — Kevin + Jeffrey

We highly recommend using Buddhist-style chicken here for its flavorful meat and rich, springy skin. (For more information on buying Buddhist-style chicken, see page 176.) Otherwise, we suggest sourcing the finest free-range chicken you can for this dish. Pandan leaves can be found both fresh and frozen (see more on page 308). While jasmine rice is traditional, any long- or medium-grain rice will work. For the sweet soy sauce, we recommend ABC brand from Indonesia.

1   For the chicken: Trim excess fat from chicken and reserve. Season chicken with salt and pepper. Bring water, scallions, garlic, ginger, and soy sauce to boil in large Dutch oven over medium-high heat. Place chicken in pot breast side up. Cover, reduce heat to medium-low, and simmer gently for 15 minutes. Off heat, let chicken sit for 15 minutes.

2   Using tongs, gently flip chicken and continue to let sit, covered, until breasts register 160 degrees and thighs register at least 175 degrees, 15 to 30 minutes.

3   Fill large pot halfway with ice and water. Using tongs and spatula, transfer chicken to ice bath and fully submerge, being careful not to tear skin. Let chicken cool for 10 minutes, then transfer to cutting board and gently pat dry with paper towels. Rub chicken with sesame oil and set aside while preparing rice.

recipe continues on next page

Chicken

- 1 (3½- to 4½-pound) whole chicken, head, feet, and giblets removed
- 1 tablespoon table salt
- ¼ teaspoon white pepper
- 10 cups water
- 6 scallions, cut into 1-inch pieces
- 6 garlic cloves, lightly crushed and peeled
- 1 (4-inch) piece ginger, sliced into thin rounds
- 1 tablespoon soy sauce
- 1 tablespoon toasted sesame oil

Rice

- 1 tablespoon vegetable oil
- 1 shallot, minced
- 1 teaspoon table salt
- 3 garlic cloves, minced
- 1 tablespoon minced fresh ginger
- 2 cups jasmine rice, rinsed
- 2 pandan leaves, folded in half crosswise and tied in knot (optional)

- 1 English cucumber, halved lengthwise and sliced thin on bias
- 1 cup coarsely chopped cilantro
- Ginger-Scallion Sauce (page 23)
- Chili-Garlic Sauce (page 23)
- Sweet soy sauce

4   Strain broth through fine-mesh strainer set over large bowl or container. Let broth settle for 10 minutes. Measure out and reserve 2½ cups broth, including as much fat that has risen to the surface as possible. Return remaining broth to now-empty Dutch oven; set aside.

5   **For the rice:** Heat oil and reserved chicken fat trimmings in large saucepan over medium-low heat until fat is mostly rendered, about 3 minutes. Increase heat to medium, add shallot and salt, and cook until shallot is softened, about 2 minutes. Stir in garlic and ginger and cook until fragrant, about 30 seconds. Discard rendered chicken trimmings.

6   Add rice and cook, stirring frequently, until edges begin to turn translucent, about 2 minutes. Stir in reserved broth and bring to boil. Reduce heat to low and nestle pandan leaves, if using, into rice. Cover and simmer gently until rice is tender and liquid has been fully absorbed, about 18 minutes. Off heat, lay clean dish towel underneath lid and let sit for 10 minutes. Remove pandan leaves and fluff rice with fork.

7   Return broth to simmer and divide among small serving bowls. To carve chicken, slice breasts from bone and slice each crosswise into ½-inch pieces. Remove thigh meat and slice or shred. Leave legs and wings whole.

8   Arrange chicken on platter with rice, cucumber, and cilantro. Serve with broth, passing ginger-scallion sauce, chili-garlic sauce, and sweet soy sauce separately.

Pandan Express

Pandan leaves can be thought of as the "vanilla" of Southeast Asian cooking. They lend a unique grassy taste and floral aroma, and a little goes a long way. If you can find them fresh at a Chinese or Southeast Asian market, extra leaves can be tied in knots and stored in the freezer for future use. Frozen leaves are also available as both whole 12-inch leaves and cut pieces. If using pieces substitute four 6-inch pieces or ¼ cup, skip the tying step, and remove the pieces before serving.

Preparing Hainanese Chicken

1 After poaching chicken, use tongs and spatula to transfer chicken to ice bath, being careful not to tear skin.

2 Garlic, ginger, and pandan leaves all infuse rice with flavor as it simmers in poaching liquid.

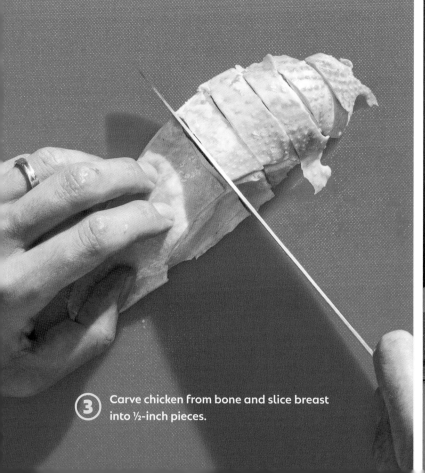

3 Carve chicken from bone and slice breast into ½-inch pieces.

4 For the accompanying Ginger-Scallion Sauce, pouring hot oil over aromatics releases their flavor, creating a supersavory relish.

On Chinese New Year

After immigrating to the United States in 1992, our family experienced our first Thanksgiving. Those were pre-Google days and we didn't quite know how to celebrate. From what we could piece together, it involved eating turkey and candied yams, watching football, and waking up early the next morning to buy discount movies on VHS. We realized: American Thanksgiving felt a whole lot like Chinese New Year.

Both holidays are steeped in rigid tradition. The same handful of dishes get served year after year, of which copious amounts are consumed. Most important, both holidays provide happy reasons for gathering, with a lot of gratitude spread around.

There's no way to pithily explain all that's involved with Chinese New Year (also known as Lunar New Year), as customs vary from region to region. Broadly speaking, the Chinese calendar is lunisolar and based on the positions of the sun and moon, and Chinese New Year celebrates the arrival of spring, as well as honoring families, elders, and those passed on. It's also a forward-looking holiday, during which we ask the spirits to grant us good fortune in the coming year. Festivities run from eight days before New Year's Day to 15 days after, and they involve parades, firecrackers, and furry lion costumes.

I can reference only my Cantonese experience. As someone who grew up with one foot in both Chinese and American cultures, my family's New Year customs didn't always make sense to me. But I was happy to participate in them.

For example, there are certain dishes we must eat. They are consumed because they're homophones of auspicious words. For example, the Chinese word for fish 魚 sounds a lot like surplus, which is great if you're hoping for a surplus of money. Fat choy 髮菜 is an algae that looks like a tangle of black hair; we eat it because it sounds like the term for prosperity. (Perhaps you've heard us Chinese wish each other good fortune with the greeting "gung hei fat choy" 恭喜發財.)

This tradition of eating food for its symbolism goes on and on: tofu squares if you want a good harvest, because they resemble a field; sesame balls (page 60) because their round shape ensures good fortune rolling into your house; noodles because their length represents longevity; pork knuckles if you're a gambler and want to improve your luck. In actuality a lot of the superstition revolves around money, and eating algae and fish *might* improve your 401(k) portfolio. I guess it can't hurt to try.

I remember snatches of Chinese New Years from my childhood. The night before the first of the year was the big meal. At the same time, my parents did all the food prep for New Year's Day proper, a day when little cooking actually gets done. (It's a vestige of not wanting to slaughter any livestock to start off the year.) On Chinese New Year's Eve, my sister and I would watch TV and play Nintendo past midnight. Staying up late extends the lives of your parents, so they say.

Then on New Year's Day we'd pay visits to elders and various aunties and uncles, who'd hand us kids red envelopes filled with cash!

Our especially wealthy relatives—the ones who probably ate more than their share of tofu squares and pork knuckles—might slip in a hundred-dollar bill. Those were magical times.

With other customs we just did as we were told. We didn't shampoo our hair on New Year's Day because that could wash away our fortune. We avoided taking out the garbage for fear we'd throw out the good luck with it. We should bring gifts to elders but please, nothing sharp (cuts into health and prosperity) or in groups of four (sounds like the word for death). If you have kids, don't scold them that day! Keep things positive, if just for 24 hours. For a Chinese kid, following all these strange rules in exchange for a red envelope filled with a few hundred bucks seemed like a magnificent deal. What's more, the food around Chinese New Year can be pretty spectacular.

As I've grown older and perhaps less cynical, I've come to appreciate Chinese New Year traditions as familiar and comforting. In years past such emphasis on customs struck me as old-fashioned. For a while I questioned why anyone would want to eat overcooked turkey on Thanksgiving when other roast meats were more delicious. (I wanted Thanksgiving porchetta to become a thing!) Now I see that I was missing the point. The goal of these holidays has always been to bring family members together and be thankful. But mostly, it's a time for lots of tasty food.

— Kevin

Photo Descriptions (from top to bottom): *Photo 1: The Pangs, Chinese New Year, 1987; Photo 2: A very festive spread; Photo 3: Jeffrey dancing under a lion costume.*

Roast Duck (page 314)

Kǎoyā 烤鸭
Roast Duck

Serves: 4 — **Total Time:** 3 hours, plus 6 hours salting — **Difficulty:** ●●●○

1 (5½- to 6-pound) Pekin duck, neck and giblets removed

2 tablespoons kosher salt, divided

1 tablespoon maltose or honey

1½ teaspoons soy sauce

Here's how it typically goes every time someone thinks of roasting a duck: They daydream about how delicious it'd taste, and this compels them to drop a pretty penny to buy a whole duck. They lovingly season the bird and roast it. As they wait they prepare some nice sauces.

Then the duck comes out of the oven chewier than an old boot.

What went wrong? The duck was cooked as if it were chicken. Duck is pretty much all dark meat and contains far more fat than does chicken or turkey. You can't just throw a duck in the oven and hope for the best. Thankfully, our colleague Lan Lam cooked through several flocks' worth to develop a two-part cooking method that yields restaurant-worthy roast duck at home. Here's what is different:

1. The skin is scored to create channels for rendered fat to escape. This also allows the salt rubbed over the skin to penetrate more deeply over a 6-hour rest.

2. We give the tougher legs a head start by submerging the bottom half of the duck in water in a wok or Dutch oven and vigorously simmering the bird on the stove until the leg quarters register 145 to 160 degrees. Meanwhile, because the breasts don't have contact with the water, they cook more slowly.

3. Finally, we move the bird to a roasting pan and finish it in the oven, brushing the bird with a soy sauce–maltose glaze to encourage deep browning.

— Kevin + Jeffrey (+ Lan)

Pekin duck may also be labeled Long Island duck and is typically sold frozen. Thaw the duck in the refrigerator for 24 hours. This recipe was developed with Diamond Crystal kosher salt. If using Morton kosher salt, reduce the amount to 4½ teaspoons. Even when the duck is fully cooked, its juices will have a reddish hue. The leftover cooking liquid in step 4 is an excellent broth for cooking; defat and reserve for another use. The neck, giblets, and trimmings from step 1, along with the carved duck carcass, can also be reserved for making more broth (see page 25).

1 Using hands, remove large fat deposits from bottom of cavity. Using kitchen shears, trim excess neck skin from top of breast; remove tail and first 2 segments from each wing, leaving only drumette. Arrange duck breast side up on cutting board.

With tip of sharp knife, cut slits spaced ¾ inch apart in crosshatch pattern in skin and fat of breast, being careful not to cut into meat. Flip duck breast side down. Cut parallel slits spaced ¾ inch apart in skin and fat of each thigh (do not crosshatch).

2 Rub 2 teaspoons salt into duck cavity. Rub 1 teaspoon salt into breast, taking care to rub salt into slits. Rub remaining 1 tablespoon salt into skin of rest of duck. Align skin at bottom of cavity so 1 side overlaps other by at least ½ inch. Use sturdy toothpick to pin skin layers to each other to close cavity. Place duck on large plate and refrigerate uncovered for at least 6 hours or up to 24 hours.

3 Place duck breast side up in 14-inch flat-bottomed wok or Dutch oven. Add water until at least half of thighs is submerged but most of breast remains above water, about 6 cups. Bring to boil over high heat, then reduce heat to maintain vigorous simmer. Cook, uncovered, until thermometer inserted into thickest part of drumstick to bone registers 145 to 160 degrees, 45 minutes to 1 hour. After 20 minutes of cooking, adjust oven rack to lower-middle position and heat oven to 425 degrees. Combine maltose and soy sauce in bowl.

4 Crumple 20-inch length of aluminum foil into loose ball. Uncrumple foil and place in roasting pan. Set V-rack on foil and spray with vegetable oil spray. Using tongs and spatula, lift duck from wok, allowing liquid to drain, and transfer to V-rack breast side up. Brush breast and top of drumsticks with one-third of maltose mixture. Flip duck and brush remaining mixture over back and sides. Roast until back is golden brown and breast registers 140 to 150 degrees, about 20 minutes.

5 Remove roasting pan from oven. Using tongs and spatula, flip duck breast side up. Continue to roast until breast registers 160 to 165 degrees, 15 to 25 minutes. Transfer duck to carving board and let rest for 20 minutes. Carve duck and serve.

Test Kitchen Tip

See page 177 for how to chop up a duck. Serve with rice and vegetables, or make it a centerpiece by adding several dishes, such as Steamed Whole Fish with Scallions and Ginger (page 198), Spicy Cold Tofu (page 238), Stir-Fried Tender Greens with Garlic (page 209), and bowls of rice. Or carve the meat off the bone and serve with Spring Pancakes (page 192), Plum Sauce (page 24), sweet bean sauce, scallions cut into matchsticks, and sliced cucumbers.

Preparing a Duck for Roasting

1 Using kitchen shears, trim excess neck skin from top of breast, then remove tail and first 2 segments from each wing, leaving only drumette.

2 With tip of sharp knife, cut crosshatch pattern in skin and fat of breast. Cut parallel slits in skin and fat of each thigh. Rub salt into cavity and deep into scored skin and fat.

3 Align skin at bottom of cavity so 1 side overlaps other; use toothpick to pin layers to each other to close cavity. Refrigerate for 6 to 24 hours.

Hóngshāoròu 紅燒肉
Red-Braised Pork Belly

Serves: 6 to 8 — **Total time:** 2 hours — **Difficulty:** ●●○○

2 tablespoons vegetable oil

¼ cup (2 ounces) rock sugar, crushed

2 pounds skin-on center-cut fresh pork belly, cut into 2-inch pieces

1 (4-inch) piece ginger, sliced into thin rounds

2 tablespoons soy sauce

1 tablespoon dark soy sauce

2 star anise pods

2 cinnamon sticks

¼ teaspoon table salt

5 cups water

2 scallions, sliced thin

Public Service Announcement

We brought this dish to a friend's house once. The next day he reported not feeling so great. Turns out he ate half the pot in one go, shoveling it in his mouth by the spoonful as if it was beef stew! This would be a good time to mention that we treat meat a bit like a condiment: Not meant to be consumed by itself, it is used more as a flavoring agent between bites of noodles, rice, and breads. (Red-braised pork belly is best with lots of steamed rice.)

To fully appreciate this quintessential Hunanese dish, you must view pork fat as a feature, not a bug. The dish requires the type of person who savors prosciutto fat melting in your mouth and who tolerates bacon on the flabbier side, because the red-braised method celebrates the richness of pork belly in its most gelatinous, jiggly, maximally decadent way.

Developer Carmen Dongo is justly proud of her superb recipe. There's no subtlety about what you're enjoying: distinct striations of skin-fat-meat-fat-meat on the pork, enrobed in a warmly spiced, caramelized, and sweet deep-red glaze so luxuriant it would make rubber tires taste good.   — Kevin

Look for pork belly that is sold as one whole piece, about 2 inches thick, with a decent amount of fat. We prefer skin-on pork belly to achieve traditional textures and flavors; if you cannot find skin-on pork, you can use skin-off.

1   Heat empty 14-inch flat-bottomed wok over high heat until just beginning to smoke. Reduce heat to medium-high, drizzle oil around perimeter of wok, and heat until just smoking. Add rock sugar and cook, stirring constantly, until sugar has melted and mixture is amber-colored, about 1 minute. Carefully add pork belly and cook, tossing slowly but constantly, until fat begins to render and pork begins to brown, about 7 minutes.

2   Stir in ginger, soy sauce, dark soy sauce, star anise, cinnamon sticks, and salt and cook, stirring frequently, until fragrant, about 30 seconds. Stir in water and bring to boil. Reduce heat to medium-low, cover, and simmer until paring knife inserted into pork offers no resistance, 70 to 80 minutes, flipping pork pieces halfway through cooking.

3   Increase heat to medium-high and vigorously simmer, uncovered, stirring frequently, until sauce is thickened and begins to coat pork, 10 to 25 minutes.

4   Off heat, let pork rest for 5 minutes. Using wide, shallow spoon, skim excess fat from surface of sauce and remove ginger, star anise, and cinnamon sticks. Sprinkle with scallions and serve.

Cuìpí Shāoròu 脆皮燒肉

Crispy Roast Pork Belly

Serves: 8 to 10 — **Total Time:** 4 hours, plus 12 hours salting — **Difficulty:** ●●●○

1 (3-pound) skin-on center-cut fresh pork belly, about 1½ inches thick

2 tablespoons kosher salt, plus extra as needed

2 tablespoons packed dark brown sugar

1 teaspoon five-spice powder

Vegetable oil

Unless you have a commercial gas-powered vertical roaster at home—we're guessing you don't—replicating the crispy wonders of Cantonese roast pork is next to impossible. Fortunately, "impossible" is a four-letter word at America's Test Kitchen (actually it's 10 but you get our drift).

This innovative technique comes from *Cook's Illustrated* editor in chief Dan Souza, who figured out that roasting the pork belly low and slow (rather than using high heat) keeps the meat supremely juicy. As for the all-important crunchy skin: Scoring it before air-drying in the fridge overnight, and then frying the pork belly in rendered pork fat, causes the skin to puff up and crisp dramatically.
– Kevin + Jeffrey (+ Dan)

Look for pork belly that is sold as one whole piece, about 1½ inches thick, with roughly equal amounts of meat and fat. Serve with hoisin and hot mustard.

1 Using sharp chef's knife, slice pork belly lengthwise into 2- to 2½-inch-wide strips, then make ¼-inch-deep crosswise cuts, spaced ½ inch apart, through skin and into fat. Combine salt, sugar, and five-spice powder in bowl. Rub salt mixture into bottom and sides of pork belly (do not rub into skin). Season skin of each strip evenly with extra salt. Place pork belly skin side up in 13 by 9-inch baking dish and refrigerate, uncovered, for at least 12 hours or up to 24 hours.

2 Adjust oven rack to middle position and heat oven to 250 degrees. Line rimmed baking sheet with aluminum foil, set wire rack in sheet, and spray rack with vegetable oil spray. Transfer pork belly skin side up to prepared wire rack and roast until pork registers 195 degrees and paring knife inserted in pork meets little resistance, 3 to 3½ hours, rotating sheet halfway through roasting.

3 Transfer pork belly skin side up to large plate. (Pork belly can be held at room temperature for up to 1 hour.) Pour fat from sheet into 1-cup liquid measuring cup. Add vegetable oil as needed to equal 1 cup and transfer to 12-inch skillet. Arrange pork belly skin side down in skillet (strips can be sliced in half crosswise if whole strips won't fit) and place over medium heat until bubbles form around pork belly. Continue to fry, tilting skillet occasionally to even out hot spots, until skin puffs, crisps, and turns golden, 6 to 10 minutes. Transfer pork belly skin side up to carving board and let rest for 5 minutes. Flip pork belly on its side and slice ½ inch thick (being sure to slice through original score marks). Reinvert slices and serve.

Chāshāo 叉燒
Char Siu

Serves: 12 to 14 — **Total Time:** 1¼ hours, plus 10 hours marinating — **Difficulty:** ●●●○

If up to this point this cookbook has been a sweeping culinary adventure, we've now arrived at the dramatic high point of our tale, where our father-son protagonists prove themselves either heroes or mere fools.

This is the recipe that makes or breaks our reputation. It's our real-deal version of char siu, the extraordinary Cantonese barbecue pork. Sweet and caramelized, juicy and mouthwatering, char siu is endlessly versatile. It's fantastic chopped in fried rice, satisfying shingled over steamed rice, or great nestled in a bowl of noodles. Of course, it's at peak deliciousness hot from the roaster, freshly sliced, the fattiest and crustiest piece selected, plopped straight into the mouth.

While many Western recipes for char siu get away with using just soy sauce and hoisin, our version is rooted in the traditions of Hong Kong meat roasters and requires several key ingredients easily found at Chinese grocers. Fermented bean curd, maltose, rose cooking liquor, and sesame paste add a deeply savory, subtle floral character to the pork. Our goal wasn't a recipe that makes us just say: "This is pretty good." We want to be able to say: "This is legit." — Kevin + Jeffrey

---

Pork butt roast is often labeled Boston butt in the supermarket. Look for pork butt that is sold as one whole piece with a decent amount of fat. The combination of red food coloring and pink curing salt provides the crimson appearance of char siu. Pink curing salt #1, which can be purchased online or in stores specializing in meat curing, is a mixture of table salt and nitrites; it is also called Prague Powder #1, Insta Cure #1, or DQ Curing Salt #1. Honey can be used in place of the maltose.

---

1 Cut pork crosswise into ¾-inch-thick steaks. Divide pork between 2 one-gallon zipper-lock bags. Whisk soy sauce, sugar, hoisin, mei kuei lu chiew, ginger, sesame paste, fermented bean curd and liquid, garlic, food coloring, if using, five-spice powder, and pepper in bowl until smooth. Measure out and reserve 1 cup marinade. Whisk pink curing salt, if using, into remaining marinade; divide equally between bags and rub to distribute evenly over pork. Press out as much air as possible from bags and seal; refrigerate pork for at least 10 hours or up to 16 hours.

- 1 (4- to 4½-pound) boneless pork butt roast
- 1 cup soy sauce
- ½ cup sugar
- ½ cup hoisin sauce
- ¼ cup mei kuei lu chiew (rose cooking liquor)
- ¼ cup grated fresh ginger
- ¼ cup Chinese sesame paste
- 1½ tablespoons (1¼ ounces) red or white fermented bean curd, mashed to paste, plus 2 teaspoons fermented bean curd liquid
- 4 garlic cloves, minced
- 1 tablespoon red food coloring (optional)
- 2 teaspoons five-spice powder
- ½ teaspoon white pepper
- ⅛ teaspoon pink curing salt #1 (optional)
- ½ cup maltose

recipe continues on next page

2   While pork marinates, cook maltose with reserved marinade in medium saucepan over medium heat, stirring frequently, until glaze is reduced to 1 cup, 4 to 6 minutes. (Glaze can be refrigerated for up to 24 hours.)

3   Adjust oven rack to middle position and heat oven to 400 degrees. Line rimmed baking sheet with aluminum foil and set wire rack in sheet. Spray rack with vegetable oil spray.

4   Remove pork from marinade, letting excess drip off, and place on prepared rack. Bake until pork registers 165 degrees, 25 to 30 minutes. Let pork rest on rack for 10 minutes.

5   Heat broiler. Brush both sides of pork with half of glaze. Broil until top is mahogany, 2 to 4 minutes. Flip pork and broil until second side is mahogany, 2 to 4 minutes. Brush both sides with remaining glaze and continue to broil until top is dark mahogany and lightly charred, 2 to 4 minutes. Transfer pork to carving board, charred side up, and let rest for 10 minutes. Slice pork crosswise into ½-inch-thick strips and serve.

Shine On, You Crazy Pork Butt

Char siu is ruby red with deeply browned crusty edges and a sticky glazed exterior. Traditional recipes roast the meat on metal rods inside refrigerator-size ovens so the heat hits from all sides. To achieve similar results, we slice pork butt into steaks, creating plenty of surface area for receiving marinade and developing a crust. After roasting the meat, we brush on a maltose-sweetened glaze in two stages, running the meat under the broiler after each, until the crust takes on a lacquered appearance and reaches crispy, sticky, toothsome perfection.

Sìchuān Shuǐzhǔ Yú 四川水煮魚
Sichuan Boiled Fish

Serves: 4 to 6 — **Total Time:** 1¼ hours, plus 30 minutes marinating — **Difficulty:** ●●●●

1 tablespoon Shaoxing wine

1 large egg white

2 teaspoons cornstarch

½ teaspoon table salt

¼ teaspoon white pepper

1 pound skin-on black sea bass fillets, sliced crosswise ½ inch thick on bias

¾ ounce (⅔ cup) small dried Sichuan chiles, stemmed and seeds removed, plus extra for garnish

7 tablespoons vegetable oil, divided

6 garlic cloves, peeled (3 sliced thin, 3 lightly crushed)

2 teaspoons Sichuan peppercorns

3 scallions, white parts cut into 1-inch pieces, green parts sliced thin

1 (2-inch) piece ginger, sliced into thin rounds

3 tablespoons doubanjiang (broad bean chile paste)

2 teaspoons Sichuan chili flakes

4 cups water

4 ounces (2 cups) bean sprouts

8 ounces Chinese celery, cut into 2-inch lengths (2 cups)

½ cup fresh chopped cilantro leaves and tender stems

Like Dry Chili Chicken in the previous chapter (page 282), this showpiece Sichuanese dish appears more foreboding than it tastes. What arrives is a seething caldera of red chile pods, green cilantro and scallions, and white bean sprouts and celery, still emitting steam after a douse of sizzling hot oil. All of that, however, is window dressing for the meltingly delicate fillets of fish just beneath the surface.

It might seem like a lot of trouble to flavor slices of fish, but what beautiful trouble the dish reveals itself to be. And the spicy, numbing, toasty perfume imparted to the fish is hard to replicate any other way. Want to simultaneously intimidate and impress your dinner guests? Look no further.   — Kevin

---

For the best presentation, use a wide, shallow serving bowl that holds at least 2 quarts. We prefer the narrow stalks of Chinese celery here; if using celery with thick stalks, we recommend slicing them thin on bias instead of cutting into lengths. Flounder and fluke are good substitutes for the sea bass. While the broth in this dish may tempt you to slurp it, the liquid is intensely flavored and better used as a seasoning that coats the fish and vegetables.

---

1   Whisk Shaoxing wine, egg white, cornstarch, salt, and pepper together in large bowl. Add sea bass and gently toss to coat. Cover and refrigerate for 30 minutes.

2   Halve 5 chiles; set aside. Chop remaining chiles. Add 3 tablespoons oil, chopped chiles, sliced garlic, and peppercorns to 14-inch flat-bottomed wok and cook over medium-low heat, tossing constantly, until garlic edges turn golden and chiles and peppercorns are fragrant, about 3 minutes. Using slotted spoon, transfer chile-garlic mixture to bowl; set aside.

3   Increase heat to medium, add halved chiles, crushed garlic, scallion whites, and ginger, and cook, tossing constantly, until garlic and scallions are softened and beginning to brown, about 2 minutes. Add doubanjiang and chili flakes and cook, tossing constantly, until darkened and oil begins to separate, about 1 minute. Carefully add water (oil will crackle), scraping up any browned bits, and bring to boil. Reduce heat to low, cover, and simmer for 15 minutes.

4   Using spider skimmer or slotted spoon, discard solids. Increase heat to high and bring broth to boil. Add bean sprouts and celery and cook until vegetables are crisp-tender, about 1 minute. Using spider skimmer, transfer vegetables to large

shallow serving bowl. Return broth to boil, gently stir in sea bass, and simmer until opaque throughout, about 2 minutes. Using spider skimmer, remove sea bass from broth and arrange on top of vegetables. Return broth to boil, then gently ladle over sea bass. Top with extra chiles and sprinkle with scallion greens and chile-garlic mixture.

5   Heat remaining ¼ cup oil in 8-inch skillet over high heat until just smoking. Quickly drizzle oil over chiles, scallions, and chile-garlic mixture (oil will crackle). Top with cilantro and serve.

Jiāngcōng Lóngxiā 薑葱龍蝦
Ginger-Scallion Lobster

Serves: 4 to 6 — **Total Time:** 45 minutes — **Difficulty:** ●●●●

¼ cup cornstarch

½ teaspoon table salt

2 (1½- to 2-pound) live lobsters, each cut into 14 pieces (6 tail pieces, 4 halved knuckles, 4 halved claws), head and legs discarded

2 cups peanut or vegetable oil, for frying

¼ cup chicken broth

2 tablespoons Shaoxing wine

1 tablespoon soy sauce

1 teaspoon sugar

3 scallions, cut into 2-inch lengths, white and green parts separated

1 (2-inch) piece ginger, sliced into thin rounds

Test Kitchen Tip

Recipe developer Hannah Fenton notes: "When removing the lobster from the frying oil, try to aim for and remove tail pieces before the claw pieces. The claws take a little longer to cook since they are more encased in shell. This will ensure that the claws and tails are properly cooked at the same time."

The Cantonese exclamation for "whoa" is a comically drawn-out "waaaaaaaah!" The more impressed you are, the higher your pitch and the more a's you add.

This presentation of stir-fried lobster with ginger and scallions has never failed to elicit an outsized "waaaaaaaah!" with us Chinese. Glistening orange hunks of lobster come to the table piled high on the plate, a gastronomic status symbol of opulence. At finer restaurants you might find the whole lobster head—antennae and all—perched on one end of the platter to resemble a dragon, supposedly bringing strength and good fortune to those who eat it. (The Chinese translation of lobster happens to be "dragon shrimp.")

Derive as much symbolism as you like, but we just find this dish extravagant and delicious. The flash frying of lobster pieces is intended not to make it crispy but rather to give the luxurious sauce something to cling to. Extracting the meat and slurping on the sauce-laden shells are among the dish's enduring pleasures. — Kevin

Although you can cut the lobsters into pieces at home using a cleaver or a chef's knife and meat pounder (we'll show you how on page 328), we find it much easier to ask our fishmonger to do this for us.

1 Set wire rack in rimmed baking sheet and line rack with triple layer of paper towels. Whisk cornstarch and salt together in large bowl. Add lobster and toss to coat evenly. Add oil to 14-inch flat-bottomed wok and heat over medium-high heat to 400 degrees.

2 Using spider skimmer or slotted spoon, carefully add one-third of lobster pieces to hot oil (oil will crackle). Fry, stirring slowly but constantly, until meat turns opaque and shells turn bright red, about 45 seconds. Adjust burner as needed to maintain oil temperature between 375 and 400 degrees. Using spider skimmer, transfer lobster to prepared rack. Return oil to 400 degrees and repeat with remaining lobster in 2 more batches; transfer to prepared rack.

3 Whisk broth, Shaoxing wine, soy sauce, and sugar together in small bowl. Measure out and reserve 1 tablespoon frying oil; discard remaining oil or save for another use. Wipe wok clean with paper towels.

4   Heat now-empty wok over high heat until just beginning to smoke. Drizzle reserved oil around perimeter of wok and heat until just smoking. Add scallion whites and ginger and cook, stirring frequently, until fragrant, about 30 seconds. Add lobster, drizzle Shaoxing wine mixture around perimeter of wok, and toss to combine. Cover and cook until lobster is cooked through and sauce is bubbling, about 2 minutes. Uncover and continue to cook, tossing slowly but constantly, until sauce has thickened and coats lobster, about 30 seconds. Off heat, add scallion greens and toss to combine. Serve.

turn to see how to prep lobster for stir-frying

Preparing Lobster for Stir-Frying

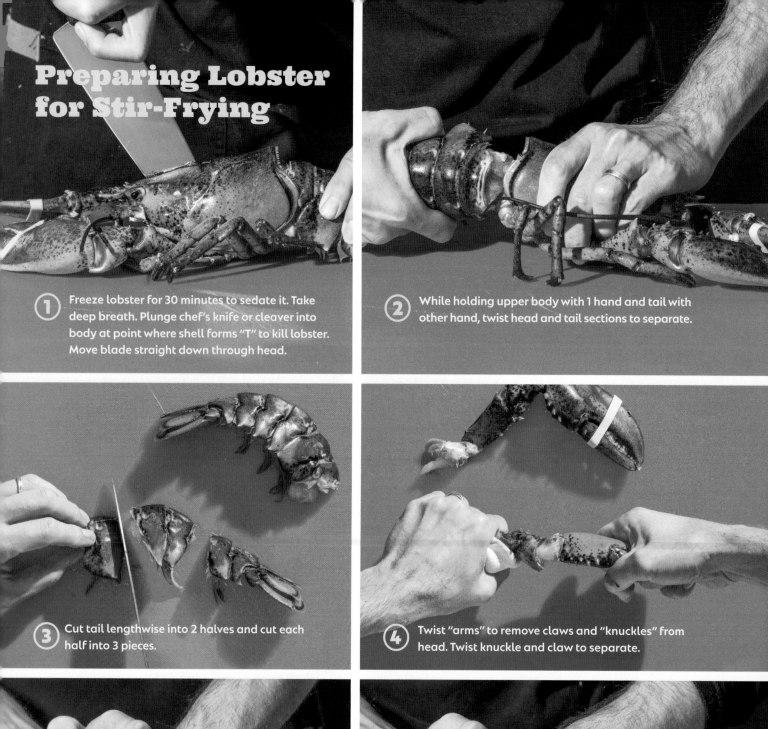

① Freeze lobster for 30 minutes to sedate it. Take deep breath. Plunge chef's knife or cleaver into body at point where shell forms "T" to kill lobster. Move blade straight down through head.

② While holding upper body with 1 hand and tail with other hand, twist head and tail sections to separate.

③ Cut tail lengthwise into 2 halves and cut each half into 3 pieces.

④ Twist "arms" to remove claws and "knuckles" from head. Twist knuckle and claw to separate.

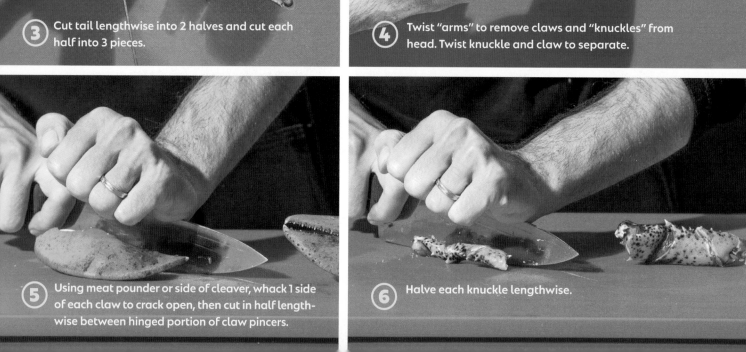

⑤ Using meat pounder or side of cleaver, whack 1 side of each claw to crack open, then cut in half lengthwise between hinged portion of claw pincers.

⑥ Halve each knuckle lengthwise.

ALL DAY BREAKFAST

There seems to be a law stating cookbooks are obligated to end with a chapter on desserts. We won't. Instead, we'll complete our journey together through Chinese cooking with a collection of soul-satisfying breakfast foods, with an emphasis on our hometown, Hong Kong. There are plenty of sweet foods we'll enjoy in the morning, but also savory breakfast traditions that are fried, baked, or long-simmered. The delicious dishes in this chapter all say: "And a good day to you."

Gǎngshì Nǎichá 港式奶茶

Milk Tea

Serves: 4 — **Total Time:** 30 minutes — **Difficulty:** ●○○○

1½ quarts water

2 tablespoons Ceylon tea leaves

2 tablespoons Assam tea leaves

1 (12-ounce) can evaporated milk

¼ cup sweetened condensed milk, plus extra as needed

Our Preferred Evaporated Milk

Any evaporated milk brand will work, but in Hong Kong the Black & White brand is the go-to used by all the tea houses and cafés. Stateside, we're fond of the organic evaporated milk from Whole Foods' 365 brand.

However we may feel about our former British colonial rulers, there remains a bit of Anglophile in every Hong Konger. A one-two punch of milk tea and condensed milk toast in the morning perfectly captures that lingering influence.

I begin every day with Hong Kong–style milk tea. It is simply exquisite. Robust, roasty black tea splashed with the dairy creaminess of evaporated and condensed milk is breakfast alchemy. Proper diners in Hong Kong will strain the tea multiple times through a sackcloth bag (it looks like stockings with a handle), introducing air to the tea and giving it a smooth, velvety quality. While you might choose to skip this step, I do find that it makes a subtle textural difference.

Then there's condensed milk toast, a Texas toast–thick slab of white bread, toasted golden on a griddle with butter, topped with even more butter and generously slathered with condensed milk. Rule, Britannia, indeed.   — Kevin

English Breakfast tea may be substituted for the Ceylon and Assam teas.

1 Bring water to boil in medium saucepan over high heat, then stir in tea leaves. Reduce heat to low, cover, and simmer for 5 minutes.

2 Line fine-mesh strainer with single layer of cheesecloth and set in heat-resistant pitcher, 8-cup liquid measuring cup, or second saucepan. Working in continuous motion, slowly pour tea into strainer while lifting pot away from strainer to increase length and arc of tea stream. Remove strainer and repeat pouring between saucepan and pitcher 3 more times, ending in saucepan. Stir in evaporated milk and condensed milk. Adjust sweetness of tea with extra condensed milk as needed. Serve.

Nǎiyóu Duō 奶油多
Condensed Milk Toast

Serves: 1
Total Time: 15 minutes
Difficulty: ●○○○

Milk bread is traditionally used here; however, other enriched breads such as brioche or challah will work. This recipe can be easily doubled in a 10- or 12-inch skillet.

- 1 tablespoon unsalted butter, softened, plus extra for serving
- 1 (1- to 1½-inch-thick) slice milk bread, crust removed
- 1 tablespoon sweetened condensed milk

Spread butter evenly over both sides of bread. Place bread in 8- or 10-inch nonstick skillet and cook over medium heat until golden brown and crisp, about 4 minutes per side, adjusting heat as needed to prevent scorching. Transfer toast to plate and drizzle with condensed milk. Serve with extra butter, if desired.

Dòujiāng 豆漿
Soy Milk

Makes: 4 cups — **Total Time:** 1½ hours, plus 2 hours soaking and chilling — **Difficulty:** ●●○○

Centuries before soy milk became new-agey fodder and sold for $17 at the cruelty-free co-op, the Chinese were drinking the stuff. Making it at home is all upside: It's cheap, healthful, refreshing, delicious. Serve it warm or cold, savory or sweet, by itself in a tall glass or as the base for something else. Why buy it, when it's easier to make than you'd think? — Kevin

The longer the soybeans soak, the richer the milk will be. Omit the sugar if you'll be using the soy milk for cooking.

1   Place soybeans in bowl and add water to cover by 2 inches. Soak soybeans at room temperature for at least 1 hour or up to 24 hours. Drain and rinse well.

2   Bring soaked soybeans and 4½ cups water to simmer in medium saucepan. Partially cover and cook over medium-low heat until soybeans are tender, 30 to 40 minutes.

3   Line fine-mesh strainer with triple layer of cheesecloth overhanging edges; set aside. Carefully transfer soybeans and cooking liquid to blender. Add sugar, if using, and salt and process until mostly smooth, about 3 minutes. Strain blended soybean mixture through prepared strainer into 4-cup liquid measuring cup or large bowl, stirring occasionally, until liquid no longer runs freely and mixture is cool enough to touch, about 30 minutes. Pull edges of cheesecloth together and firmly squeeze pulp until liquid no longer runs freely; discard pulp. Transfer milk to airtight container and refrigerate until well chilled, about 1 hour. Serve. (Soy milk can be refrigerated for up to 4 days; stir to recombine before serving.)

½ cup dried soybeans, picked over and rinsed

2 teaspoons sugar (optional)

⅛ teaspoon table salt

Zhōu 粥

Congee

Serves: 4 to 6 — **Total Time:** 1 hour   **Difficulty:** ●○○○

¾ cup jasmine rice, rinsed

9 cups water

1 cup chicken broth

¾ teaspoon table salt

Scallions, sliced thin

Fresh cilantro leaves

Dry-roasted peanuts, chopped coarse

Chili oil

Soy sauce

Chinese black vinegar

White pepper

Topper of the Morning

Congee toppings are more than just accents; they're the focal point. They can be as simple as fresh herbs, peanuts, soy sauce, and chili oil or as substantial as fried shallots (see page 24) or strips of pork loin with century eggs (in a pinch, jammy eggs are a fine substitute). The key is to be creative with a wide variety of textures and flavors.

Every culture has its chicken soup for the soul. This is ours. Congee—known as zhou, xifan, or juk, depending on the part of the country—is what the Chinese call its rice porridge. Rice gets cooked down until the grains are barely intact while gently bound by their silky cooking liquid.

There's not much art to it. It's a soft, creamy, straightforward prescription for what ails you. It's comforting plain and unadorned, or dressed to the nines with, say, chicken and abalone, or fish fillet and scallions. It practically begs for a freshly fried dough stick, Youtiao (page 346).

Not feeling 100 percent? Seeking a bowl that warms you from the inside out? Want to start your day right? Congee is the answer.   — Kevin

To prevent the congee from boiling over, we rinse excess starch from the raw rice and wedge a wooden spoon between the lid and the rim of the pot, giving the water bubbles a chance to escape. For vegetarian congee, substitute water for the chicken broth. Other kinds of long-grain rice can be substituted for jasmine; do not use basmati.

1 Place rice in Dutch oven. Add water, broth, and salt and bring to boil over high heat. Reduce heat to maintain vigorous simmer. Cover pot, tucking wooden spoon horizontally between pot and lid to hold lid ajar. Cook, stirring occasionally, until mixture is thickened, glossy, and reduced by half, 45 to 50 minutes.

2 Serve congee in bowls, passing scallions, cilantro, peanuts, chili oil, soy sauce, vinegar, and pepper separately.

Xiàzhōu Ròusuì 下粥肉碎

Stir-Fried Ground Pork Topping

Makes: about 1 cup
Total Time: 25 Minutes
Difficulty: ●○○○

Stir-fried ground pork makes a quick, hearty topping for congee. Mixing in a little baking soda helps the pork stay juicy during cooking. We season the meat with soy sauce, Shaoxing wine, white pepper, and a touch of sugar and add a little cornstarch to thicken the sauce.

  8 ounces ground pork
  1 tablespoon water
  ¼ teaspoon table salt
  ⅛ teaspoon baking soda
  1 garlic clove, minced
  1 teaspoon grated fresh ginger
  1 teaspoon soy sauce
  1 teaspoon Shaoxing wine
  1 teaspoon cornstarch
  ½ teaspoon sugar
  ¼ teaspoon white pepper
  1 teaspoon vegetable oil

1 Toss pork, water, salt, and baking soda in bowl until thoroughly combined. Add garlic, ginger, soy sauce, Shaoxing wine, cornstarch, sugar, and pepper and toss until thoroughly combined.

2 Heat empty 14-inch flat-bottomed wok over high heat until just beginning to smoke. Drizzle oil around perimeter of wok and heat until just smoking. Add pork mixture and cook, breaking meat into ¼-inch pieces with spatula, until pork is no longer pink and is just beginning to brown, about 5 minutes. Spoon over congee to serve.

Waiting for Good Dough

We can't talk about Chinese bakeries without mentioning Shanghai. The city was a hub of Western culture in the early 20th century, with neighborhoods carved out by European and American colonial presence. Shanghai became home to ritzy nightclubs and restaurants that led to its "Paris of the East" moniker.

Europeans in Shanghai brought a culinary art form that the Chinese continue today: the pâtisserie. Cream-filled cakes, palmiers, éclairs, and more became ingrained in Shanghainese food culture. The Chinese learned from the French pâtissiers, and their recipes found their way south to Guangzhou and Hong Kong, and eventually to Chinatown bakeries around the globe.

Chinese bakers, of course, added their own twists along the way. A brioche-like bao would get filled with char siu. A popular snack is the baked bun wrapped around a frankfurter, a self-contained hot dog. My favorite will always be Egg Tarts (page 350), so important to Chinese bakeries that their reputation rests on how well they make them.

— Jeffrey

How Our Baos Get So Fluffy
Pssst. Sneak liquid into the dough.

The bao's supermoist interior is the result of adding a tangzhong, a cooked flour and water paste that gets combined with the rest of the ingredients. This superhydrated dough yields rolls that are not just moist but also fluffy because the water converts to steam in the oven, acting as a leavener. The extra water also increases gluten development to give the buns structure.

Bōluó Bāo 菠蘿包

Bolo Bao

Makes: 20 bao — **Total Time:** 1½ hours, plus 2¼ hours rising and cooling — **Difficulty:** ●●●●

Dough

- **2** tablespoons plus 2⅔ cups (13⅓ ounces) all-purpose flour, divided
- **½** cup water, room temperature
- **½** cup whole milk, chilled
- **1** large egg
- **⅓** cup plus 4 teaspoons (3 ounces) sugar
- **3½** teaspoons nonfat dry milk powder
- **2¼** teaspoons instant or rapid-rise yeast
- **1** teaspoon table salt
- **4** tablespoons unsalted butter, cut into 2 pieces and softened

Topping

- **⅔** cup plus 2 teaspoons (3½ ounces) all-purpose flour
- **¼** teaspoon baking powder
- **¼** teaspoon table salt
- **6** tablespoons unsalted butter, softened
- **⅔** cup confectioners' sugar
- **2** large eggs, beaten
- **2** teaspoons vanilla extract

Just as walking out of a boulangerie with a fresh croissant is distinctly Parisian, it is quintessentially Hong Kong to pick up your morning bolo bao at the corner bakery. Bolo bao is also known as a pineapple bun because of its sugar-crisp crosshatched top that resembles the skin of the tropical fruit. (Our recipe has a smooth top, inspired by the dim sum chain Tim Ho Wan.) Though Cantonese, this yeasted bun feels very European. Its interior is supermoist and fluffy, as soft and as subtly sweet as a Parker House roll if it resided on the dessert menu.

Bolo baos are deliciously versatile. They're great solo or as sandwich bread; in Macau I had one with a fried pork chop nestled between. The pro move, though, is slicing the center of a warm bolo bao almost all the way through, then tucking in a playing-card-size slice of cold salted butter.   — Kevin

1 **For the dough:** Whisk 2 tablespoons flour and water in microwave-safe bowl until smooth. Microwave, whisking every 20 seconds, until mixture thickens to stiff, smooth, pudding-like consistency and registers at least 150 degrees, 40 to 60 seconds. Whisk in milk until smooth, then whisk in egg until smooth.

2 In bowl of stand mixer, whisk together remaining 2⅔ cups flour, sugar, milk powder, yeast, and salt. Add cooked flour mixture. Fit stand mixer with dough hook and mix on low speed until all flour is moistened, 1 to 2 minutes. Increase speed to medium-high and knead until dough is smooth and elastic and clears sides of bowl, 10 to 12 minutes.

3 Fit stand mixer with paddle. With mixer on medium speed add butter, 1 piece at a time, beating for 30 seconds after each addition. Continue to mix until butter is fully incorporated and dough is no longer shiny, 1 to 2 minutes.

4 Transfer dough to very lightly floured counter. Knead dough briefly to form ball and transfer seam side down to lightly greased large bowl. Cover with plastic wrap and let rise until doubled in size, 1 to 1½ hours.

5 **For the topping:** Meanwhile, whisk flour, baking powder, and salt together in small bowl. Using clean, dry mixer bowl and paddle, mix butter and confectioners' sugar on low speed until combined, about 1 minute. Increase speed to medium-high and beat until light, pale, and fluffy, about 3 minutes. With mixer running, gradually add eggs, then vanilla; mix until smooth, scraping down bowl as needed, about 2 minutes. Add flour mixture and mix on low speed until combined, about 30 seconds. Scrape down bowl, then fold ingredients by hand to mix fully. Transfer mixture to 1-quart heavy-duty zipper-lock bag and snip off 1 corner, making hole no larger than ¼ inch (alternatively, transfer to pastry bag fitted with ¼-inch piping tip); set aside until ready to use (do not refrigerate).

6 Line 2 rimmed baking sheets with parchment paper. Transfer dough to counter and divide into 20 equal pieces (about 1½ ounces each); cover loosely with plastic. Working with 1 piece of dough at a time (keep remaining pieces covered), form into rough ball by stretching dough around thumbs and pinching edges together so top is smooth. Place ball seam side down on counter and, using cupped hand, drag in small circles until dough feels taut and round. Space 10 balls evenly on each prepared sheet, keeping balls covered with plastic while rolling remaining dough. Lightly spray tops of buns with vegetable oil spray, cover with plastic, and let rise until doubled in size, about 1 hour. Adjust oven rack to middle position and heat oven to 375 degrees.

7 Pipe about 2 tablespoons topping in tight spiral on top of each bun (topping should form circle roughly 2 inches in diameter and ¼ inch thick). Bake, 1 sheet at a time, until topping is golden brown, 14 to 16 minutes, rotating sheet halfway through baking. Transfer buns to wire rack and let cool for at least 10 minutes. Serve. (Buns can be individually wrapped in plastic and frozen for up to 2 weeks; thaw frozen buns at room temperature before reheating. To reheat, place buns on rimmed baking sheet and bake in 400-degree oven until tops are dry but not browned and centers are warmed through, 4 to 6 minutes.)

turn to see bao fillings

Piping Topping onto Bolo Bao

Pipe about 2 tablespoons topping in tight spiral on top of each bun (topping should form circle roughly 2 inches in diameter and ¼ inch thick).

Chāshāo Bōluó Bāo　叉燒菠蘿包
Char Siu Bolo Bao

As if a bolo bao isn't magical enough, it's even tastier with barbecued pork. You'll find char siu in most Cantonese delis if you live near a Chinatown. Or, use our recipe on page 321.

Chop 1¼ pounds char siu. After dividing dough into pieces in step 6, cover with plastic wrap. Working with 1 piece of dough at a time, press dough into 4-inch round on lightly floured counter and drape in muffin tin to form cup shape, covering each dough cup with plastic while pressing remaining dough. Fill 1 dough cup with about 1½ tablespoons char siu. Pull edges of dough to center and pinch tightly to seal. Transfer bun to counter seam side down and rotate gently to form round shape. Repeat with remaining dough cups and remaining pork. Space balls on prepared sheet and proceed with recipe as directed.

Nǎihuáng Bōluó Bāo　奶黃菠蘿包
Bolo Bao with Custard Filling

You can also take your bolo bao in a nonmeaty direction by filling it with sweet pastry cream. Hoo-boy.

- 5　large egg yolks
- ½　cup sugar, divided
- 3　tablespoons cornstarch
- 2　cups milk
- 　　Pinch table salt
- 4　tablespoons unsalted butter
- 1½　teaspoons vanilla extract
- 1　recipe Bolo Bao, baked and cooled

1 Whisk egg yolks, 2 tablespoons sugar, and cornstarch in medium bowl until mixture is pale yellow and thick, about 1 minute; set aside.

2 Heat milk, remaining 6 tablespoons sugar, and salt in medium saucepan over medium heat until simmering, stirring occasionally to dissolve sugar. Gradually whisk half of milk mixture into yolk mixture to temper.

3 Pour milk-yolk mixture into saucepan. Return to simmer over medium heat and cook, whisking constantly, until mixture is thickened and 3 or 4 bubbles burst on surface, about 1 minute. Off heat, whisk in butter and vanilla. Transfer mixture to clean bowl, press parchment paper directly onto surface, and refrigerate until set, at least 3 hours or up to 2 days.

4 Fit pastry bag with ¼-inch piping tip. Fill pastry bag with pastry cream. Working with 1 baked and cooled bun at a time, twist paring knife into center of bottom of bun to create ½-inch-deep hole. Insert tip of pastry bag into hole and fill with about 3 tablespoons pastry cream.

Làchángjuǎn 臘腸卷
Lap Cheong Rolls

Makes: 10 rolls — **Total Time:** 1¼ hours, plus 1½ hours rising and cooling — **Difficulty:** ●●●○

¾ cup warm whole milk
   (110 degrees)

3 tablespoons sugar

1 teaspoon instant or
   rapid-rise yeast

1 tablespoon vegetable oil

2 cups (10 ounces) all-purpose flour

2 tablespoons cornstarch

1 teaspoon baking powder

⅛ teaspoon table salt

10 lap cheong (Chinese sausage)

Lap cheong rolls are the Chinese version of pigs in a blanket. A snow-white yeasted dough is twirled around a cured Chinese sweet sausage, and the buns are steamed until the dough turns fluffy and firm. The snap of the rich sausage when you bite into the pillowy, slightly sweet bun is supersatisfying.

   This recipe was developed by Jacqueline Church, who leads food and culture tours in Boston's Chinatown.   — Jeffrey

Using bleached all-purpose flour will create the bright-white color that is traditional and prized for these buns; you can also use unbleached all-purpose flour, though the rolls will be less bright-white. Look for lap cheong that are about 6 inches long.

1   Whisk milk, sugar, and yeast together in 2-cup liquid measuring cup until sugar has dissolved, then let sit until foamy, about 5 minutes. Whisk in oil. Pulse flour, cornstarch, baking powder, and salt in food processor until combined, about 3 pulses. With processor running, slowly add milk mixture and process until no dry flour remains, about 30 seconds.

2   Transfer dough to lightly floured counter and knead by hand to form smooth, round ball, about 30 seconds. Transfer dough to lightly oiled large bowl, turning to coat dough ball in oil and arranging dough seam side down. Cover with plastic wrap and let rise until doubled in size, about 1 hour.

3   Bring 4 cups water to boil in 14-inch flat-bottomed wok. Place plate in 10-inch bamboo steamer basket, arrange sausages in single layer on plate, and cover basket. Reduce heat to maintain vigorous simmer, and set steamer in wok. Steam until sausages are plump and color is muted, 10 to 15 minutes. Set aside plate with sausages and let cool completely. Remove basket from simmering water and set aside; discard water.

4   Cut ten 6 by 4-inch rectangles of parchment paper; set aside. Press down on dough to deflate. Transfer to counter and portion into 10 equal pieces (about 2 ounces each); cover loosely with plastic. Working with 1 piece of dough at a time (keep remaining pieces covered), form into rough ball by stretching dough around thumbs and pinching edges together so top is smooth. Place ball seam side down on counter and, using cupped hand, drag in small circles until dough feels taut and round. Cover dough balls with plastic while rolling remaining dough.

5 Working with 1 dough ball at a time (keep remaining pieces covered) and starting at center, gently and evenly roll and stretch dough into 10-inch-long rope. Wrap dough around 1 cooled sausage, starting 1 inch from 1 end of sausage (dough should wrap around sausage at least 3 times and be roughly centered on sausage), and place in 10-inch bamboo steamer basket on 1 prepared parchment rectangle, tucking ends of dough underneath sausage. Cover with damp dish towel while forming remaining rolls, spacing rolls about 1 inch apart in 2 baskets. Let rolls sit until slightly puffy, about 20 minutes.

6 Remove towels, stack baskets, and cover. Set steamer over 4 cups cold water in now-empty wok. Bring water to simmer over high heat and, once steam begins to escape from sides of basket, reduce heat to medium and steam until rolls are puffy and firm, 10 to 15 minutes. Remove basket from simmering water and let rolls cool for 5 minutes before serving.

Yóutiáo 油條
Youtiao

Makes: 12 — **Total Time:** 1½ hours, plus 2¾ hours resting — **Difficulty:** ● ● ● ●

- 3½ cups (17½ ounces) all-purpose flour, plus extra for dusting
- 1 tablespoon baking powder
- 1¼ teaspoons instant or rapid-rise yeast
- 1 teaspoon table salt
- 1½ cups (12 ounces) water
- 1½ tablespoons vegetable oil
- 2 quarts peanut or vegetable oil for frying

At some point in any gastronomic culture, an enterprising cook will discover that frying dough in oil creates something remarkably tasty. Zeppoles, paczkis, beignets, funnel cakes—all are magical in their own crispy way. The Chinese offering to the genre is the mighty youtiao, the crackly-puffy fried dough stick that vastly improves your mornings. It can be dipped in congee and soy or condensed milk, wrapped with sticky rice and pork floss, or draped in rice noodle sheets and served with soy sauce.

Know that few in Hong Kong bother to make youtiaos at home. It's easier to buy from street stalls specializing in them. But the highs of a first-rate youtiao are stratospheric, and we really wanted the recipe for this book. That's why we enlisted Faye Yang (her Taiwanese Beef Noodle Soup is on page 166), formerly on the pastry team at a Michelin three-star restaurant in New York. After months of diligence, Faye cracked the youtiao code. She deserves a Nobel Prize. — Kevin

---

Once cooled, youtiao can be wrapped individually and frozen for up to 2 months. To reheat frozen youtiao, adjust an oven rack to the middle position and heat the oven to 400 degrees. Place frozen youtiao on a wire rack set in a rimmed baking sheet and bake until heated through and the exterior crisps, about 8 minutes.

---

1 Whisk flour, baking powder, yeast, and salt together in large bowl. Using rubber spatula, fold water and vegetable oil into flour mixture until cohesive dough forms and no dry flour remains. Transfer dough to lightly floured counter and knead by hand to form ball, about 1 minute. Place dough in lightly greased bowl, cover tightly with plastic wrap, and let rest for 20 minutes.

2 Transfer dough to lightly oiled counter. Gently stretch and press dough into 18 by 12-inch rectangle, with short side parallel to counter edge. Starting at bottom of dough, fold into thirds like business letter, using bench scraper or metal spatula to release dough from counter. Press edges of dough firmly to seal folds. Turn dough 90 degrees counterclockwise. Stretch and press dough into 18 by 12-inch rectangle and repeat folding into thirds and pressing edges to seal. Repeat rotating, pressing, and folding dough into thirds 1 more time. Transfer dough to lightly greased rimmed baking sheet and cover loosely with greased plastic. Let dough rest at room temperature for 2 hours. (Alternatively, refrigerate dough for at least 12 hours or up to 24 hours; bring to room temperature before proceeding.)

3 Transfer dough seam side down to well-floured counter and dust top with flour. Stretch and roll dough into rough 13-inch square. Using pizza cutter or sharp knife, trim edges of dough to form uniform 12-inch square. Cut dough into two 12 by 6-inch rectangles, then cut each rectangle crosswise into twelve 1-inch-wide strips.

4 Separate strips and use pastry brush to lightly dust tops and sides with flour. Using bench scraper or edge of metal ruler, press lengthwise down center of 12 strips to create crease, making sure not to cut through dough. Arrange remaining 12 uncreased dough strips on top of creased strips and use bench scraper to create second crease that adheres dough strips to each other. Cover youtiao with plastic and let rest for 20 minutes.

5 Set wire rack in second rimmed baking sheet and line with triple layer of paper towels. Add peanut oil to large Dutch oven until it measures about 1½ inches deep and heat over medium-high heat to 400 degrees.

6 Working with 1 youtiao at a time, hold at each end and gently stretch to 11 inches. While still holding youtiao at each end, gently and carefully lower, middle first, into hot oil. Cook, using tongs or cooking chopsticks to flip continuously until dough puffs and begins to turn light golden brown, about 30 seconds. Continue to fry without flipping until deep golden brown on 1 side, about 30 seconds. Flip and continue to fry until deep golden brown on second side, about 30 seconds. Adjust burner as necessary to maintain oil temperature of 400 degrees. Transfer youtiao to prepared rack. Return oil to 400 degrees and repeat with remaining youtiao; transfer to rack. Serve.

The Tearable Twos

The reason you press the crease down the center of the youtiao is so you can tear it. After frying, pull it apart lengthwise—you'll have two crisp sticks the perfect width for dipping. If you prefer to keep the youtiao whole, you can snip it at regular intervals, creating golden butterfly-shaped wedges that can be tossed into savory or sweet soy milk, soups, and congee.

Shaping Youtiao

1 Cut dough into two 12 by 6-inch rectangles, then cut each rectangle into twelve 1-inch-wide strips.

2 Using bench scraper, press lengthwise down center of 12 strips to create crease.

3 Arrange remaining strips on top of creased strips and create second crease that adheres dough strips to each other.

Youtiao
(page 346)

Egg Tarts (page 350)

Dàntà 蛋撻

Egg Tarts

Makes: 12 tarts — **Total Time:** 1¾ hours, plus 1¾ hours refrigerating and cooling — **Difficulty:** ●●●○

Crust

1½ cups (7½ ounces) all-purpose flour

1 tablespoon sugar

½ teaspoon table salt

10 tablespoons unsalted butter, cut into ½-inch pieces and chilled

6 tablespoons ice water

Custard

1 cup warm water (110 degrees)

½ cup (3½ ounces) sugar

2 large eggs plus 2 large yolks

½ cup evaporated milk

1 teaspoon vanilla extract

⅛ teaspoon table salt

That specific hue of sunflower yellow on the previous page triggers an immediate emotional response for the Cantonese. This color, especially in the round, can belong to one item only: egg tarts. A brief flash of that yellow and we're transported to dim sum parlors, teahouses, cafés, and bakeries, and to visits with aunties and uncles while bearing a box of a dozen egg tarts. It's just that visually iconic.

Popularized in Guangzhou in the early 20th century, egg tarts are steeped in both European and Chinese traditions—as are many baked goods of the region. There's a bit of English in the baked custard filling, some French in the short crust or puff pastry shell, and surely some Portuguese from the very similar pastel de nata. And the Cantonese love a steamed egg custard (see page 260).

All those influences come together in a flaky, sweet, not-too-indulgent pastry. Egg tarts are something you can eat one or two of every day without feeling too much guilt. — Jeffrey

Test kitchen recipe developer Hannah Fenton came up with this recipe using twelve individual 3-inch egg tart pans or other 3-inch tart pans (fluted and smooth pans work), widely available online or in kitchen supply stores. A 12-cup muffin tin can be substituted for individual pans; you will need to pleat the dough disks around the edge to create a uniform fit. If the dough becomes too soft at any point while shaping, refrigerate until firm to the touch, about 10 minutes, before proceeding. To best enjoy the crisp crust and silky custard, eat them on the day they're baked; store leftovers in the refrigerator for up to 2 days.

1 **For the crust:** Process flour, sugar, and salt in food processor until combined, about 5 seconds. Scatter butter over top and pulse until butter pieces are size of small peas, about 10 pulses. Continue to pulse, slowly streaming in ice water, until dough begins to form small curds that hold together when pinched with fingers, about 10 pulses.

2 Transfer mixture to lightly floured counter and gather into rectangular-shaped pile. Starting at farthest end, use heel of lightly floured hand to smear small amount of dough against counter. Continue to smear dough until all crumbs have been worked. Gather smeared crumbs together in another rectangular-shaped pile and repeat process. Form dough into 5-inch square, wrap tightly in plastic wrap, and refrigerate for at least 1 hour or up to 2 days.

3 Evenly space twelve 3-inch metal tart pans on parchment paper–lined rimmed baking sheet and spray with vegetable oil spray; set aside. Divide dough in half. Working with 1 half of dough at a time, roll into 12 by 8-inch rectangle on lightly floured counter. Using 4-inch round dough cutter, cut out 6 dough rounds. Working with 1 round at a time, center in prepared tart pan and use fingers to press dough evenly into bottom and up sides of pan. Trim any overhang ¼ inch beyond lip of pan. Repeat with remaining 5 dough rounds and then repeat rolling and shaping 6 more rounds with remaining dough half. Lightly prick shells all over with fork, cover loosely with plastic, and refrigerate until dough is firm, about 15 minutes.

4 **For the custard:** Adjust oven rack to lowest position and heat oven to 400 degrees. Whisk water and sugar in bowl until sugar has dissolved. Let cool to room temperature, about 10 minutes. Whisk eggs and yolks, evaporated milk, vanilla, and salt together in separate large bowl. Whisk sugar-water mixture into egg mixture until combined. Strain egg mixture through fine-mesh strainer set over 4-cup liquid measuring cup or bowl.

5 Divide custard evenly among pastry shells, leaving ¼-inch space below rim of each tart pan. (You may have extra filling.) Using fork or toothpick, pop any large bubbles on surface of custard. Carefully transfer sheet to oven and bake until shells are golden brown and crisp and edges of custard are just set and center of custard jiggles slightly when gently shaken, 20 to 25 minutes, rotating sheet halfway through baking. Let tarts cool in pans on wire rack for 10 minutes. Gently unmold tarts and let cool on wire rack for 15 minutes. Serve warm or at room temperature.

Test Kitchen Tip

Recipe developer Hannah Fenton notes: "To make picture-perfect egg tarts, use clear vanilla so that the custard stays deep yellow-gold, and make sure to pour the custard into the tart shells from a low height to ensure there are no air bubbles on the surface or under the surface that may rise during the beginning of baking. We like the look of a tart made using a fluted cutter and a smooth mini tart pan—or a smooth cutter and a fluted mini tart pan."

Assembling Egg Tarts

1 Center dough round over tart pan and use fingers to press dough evenly into bottom and up sides of pan; trim any overhang.

2 Divide custard evenly among pastry shells. Use fork to pop any bubbles on surface of custard.

Hong Kong's Greasy Spoon

Cha chaan teng 茶餐廳, meaning "tea restaurant" in Cantonese, is Hong Kong's take on the luncheonette. All people in Hong Kong, regardless of wealth or social status, can name their favorite cha chaan teng on command. (Mine is Cheung Hing in Happy Valley, open since 1951.) It's usually the restaurant they've been going to since childhood, or it's a three-minute walk from where they currently live. Cha chaan teng cafés are second homes to the Cantonese.

There's a particular ritual with almost every cha chaan teng you enter. At the door you're hit by a bone-chilling blast of air-conditioning, as Hong Kong is almost always hot and humid. It's refreshing and immediately welcoming. Talk radio drones on in the background. Then you're seated at a wooden banquette or on a folding stool at the world's tiniest Formica table. You'll order from the Chinese-only menu (despite Hong Kong being an English-speaking city) that's probably been encased beneath the laminate tabletop since the 1980s.

The food (thanks again to the British) can feel very Western. Scrambled egg sandwich. Macaroni and deli ham soup. Warm bolo bao with a thick hunk of butter nestled within. The food is also very Chinese. Pork and century egg congee with youtiao. Singapore noodles and beef ho fun. The restaurant will cook instant soup noodles straight from the packet and top them with Spam luncheon meat and a fried egg.

There will be milk tea, of course. Or you can order yuen yeung 鴛鴦, which is milk tea and coffee combined. There's also soy milk, iced lemon tea, Coke with lemon, and Horlicks and Ovaltine malted milks.

Whatever welcoming "Hi, hon" hospitality you expect at American diners, expect the opposite at a cha chaan teng. Bank on brusque wait staff, slightly tacky tabletops, quickly prepared and served food, and a cheap tab. During times of peak cha chaan teng traffic you'll probably be seated with complete strangers. You'll be in and out in 20 minutes tops. And you'll be back the next day.

— Kevin

Nutritional Information for Our Recipes

To calculate the nutritional values of our recipes per serving, we used The Food Processor SQL by ESHA research. When using this program, we entered all the ingredients, using weights wherever possible. Any ingredient listed as "optional" was excluded from the analyses. If there is a range in the serving size, we used the highest number of servings to calculate nutritional values. We did not include additional salt or pepper for food that's seasoned to taste.

	CALORIES	TOTAL FAT (G)	SAT FAT (G)	CHOL (MG)	SODIUM (MG)	TOTAL CARB (G)	DIETARY FIBER (G)	TOTAL SUGARS (G)	PROTEIN (G)
Getting Started									
Chili Oil (1 tbsp)	90	10	1.5	0	50	1	1	0	0
Chili Crisp (1 tbsp)	100	11	1.5	0	75	2	1	0	0
Jeffrey's XO Sauce (1 tbsp)	70	6	1	25	115	2	0	1	2
Soy-Vinegar Dipping Sauce (1 tbsp)	15	1	0	0	310	1	0	1	1
Hoisin-Sesame Dipping Sauce (1 tbsp)	30	2.5	0	0	180	2	0	1	0
Ginger-Scallion Sauce (1 tbsp)	60	7	1	0	55	1	0	0	0
Chili-Garlic Sauce (1 tbsp)	25	0	0	0	5	5	0	2	1
Plum Sauce (1 tbsp)	50	0	0	0	200	13	0	9	0
Microwave-Fried Shallots (1 tbsp)	40	3.5	0.5	0	0	2	0	1	0
Stir-Fried Pickled Mustard Greens (1 tbsp)	25	2	0	0	20	2	0	2	0
Chicken Broth (1 cup)	45	0	0	5	436	1	0	0	9
Enriched Chicken and Pork Broth (1 cup)	45	0	0	5	436	1	0	0	9
Pressure-Cooker Chicken Broth (1 cup)	45	0	0	5	436	1	0	0	9
Finger Foods and Small Plates									
Tea Eggs (1 egg)	80	5	1.5	185	210	1	0	1	6
Sichuan Snack Peanuts (⅓ cup)	250	21	3.5	0	290	9	3	3	9
Shrimp Toast	140	9	1.5	55	270	7	1	1	8
American-Style Egg Rolls (1 roll)	250	12	3.5	30	720	25	1	2	9
Spring Rolls (Cantonese Egg Rolls) (1 roll)	120	6	0	0	250	16	1	1	2
Sesame Balls (1 ball)	260	12	2	0	45	37	2	11	4
Scallion Pancakes	310	19	3	0	340	30	1	1	4
Smashed Cucumbers	50	2.5	0	0	640	6	2	3	3
Tiger Salad	60	4	0	0	400	5	2	2	2
Mouthwatering Chicken	210	16	2.5	55	510	5	2	2	13
Char Siu–Style Spareribs	630	38	13	135	1340	36	0	30	34

	CALORIES	TOTAL FAT (G)	SAT FAT (G)	CHOL (MG)	SODIUM (MG)	TOTAL CARB (G)	DIETARY FIBER (G)	TOTAL SUGARS (G)	PROTEIN (G)
Soup and Dumplings									
Corn and Chicken Soup	130	3.5	1	75	1030	19	2	3	9
Winter Melon Soup with Meatballs	270	18	6	55	1110	11	1	2	16
West Lake Beef Soup	120	3.5	1	25	1330	10	0	2	13
Hot and Sour Soup	140	5	1	50	1330	10	1	2	13
Hong Kong–Style Wonton Noodle Soup	270	6	1.5	55	1080	36	0	2	14
Hot Water Dough Dumpling Wrappers (1 wrapper)	30	0	0	0	0	7	0	0	1
Pork Filling (1 tbsp)	20	1.5	0	5	55	0	0	0	1
Shrimp Filling (1 tbsp)	10	0.5	0	5	35	0	0	0	1
Vegetable Filling (1 tbsp)	10	0.5	0	0	35	1	0	0	0
Pot Stickers (1 dumpling)	70	3	1	5	90	7	0	0	3
Boiled Dumplings (1 dumpling)	70	3	1	5	90	7	0	0	3
Steamed Dumplings (1 dumpling)	70	3	1	5	90	7	0	0	3
Shu Mai (1 dumpling)	50	1	0	10	150	8	0	0	3
Har Gow (1 dumpling)	45	1.5	0.5	10	50	7	0	0	1
Shanghai Soup Dumplings (1 dumpling)	60	2	0.5	10	190	6	0	0	3
Shanghai Pan-Fried Pork Buns (1 bun)	150	5	1.5	10	110	20	0	0	6
Rice and Noodle Dishes									
100% Perfect Rice	230	0	0	0	5	49	1	0	4
Stovetop Steamed Long- or Medium-Grain Rice	230	0	0	0	5	49	1	0	4
Stovetop Steamed Short-Grain Rice	240	0	0	0	0	53	1	0	4
Microwave-Steamed Rice	230	0	0	0	5	53	1	0	4
Faux Leftover Rice (½ cup)	130	2.5	0	0	0	25	0	0	2
Simple Fried Rice	380	12	2.5	150	1230	49	2	2	16
Shrimp and Pork Fried Rice	360	12	2.5	120	1000	43	2	6	19
Stir-Fried Rice Cakes	360	14	3	20	480	44	1	2	13
Clay Pot Chicken Rice	440	18	4	80	1110	47	1	2	19
Rice Cooker Chicken Rice	370	9	1.5	90	1130	47	1	2	24
Sesame Noodles	330	8	1	5	1150	51	1	10	11
Scallion Oil Noodles	460	24	4	5	1540	50	1	10	10
Dan Dan Mian	660	31	7	45	1310	69	1	9	24
Pork Stir-Fried Noodles	400	12	2.5	85	1150	43	3	5	26
Zha Jiang Mian	780	38	12	45	1260	84	2	21	21
Beef Ho Fun	220	6	1.5	20	690	32	1	2	10
Singapore Noodles	410	20	4	210	1020	35	3	7	21
Flat Hand-Pulled Noodles	660	37	5	0	890	72	4	3	13
Noodle Soup with Pork and Preserved Mustard	260	5	0.5	25	1050	35	0	5	15
Taiwanese Beef Noodle Soup	480	12	2.5	55	1760	52	1	17	39

	CALORIES	TOTAL FAT (G)	SAT FAT (G)	CHOL (MG)	SODIUM (MG)	TOTAL CARB (G)	DIETARY FIBER (G)	TOTAL SUGARS (G)	PROTEIN (G)
Poultry, Meat, Fish									
Kung Pao Chicken	290	17	3	90	780	8	2	3	27
Three-Cup Chicken	280	16	3	105	850	7	0	5	24
Soy Sauce Chicken	320	16	4.5	100	1160	4	0	2	34
Stir-Fried Cumin Lamb	200	12	3.5	60	490	3	1	1	19
Mongolian Beef	400	16	4.5	80	950	36	1	24	26
Stir-Fried Beef and Gai Lan	200	13	2.5	35	700	7	3	1	14
Twice-Cooked Pork	260	16	4.5	50	350	14	2	5	16
Taiwanese Pork Rice Bowl	620	24	8	260	970	60	2	4	33
Mu Shu Pork	530	18	3.5	165	1030	54	4	5	35
Spring Pancakes (1 pancake)	70	1	0	0	0	13	0	0	2
Lion's Head Meatballs	520	34	12	140	1430	22	2	5	31
Steamed Fish Fillets with Scallions and Ginger	250	10	1.5	75	940	7	1	2	32
Steamed Whole Fish with Scallions and Ginger	240	12	2	50	800	2	0	1	29
Oil-Exploded Shrimp	160	10	1.5	120	530	3	0	1	13
Stir-Fried Clams with Black Bean Sauce	100	6	0.5	15	460	4	0	0	6
Vegetables and Tofu									
Stir-Fried Tender Greens with Garlic	50	5	0	0	190	2	1	0	2
Ong Choy with Fermented Bean Curd	80	5	1	0	410	5	2	1	4
Hot and Sour Napa Cabbage	100	4.5	0.05	0	410	9	2	5	3
Baby Bok Choy with Ginger and Garlic	80	7	1	0	320	4	1	1	2
Gai Lan with Oyster Sauce	130	8	1	0	650	11	4	4	3
Sichuan Green Beans	210	15	3	15	460	14	5	7	7
Eggplant with Black Bean Sauce	460	32	2.5	0	550	31	5	16	8
Braised Eggplant with Soy, Garlic, and Ginger	80	3	0	0	380	8	2	6	2
Sichuan Hot and Sour Potatoes	140	5	0.5	0	590	22	2	1	3
Stir-Fried Tomatoes and Eggs	310	21	4	370	1150	13	2	8	15
Homemade Tofu (1 ounce)	25	1	0	0	10	0	0	0	3
Homestyle Tofu	250	19	1.5	0	390	10	1	3	10
Spicy Cold Tofu	90	6	0	0	460	3	0	1	5
Mapo Tofu	270	16	3	25	870	9	0	3	18
Jeffrey's Greatest Hits									
Stir-Fried Chicken in Black Bean Sauce	410	32	6	120	720	6	1	3	23
Hong Kong–Style Portuguese Chicken	750	47	24	225	1420	30	3	5	54
Shrimp-Paste Fried Chicken	420	28	6	150	460	12	0	2	28
"Taste of Sichuan" Beef Shank	350	16	4	100	500	6	0	6	43
Honey-Walnut Shrimp	480	34	4	110	480	27	1	11	15

	CALORIES	TOTAL FAT (G)	SAT FAT (G)	CHOL (MG)	SODIUM (MG)	TOTAL CARB (G)	DIETARY FIBER (G)	TOTAL SUGARS (G)	PROTEIN (G)
Jeffrey's Greatest Hits *(cont.)*									
Steamed Egg Custard with Ground Pork	330	25	7	400	1050	4	0	3	20
Hakka Stuffed Tofu with Egg Dumplings	300	21	4.5	120	860	7	1	2	17
Hong Kong–Style Baked Pork Chop Rice	950	39	8	275	1930	77	2	10	67
Sticky Spareribs with Chinkiang Vinegar	430	34	9	95	250	7	0	6	19
Stir-Fried Sticky Rice	620	22	7	85	760	88	4	3	16
Radish Cake	330	14	2	40	530	33	2	5	7
Deep Fried and Delicious									
Dry Chili Chicken	290	15	2.5	105	480	14	1	2	24
General Tso's Chicken	430	18	2	85	1050	37	0	13	29
Almond Chicken	420	17	2.5	115	870	31	2	2	31
Crispy Orange Beef	540	32	1.5	120	770	20	1	6	39
Beijing-Style Sweet and Sour Pork	460	19	2	75	1590	44	0	17	26
Taiwanese Fried Pork Chops	340	14	2.5	110	610	24	0	2	27
Sichuan Deep-Fried Fish Fillets	200	11	1	35	410	13	0	1	10
Salted Egg Fried Shrimp	330	14	3	345	1920	15	0	1	18
Salt and Pepper Squid	220	11	1.5	175	760	17	1	1	13
On Special Occasion									
Hainanese Chicken Rice	580	23	5	100	1430	52	2	3	39
Roast Duck	580	48	16	140	550	3	0	3	32
Red-Braised Pork Belly	280	18	6	70	490	7	0	7	22
Crispy Roast Pork Belly	310	22	8	85	430	2	0	1	26
Char Siu	270	12	4	80	580	15	0	13	25
Sichuan Boiled Fish	130	6	1	35	370	2	1	1	16
Ginger-Scallion Lobster	110	5	0.5	85	580	4	0	1	12
All Day Breakfast									
Milk Tea	180	8	5	30	115	19	0	19	7
Condensed Milk Toast	440	22	13	85	460	54	0	15	8
Soy Milk (1 cup)	80	4	0.5	0	85	4	0	0	7
Congee	80	0	0	0	390	18	0	0	2
Stir-Fried Ground Pork Topping (1 tbsp)	40	3.5	1	10	75	0	0	0	2
Bolo Bao (1 bao)	190	6	4	45	170	27	0	10	4
Char Siu Bolo Bao (1 bao)	280	11	5	70	370	32	0	14	13
Bolo Bao with Custard Filling (1 bao)	270	11	6	130	190	35	0	16	6
Lap Cheong Rolls (1 roll)	390	2	0.5	2	780	34	0	10	17
Youtiao (1 youtiao)	200	6	0.5	0	190	30	0	0	4
Egg Tarts (1 tart)	220	12	7	90	150	23	0	10	4

Conversions and Equivalents

Some say cooking is a science and an art. We would say that geography has a hand in it, too. Flours and sugars manufactured in the United Kingdom and elsewhere will feel and taste different from those manufactured in the United States. So we cannot promise that the loaf of bread you bake in Canada or England will taste the same as a loaf baked in the States, but we can offer guidelines for converting weights and measures. We also recommend that you rely on your instincts when making our recipes. Refer to the visual cues provided. If the dough hasn't "come together in a ball" as described, you may need to add more flour—even if the recipe doesn't tell you to. You be the judge.

The recipes in this book were developed using standard U.S. measures following U.S. government guidelines. The charts below offer equivalents for U.S. and metric measures. All conversions are approximate and have been rounded up or down to the nearest whole number.

EXAMPLE:

1 teaspoon = 4.9292 milliliters, rounded up to 5 milliliters
    1 ounce = 28.3495 grams, rounded down to 28 grams

VOLUME CONVERSIONS:

U.S.	Metric
1 teaspoon	5 milliliters
2 teaspoons	10 milliliters
1 tablespoon	15 milliliters
2 tablespoons	30 milliliters
¼ cup	59 milliliters
⅓ cup	79 milliliters
½ cup	118 milliliters
¾ cup	177 milliliters
1 cup	237 milliliters
1¼ cups	296 milliliters
1½ cups	355 milliliters
2 cups (1 pint)	473 milliliters
2½ cups	591 milliliters
3 cups	710 milliliters
4 cups (1 quart)	0.946 liter
1.06 quarts	1 liter
4 quarts (1 gallon)	3.8 liters

WEIGHT CONVERSIONS:

Ounces	Grams
½	14
¾	21
1	28
1½	43
2	57
2½	71
3	85
3½	99
4	113
4½	128
5	142
6	170
7	198
8	227
9	255
10	283
12	340
16 (1 pound)	454

CONVERSIONS FOR COMMON BAKING INGREDIENTS:

Baking is an exacting science. Because measuring by weight is far more accurate than measuring by volume, and thus more likely to produce reliable results, in our recipes we provide ounce measures in addition to cup measures for many ingredients. Refer to the chart below to convert these measures into grams.

Ingredient	Ounces	Grams
Flour		
1 cup all-purpose flour*	5	142
1 cup cake flour	4	113
1 cup whole-wheat flour	5½	156
Sugar		
1 cup granulated (white) sugar	7	198
1 cup packed brown sugar (light or dark)	7	198
1 cup confectioners' sugar	4	113
Cocoa Powder		
1 cup cocoa powder	3	85
Butter†		
4 tablespoons (½ stick or ¼ cup)	2	57
8 tablespoons (1 stick or ½ cup)	4	113
16 tablespoons (2 sticks or 1 cup)	8	227

* U.S. all-purpose flour, the most frequently used flour in this book, does not contain leaveners, as some European flours do. These leavened flours are called self-rising or self-raising. If you are using self-rising flour, take this into consideration before adding leaveners to a recipe.

† In the United States, butter is sold both salted and unsalted. We generally recommend unsalted butter. If you are using salted butter, take this into consideration before adding salt to a recipe.

OVEN TEMPERATURES:

Fahrenheit	Celsius	Gas Mark
225	105	¼
250	120	½
275	135	1
300	150	2
325	165	3
350	180	4
375	190	5
400	200	6
425	220	7
450	230	8
475	245	9

CONVERTING TEMPERATURES FROM AN INSTANT-READ THERMOMETER:

We include doneness temperatures in many of the recipes in this book. We recommend an instant-read thermometer for the job. Refer to the table above to convert Fahrenheit degrees to Celsius. Or, for temperatures not represented in the chart, use this simple formula:

Subtract 32 degrees from the Fahrenheit reading, then divide the result by 1.8 to find the Celsius reading.

EXAMPLE:
"Roast chicken until thighs register 175 degrees."

TO CONVERT:
175°F – 32 = 143°
143° ÷ 1.8 = 79.44°C, rounded down to 79°C

Spicy Cold Tofu
(page 239)

Index

Note: Page references in *italics* indicate photographs.

P

Pancakes
    Scallion, 62–64, *63*
    Spring, 192, *193*
Pandan leaves
    about, 308
    Hainanese Chicken Rice, *306,* 307–9
Pastes, 18
Peanut oil, 15
Peanuts
    Chili Crisp, *20,* 21
    Kung Pao Chicken, 170, *171*
    Sichuan Snack, 46, *47*
    Tiger Salad, *68,* 69
Peas
    adding to fried rice, 134
    Shrimp and Pork Fried Rice, 136, *137*
    Simple Fried Rice, *132,* 133
    Stir-Fried Rice Cakes, 138, *139*
Peppercorns
    Sichuan, 26
    white, 26
Peppers
    adding to fried rice, 134
    Eggplant with Black Bean Sauce, 224–25, *225*
    Homestyle Tofu, *236,* 237
    Singapore Noodles, 158–59, *159*
    Stir-Fried Chicken in Black Bean Sauce, 248, *249*
    see also Chiles
Pickled Mustard
    about, 19
    see also Haam choy; Yacai; Zhacai
Pickled Mustard Greens, Stir-Fried, 24
Plum Sauce
    about, 16
    recipe for, 24
Pork
    adding to fried rice, 134
    American-Style Egg Rolls, *52,* 53–55
    Belly, Crispy Roast, 318, *319*
    Belly, Red-Braised, 316, *317*
    for braising, 30
    Buns, Shanghai Pan-Fried, *122,* 123–25
    Char Siu, *320,* 321–22, *323*

Pork *(cont.)*
    Char Siu Bolo Bao, 342, *342*
    Char Siu–Style Spareribs, 72, *73*
    and Chicken Broth, Enriched, 25
    in Chinese cooking, 30
    Chop Rice, Hong Kong–Style Baked, *266,* 267–68
    Chops, Taiwanese Fried, 292–93, *293*
    Dan Dan Mian, *149,* 150–51
    for dumpling fillings, 30
    Filling for Dumplings, 96
    Ground, Steamed Egg Custard with, 260–61, *261*
    Hakka Stuffed Tofu with Egg Dumplings, 264–65
    Hong Kong–Style Wonton Noodle Soup, *89,* 90–91
    Hot and Sour Soup, 84, *85*
    Lion's Head Meatballs, 194, *195*
    Mapo Tofu, 240, *241*
    Mu Shu, 190–91, *191*
    and Preserved Mustard, Noodle Soup with, 164–65, *165*
    Rice Bowl, Taiwanese, 188–89, *189*
    Shanghai Soup Dumplings, *116,* 117–21
    and Shrimp Fried Rice, 136, *137*
    Shu Mai, *106,* 107–9
    Sichuan Green Beans, *222,* 223
    Simple Fried Rice, *132,* 133
    Singapore Noodles, 158–59, *159*
    Sticky Spareribs with Chinkiang Vinegar, *270,* 271
    Stir-Fried Ground, Topping for Congee, 337, *337*
    Stir-Fried Noodles, 152–53, *153*
    Stir-Fried Rice Cakes, 138, *139*
    for stir-frying, 30
    Sweet and Sour, Beijing-Style, 290–91, *291*
    Twice-Cooked, 186–87, *187*
    Winter Melon Soup with Meatballs, 80, *81*
    Zha Jiang Mian, 154–55, *155*
    see also Lap cheong; Lap yuk
Portuguese Chicken, Hong Kong–Style, *251,* 252–53
Potatoes
    Hong Kong–Style Portuguese Chicken, *251,* 252–53
    Sichuan Hot and Sour, *228,* 229
Potato starch, 13
Pot Stickers, *102,* 103
Poultry, 30
    see also Chicken; Duck
Preserves, 19